contents

W9-BIM-080

southeast

day trip 01

day trip 02

south

day trip 01

southwest

day trip 01

west

day trip 01

day trip 02

day trip 03

northwest

day trip 01

day trip 02

day trip 03

day trip 04

day trips® series

day trips® from houston

second edition

 getaway ideas for the local traveler

paris permenter and john bigley

gpp®
travel
Guilford, Connecticut

All the information in this guidebook is subject to change. We recommend that you call ahead to obtain current information before traveling.

To buy books in quantity for corporate use or incentives, call **(800) 962-0973** or e-mail **premiums@GlobePequot.com.**

Editor: Kevin Sirois
Project Editor: Lauren Brancato
Layout: Lisa Reneson
Text Design: Linda R. Loiewski
Maps: Daniel Lloyd © Morris Book Publishing, LLC.
Spot photography throughout © thinkstock

ISBN 978-0-7627-8639-8

Printed in the United States of America
10 9 8 7 6 5 4 3 2

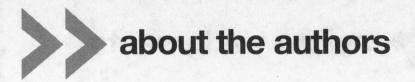

about the authors

Paris Permenter and **John Bigley** are a husband-wife team of travel writers. Longtime residents of Central Texas, they make their home in the Hill Country west of Austin, near Lake Travis. Both John and Paris are members of the prestigious Society of American Travel Writers.

John and Paris have authored numerous books including *Day Trips from Austin, Day Trips from San Antonio, Insiders' Guide to San Antonio, Adventure Guide to Jamaica, Caribbean with Kids, National Parks with Kids,* and many others. The team also edits *Lovetripper .com Romantic Travel* magazine, an online look at romantic destinations around the globe.

Paris and John are also dog travel experts. They publish DogTipper.com, named Best Dog Blog 2012, and host the weekly "DogTipper.com's Dog Travel Experts" Internet radio show. The one-hour live show (dogtravelexperts.com) features destinations, tips, and products for travelers and their dogs.

acknowledgments

To write a guidebook doesn't just take a village; it involves whole metropolitan areas. In the course of updating this guide book, we've talked with more of our fellow Texans than we can possibly thank here, from innkeepers and tourism officials to shopkeepers and festival planners. Most importantly, we talked with the people who really know what makes a good day trip: the residents and travelers of the region. They shared their out-of-the-way finds as well as their long-time favorites with us, guiding our explorations, and for that we are grateful. We're also immensely grateful for the staff at Globe Pequot Press, who brought together another book that we know will cause our hearts to skip a beat when we see it on bookstore shelves. And, finally, we'd like to thank our dogs, Irie and Tiki, for traveling many of these miles with us, reminding us that slow travel, close to home, is sometimes the best travel of all.

introduction

There's a lot to love about Houston: Great food. World-class museums. Sports teams with serious heart. Beautiful parks. Stores galore. Friendly people. Warm weather. Most of the time, that's enough to make you want to stay put.

Every now and then, though, it happens: You start growing restless and crave a change of scenery. This, believe it or not, actually makes for another reason to love Houston: You can drive just an hour or two (or even a half-hour) in any direction, and you're likely to find yourself in a town with an enchanting history, culture, and scenery of its own. Drive an hour north, for instance, and you'll find yourself walking in General Sam Houston's footsteps in Huntsville. Drive an hour south and you'll find people splashing around in the Gulf of Mexico and gazing at the seemingly countless species of birds in Freeport. Or drive just under 2 hours to Orange and you'll discover beautiful botanical gardens, vineyards, Cajun cooking, and southern hospitality galore.

If those options don't appeal to you, worry not: This book encompasses dozens of small Texas towns, each with different personalities, histories, terrains, restaurants, shops, and attractions. Most of them offer a variety of things to see and do, so you can focus on the activities that appeal to you.

In the pages that follow, you'll find 21 trips—all 2 hours or less from downtown Houston by car. Some include a single attraction-packed town like Beaumont or Columbus; others include a few stops, some with more to see than others. Each trip includes restaurants and attractions like museums, parks, and historical sites; many stops also include places to shop and places to sleep if you want to stretch your trip out. Most trips include too many attractions to visit in the course of one day, so pick and choose as you please. You might even decide to disregard some of the stops in trips contained here or to combine day trips. Go for it: There's no better way to create a new adventure.

Just be sure to get your hands on a good Texas map before you go. (We recommend the one from the Texas Department of Transportation, whose contact details you can find in the Additional Resources section below). Even if you have a GPS system, a paper map is often helpful. As you navigate some of the tinier towns and newer roads, you'll discover that your GPS system or Google Maps don't include all the roads.

No matter where your journeys take you, keep in mind that many establishments listed here are open only for a few days and hours each week. So before you hit the road, it's a good idea to chart out what you want to do. It's also a good idea to call and make sure the sites you plan to see will be open. Many small-town businesses and attractions, after all,

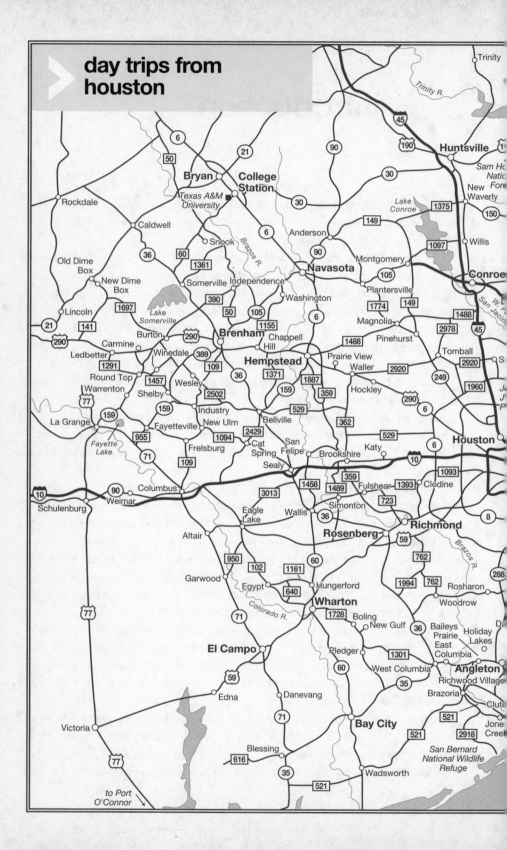

day trips from houston

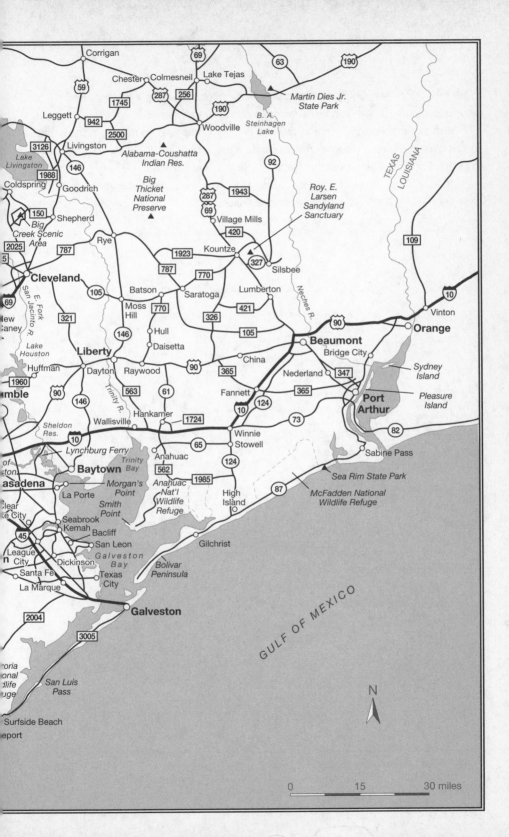

close their doors temporarily or even permanently without much of a warning. And it's not unusual for them to change hours seasonally or even on a whim.

With that in mind, go forth and day trip: Enjoy your reprieve from the big city, breathe in some fresh air, spy on some unusual plants and animals, admire Victorian architecture, and stand amazed at the sites that played a role in Texas's birth.

Then, after you've settled back into your big-city ways, pull out your map and do it all over again—only this time, try a different destination.

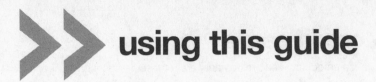

using this guide

This guide is organized starting with destinations north of Houston and working clockwise around the compass. Each day trip is designed to introduce you to the best attractions in a single 24-hour period. Or you may wish to group two or three day trips together for a weekend trip.

We have selected activities ("Where to Go"), shops ("Where to Shop"), and restaurants ("Where to Eat") with a wide range of travelers in mind—from couples looking for a romantic getaway to friends on an adventure or to families with young children. Listings are organized in alphabetical order.

scheduling your day trip

If you're day-tripping on the weekend, it's often better to schedule your trip for Saturday rather than Sunday. While the majority of attractions, restaurants, and shops included here are open for at least a few hours on Sunday, there are still many businesses in small-town Texas that close their doors. So to increase your chances of seeing all of a town's best offerings, you may be better off visiting on Saturday. (That said, beware: Some attractions, shops, and restaurants are open only on weekdays.)

hours of operation

Because many businesses change their hours of operation frequently or seasonally, these details are often not included in the pages that follow. Instead, you'll find the corresponding telephone numbers and, when available, websites so that you can call or go online to find out the current hours before your visit. Far more often than you might expect, small-town businesses move or change their phone numbers. If you call an attraction listed here and discover it's no longer a working number, try calling information. Our personal preference is to use (800) GOOG-411 since it's free. Also note that many businesses are closed on major holidays such as Thanksgiving, Christmas, Easter, and Independence Day, even though this information may not be noted in this book.

prices & credit cards

The price codes for accommodations and restaurants are represented as a scale of one to three dollar signs ($–$$$). You can assume that all establishments listed accept major credit cards unless otherwise noted. For details, contact the locations directly.

restaurant pricing

The price code used here is based on the average price of dinner entrees for two, excluding drinks, appetizers, dessert, tax, and tip. You can typically expect to pay a little less for lunch and/or breakfast, where applicable.

$	less than $15
$$	$15 to $30
$$$	more than $30

attraction pricing

While some attractions include sales tax in their published prices, many do not. Be aware of this and be prepared for the possibility of paying state sales tax of 6.25 percent on top of city and county taxes, which may range from 0.25 percent to 2 percent and 0.5 percent to 1.5 percent, respectively.

accommodation pricing

This book is geared primarily toward travelers who want to escape the city for just a few hours. However, accommodations are included in some sections for those travelers who want to stretch their trips out and see a little more of the area. The accommodations listed here are almost all B&Bs and local hotels. National chains are typically not included. However, you can find a large chain hotel in almost every town included in this book.

Each day trip does not include "Where to Stay" recommendations for every stop. Accommodation suggestions are typically included for at least one stop on each day trip, though, so consult these sections accordingly. With few exceptions, most towns in each trip aren't more than 30 minutes apart, and many are much closer.

The following price code is used for accommodations throughout this book. It is based on the average price of a 1-night stay in a standard, double-occupancy room, before taxes. This price code does not include the Texas hotel tax (currently 6 percent) or local hotel taxes, which can be as high as 7 percent but are typically much lower in small towns. Keep in mind that nightly hotel rates are often a little lower on weekdays than they are on weekends and during the summer or special events.

$	less than $100
$$	$100 to $200
$$$	more than $200

driving tips

While more suburban areas like The Woodlands, Spring, and the Bay Area tend to be well lit at night, this isn't the case with some of the more distant and smaller towns in this book. Many roads in these areas could use some paving, and others have curves that can be hard to see, particularly if you're unfamiliar with the area. So be sure to drive cautiously when traveling through less populous areas after dark.

To find out about road conditions, call the Texas Department of Transportation's 24-hour hotline at (800) 452-9292.

Also, keep in mind that speed limits often change abruptly from one town or stretch of highway to the next. While it's important to heed speed limits no matter where you're driving, be particularly cautious as you enter small towns. Police officers often sit waiting near the city limits signs, hoping to catch drivers who haven't slowed down from the 70 mph that they were driving (legally, in many cases) right outside of town.

highway designations

For consistency's sake, this book typically refers to state highways with "TX" followed by the highway number (e.g., TX 105). Beware, however, that other sources and maps may refer to Texas highways using any of the following designations: State Highway 105, SH 105, Texas 105, TX-105, or Texas Highway 105. (TX 105 here is used here merely as an example. It is a highway north of Houston near Conroe.)

In some situations, multiple highways run along the same path. In Beaumont, for instance, there's a stretch known as US 69/96/287. Typically, when using a GPS or a mapping service like Google Maps, it is not necessary to include all three highway numbers. Instead, you can enter the address with just one of these highways.

area codes

The area codes 713, 832, and 281 cover Houston, of course, as well as outlying suburbs such as Pasadena, Alvin, Baytown, Cleveland, Humble, Katy, Kemah, La Porte, Rosenberg, Richmond, Seabrook, Spring, and Sugar Land. The code 409 covers many of the areas in this book, including Galveston, Beaumont, Port Arthur, Orange, Kountze, Silsbee, Lumberton, Anahuac, and Woodville. The code 936 covers the area around Conroe and Huntsville, including Liberty, Livingston, Montgomery, and Washington. Area code 979 covers College Station, Bryan, Lake Jackson, Bellville, Brenham, Burton, Chappell Hill, Columbus, La Grange, San Felipe, Schulenburg, West Columbia, and the surrounding areas.

additional resources

Day Trips from Houston attempts to cover a variety of bases and interests, but those looking for additional material can contact the following agencies by phone, mail, or on the web. Regarding the latter, when checking out the various destinations, please be aware that online reviews may be contradictory and conflicting. Everyone's experience can be different, and the Internet allows for many forums for these diverse opinions. So call the place directly and heed ratings by the likes of AAA and the Better Business Bureau. Many of the areas have chain hotels and restaurants, which are generally not included in the listings in each chapter. At the end of the book, we provide contact information for chambers of commerce and/or convention and visitor bureaus. Below are some additional resources.

for general travel information

AAA Texas

PO Box 630588, Irving, TX 75063

(888) 765-0766 (travel planner and tour book)

(800) AAA-HELP (roadside assistance, with paid membership)

texas.aaa.com

East Texas Tourism Association

PO Box 1592, Longview, TX 75606

(903) 757-4444

(800) 766-3349

easttexasguide.com

Texas Department of Transportation, Travel and Information Division

PO Box 5064, Austin, TX 78714-9248

(800) 888-8-TEX (request a free packet, including an official Texas travel map, events calendar, and accommodations and attractions guides)

(800) 452-9292 (travel assistance)

traveltex.com

Texas Highways: The Travel Magazine of Texas

PO Box 141009, Austin, TX 78714-1009

texashighways.com

Texas Monthly travel section

PO Box 1569, Austin, TX 78767-1569

texasmonthly.com

Texas Travel Industry Association

25132 Oakhurst Dr., Ste. 201, Spring, TX 77386

(713) 942-7676 (request brochures about different regions of the state)
tourtexas.com

for accommodations recommendations

Texas Bed & Breakfast Association
PO Box 301596, Austin, TX 78703
(512) 371-9884
(800) 428-0368
texasbb.org

for outdoor recreation, including birding, hunting, camping & park-going

Houston Audubon Society
440 Wilchester Blvd., Houston, TX 77079
(713) 932-1639
(713) 461-2911
(281) 992-2757 ("Texas Rare Bird Alert" hotline)
houstonaudubon.org

Texas Parks and Wildlife Department (for information on parks, camping, hunting, fishing, and the Great Texas Coastal Birding Trail)
4200 Smith School Rd., Austin, TX 78744
(512) 389-8900 (park and campsite reservations)
(800) 792-1112 (information)
tpwd.state.tx.us

for information on historical markers & sites

Texas Historical Commission
1511 Colorado St., Austin, TX 78701
(512) 463-6100
thc.state.tx.us

for information on wineries, pick-your-own fruit and produce farms, farmers' markets & Christmas tree farms

Texas Department of Agriculture
1700 N. Congress Ave., 11th Fl., Austin, TX 78701
(512) 463-7476
texasagriculture.gov

north

day trip 01

a suburban retreat:
spring, the woodlands

spring

Driving north on I-45, you might not even realize you've left Houston and entered Spring—at least not until you exit the freeway and take a detour into Spring proper. After all, Spring is a predominately residential area with a growing population. But out of the big city you are.

Once home to the Orcoquiza Indians, Spring was settled by German immigrants in 1840. Near the turn of the 20th century, the Great Northern Railroad built its rail yards just down the street, a fact that remains central to Spring's identity. Today, the heart of this old railroad town is known as Old Town Spring. The downtown area is home to a number of quaint restaurants, galleries, and museums, and about 150 shops housed in Victorian-style buildings. Several festivals take place here throughout the year.

getting there

Located 25 miles north of downtown Houston on I-45, Old Town Spring sits about a mile east of the freeway. Take exit 70A toward Tomball/FM 2920, and then take a right at Spring Cypress Road and a slight left at Main Street. Most of the restaurants and shops are on Main Street and the parallel Midway Street, as well as a few cross streets.

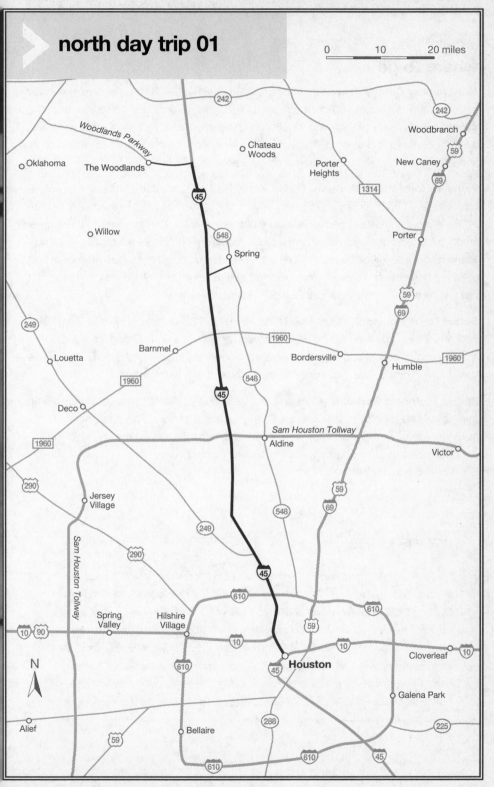

0   10   20 miles

242

242

Woodbranch

Woodlands Parkway

Chateau
Woods

Porter
Heights

New Caney

59

Oklahoma

The Woodlands

69

45

1314

Willow

548

Porter

Spring

59

69

249

1960

Louetta

Barnmel

Bordersville

Humble

1960

1960

548

Deco

Sam Houston Tollway

1960

Aldine

Victor

290

Jersey
Village

59

249

69

290

548

Sam Houston Tollway

45

610

610

Spring
Valley

Hilshire
Village

59

Cloverleaf

10

10   90

10

10

610

45

Houston

N

Galena Park

Alief

Bellaire

288

225

59

610

610

45

where to go

Montgomery County Preserve. 1122 Pruitt Rd.; (281) 367-7283; springcreekgreenway
.org/mcp.htm. Aptly nicknamed "The Little Thicket," this 71-acre land preserve runs along
Spring Creek. Take a hike through the pine and hardwood forest and get a close-up look at
a variety of plants and animals. Throughout the year, the preserve offers free guided tours
and educational programming. There's no admission fee.

Pioneer Homestead Museum. 20634 Kenswick Dr.; (281) 446-8588. At this unique
museum, you'll discover how some of the area's earliest settlers lived. Highlights include an
1830s pioneer homestead and an Akokisa Indian homestead. The homesteads themselves
aren't authentic, but they are very similar to the real thing. You'll have the chance to explore
a smokehouse, log cabin, corn crib, log barn, and other buildings that would have been part
of an old homestead. The museum is located off FM 1960 East. Call ahead for hours; the
buildings are open only a few hours a week. Admission is free.

SplashTown Houston. 21300 I-45 North; (281) 355-3300; splashtownpark.com. Stay
cool and let the kids blow off steam at this popular water park. You'll find waterslides that
are long and short, fast and slow, as well as net ladders waiting to be climbed on Treehouse
Island, "river" rafting, and the chance to ride in the eye of a wild tornado.

Spring Historical Museum. 403 Main St.; (281) 353-9310. Want to learn more about
this old railroad town? Pay a visit to the Spring Historical Museum, where you can get the
historical scoop on the town—and its railroads, lumber mills, and sawmills—by looking at
old documents, pictures, and other memorabilia. The museum is open Thursday through
Sunday, and admission is free.

crawfish rules

*Do your stomach (and ears) a favor and visit Spring during the last 2 weekends
of April. That's when this historic town hosts the South's largest crawfish festival.
Dubbed the* **Texas Crawfish & Music Festival,** *this family-friendly affair serves
up more than 25 tons—yes, you read that right—of spice-laden crawfish. Musicians from around the country (and the Houston area) play country, zydeco, and
rock music on three different stages. There are even carnival rides and midway
games for the kids. The festival gates are located at 130 Spring School Rd. in
Preservation Park. Call (800) 653-8696 or visit texascrawfishfestival.com for more
information on this area favorite.*

where to shop

Old Town Spring is home to more than 100 shops. A small sampling of these stores can be found below. Wander the streets of Old Town to find some more to your liking, or plan ahead by checking out the complete list of shops at shopspringtexas.com.

Amish Barn. 200 Main St.; (281) 651-9209; amishbarn.com. The Amish Barn sells jellies, sauces, gifts, and handcrafted furniture from more than 100 Amish furniture craftspeople.

Anthony's Decor. 26403 Preston Ave.; (832) 877-1552. If you're looking for tin home decor, including wall hangings, this is the place to find it.

B. Persnickety. 318-C Main St.; (832) 592-1104; b-persnickety.com. Satisfy your stationery addiction here. This chic stationery shop also sells some unique gifts.

Connie's Bath Shack. 211 Midway, Building E; (281) 288-9595; conniesbathshack.com. Founder and owner Connie Putnam creates a host of handmade soaps, bath salts, and lotions in her Old Town Spring shop. You'll also find bath accessories and gifts, not to mention her array of rubber duckies. She also conducts lotion-making classes.

German Gift House. 210-B Gentry St.; (281) 528-8877; germangifthouse.com. This German-themed gift shop sells all sorts of German kitsch and paraphernalia, including nutcrackers, CDs, beer steins, and flags.

Haute Dogs & Glitzy Paws Boutique & Spa. 1609 Spring Cypress Rd.; (281) 353-4347; hautedogsglitzypaws.com. Come here to pamper your favorite canine with treats, toys, and beds fit for a four-legged queen. Then, if you've got money to spare, sign your furry pal up for a doggie spa day or obedience training.

Home Sweet Home Etc. 417-C Gentry St.; (281) 288-4233; homesweethomeetc.com. Grab a cup of coffee and a pastry here; then shop for holiday decorations, collectibles, fragrance lamps, and other gifts.

Just for the Birds. 209 Main St.; (281) 288-9019; justforthebirds.com. Here's a store sure to satisfy bird lovers. Just for the Birds touts an extensive collection of birding books and CDs, bird feeders and houses, butterfly and bat houses, and all sorts of bird-inspired gifts. Closed Monday.

PTL Gallery. 315 Gentry St., No. B3; (281) 367-4901; ptlgallery.com. Specializing in artists who celebrate the glories of the natural (and spiritual) world, this gallery features works by Thomas Kinkade, Mark Keathley, Jack Dawson, June Dudley, and many others. The gallery is open Tuesday through Saturday and by appointment on Monday.

Tuscany Accents. 21127 Spring Towne Dr.; (832) 576-4930; tuscanyaccents.com. Find an extensive selection of unique gift baskets and cookie bouquets at this Old Town Spring shop.

Vamp Vintage Wear. 111 Main St.; (281) 528-8500; vampvintagewear.com. Scour the racks at this boutique to find vintage high-end women's fashion spanning from the 1950s to today. The sales staff can help you put together an outfit for any occasion.

Wild Goose Chase. 118 Midway St.; (281) 288-9501; wildgoosechase.com. This country store sells a little of everything for your home and gift needs. Among the things you'll find here are linens, scented candles, potpourri, wreaths, garden and home decor, and seasonal items. Closed Monday.

where to eat

Crescent Moon Wine Bar. 440 Rayford Rd., No. 115A; (281) 364-9463; crescentmoon winebar.com. Don't be fooled by Crescent Moon's strip mall location. Inside, you'll find a classy, Tuscan-inspired restaurant and wine bar. While the extensive wine list is a big draw, the food menu also commands attention. It's filled with cheese flights; rich desserts; and unusual dishes such as the lamb chop lollipops and a pizza with chorizo, Manchego cheese, peppers, and almonds. On Wednesday night, Crescent Moon serves steak and salmon dinners, and there's live music many nights. Closed on Sunday and Monday. $$–$$$.

Ellen's Cafe. 307 Gentry St., (282) 353-9229; ellensofoldtownspring.com. Ellen's Cafe is a convenient spot for lunch while you're scouting bargains and collectibles in Old Town Spring. Choose from sandwiches, quiches, salads, and soups and leave plenty of room for some homemade desserts. $.

English John's Pub. 26607 Keith St.; (281) 528-5055. Down authentic English pints while eating traditional pub food at this popular hangout. You can also play a game of darts or shoot some pool. $–$$.

Hyde's Cafe. 26608 Keith St.; (281) 350-8530. Owners David and Belinda Hyde have worked hard to make this rustic joint a fun place to stop in for lunch or dinner while walking

jailhouse rock

*If you're looking for some after-dinner fun, head to the **Jailhouse Saloon** at 310 Preston St. (281-288-0255; jailhousesaloontx.com). Here you'll find music, beer and wine, and fun in the building that once housed the Old Town Spring jail. There's live music on Saturday nights and karaoke on Friday evenings. Open mic night is held every Sunday.*

around Old Town Spring. The menu includes some great burgers, chicken-fried steak, salads, and pecan pie. Sit on the swing on the porch or play video games while you wait, and let the kids run in the yard. There's live music on Sunday. $.

Pho Be. 314 Sawdust Rd.; (281) 465-9598. This Vietnamese restaurant might not be the best-looking place in town, but the food gets high marks. Try the Vietnamese soup, *pho,* or noodles. $–$$.

Pizza Tonight. 27190 Glen Loch Dr.; (281) 465-4774. Fresh, gourmet ingredients and a thin New York–inspired crust make this some of the best pizza in The Woodlands–Spring area. Pizza Tonight also serves salad, pasta, wings, and subs. Unfortunately, there's no seating, so you'll have to grab your food to go, or if you're staying in the area, get it delivered. $$.

Puffabellys Old Depot & Restaurant. 100 Main St.; (281) 350-3376; puffabellys.com. If you're looking for a rustic joint that serves peanuts at your table and invites you to throw the shells on the floor, this is the place to go. Puffabellys' menu includes southern favorites such as chicken-fried steak, burgers, beer-battered onion rings, fried green tomatoes and pickles, fully loaded baked potatoes, and seafood. They even sell casseroles—think southwestern chicken and beef lasagna—for you to take home. On Wednesday and Saturday evenings, Puffabellys hosts concerts by Texas musicians. $–$$.

Rudy's Country Store & Bar-B-Q. 20806 I-45; (281) 288-0916; rudysbbq.com. The Spring location of this famed Texas barbecue joint may not get as much praise as the original Rudy's in San Antonio, but you can count on it to serve up the usual suspects: brisket, turkey breast, jalapeño sausage, and ribs by the half pound covered in Rudy's famous sauce. Other options for your feast include Rudy's popular sides and desserts like corn on the cob, green chili stew, pies, puddings, and cobblers. $.

Thep Thai. 421 Sawdust Rd.; (281) 419-7619; thep-thai.com. Don't be deterred by the decor, the strip mall location, or the lack of customers here. Thep Thai is considered one of the best Thai restaurants in the area, thanks to a menu filled with authentic curries, stir-fries, panfried noodle dishes, fried duck, Thai soups and salads, vegetarian dishes, and a delicious Thai iced tea. The chef will make your meal as spicy or as mild as you request. Thep Thai is open for lunch and dinner. $$.

The Whole Cake and Kaboodle. 417-N Gentry St.; (281) 353-7878; houstonreservations .info/wholecake.htm. This bakery is best known for its immaculate custom cakes, but you can also satisfy smaller sugar cravings here. Each day the bakery sells fresh cupcakes, several kinds of cookies, fudge, peanut brittle, pralines, and truffles. $.

the woodlands

Spring and The Woodlands may be neighbors, but they've got their share of differences: Whereas Spring feels like a quaint historic town, The Woodlands exudes a cosmopolitan yet serene aura, making this master-planned community a popular place to call home.

It's also a great place to take a day trip. The Woodlands' well-manicured, wooded setting makes a scenic backdrop for golfing, relaxing at a spa, kayaking, museum-going, and listening to live music at the Cynthia Woods Mitchell Pavilion. The Woodlands Mall and the outdoor shopping area known as Market Street also make The Woodlands a good place to shop. In fact, *Southern Living* named this Houston suburb one of the South's 10 best shopping districts in 2009.

Don't come here expecting lots of small, family-owned spots, though. Most of the stores, restaurants, and hotels in The Woodlands are large chains. To give you more of a local taste, the Where to Eat, Where to Shop, and Where to Stay sections in this chapter include a few less-prominent chains, as well as some of the area's independent businesses. Additional shops and restaurants can be found online at thewoodlandscvb.com.

getting there

From Spring, return to I-45 North and drive about 9 miles north. Take exit 76B onto Woodlands Parkway. On your right, you'll see The Woodlands Town Center, where restaurants, shops, and family-friendly activities abound.

where to go

Cynthia Woods Mitchell Pavilion. 2005 Lake Robbins Dr.; (281) 363-3300; woodlands center.org. Take in some of music's biggest names at this popular outdoor amphitheater surrounded by towering pines. Recent acts have included Journey, Iron Maiden, and Jason Mraz, though the Houston Symphony and Houston Ballet also put on shows here from time to time. Bring a blanket and sit on the grass, or pay a little more and opt for an assigned seat in the covered area. You can purchase tickets through Ticketmaster (ticketmaster .com; 800-745-3000) or at the pavilion box office. Paid parking is available in several lots near the pavilion.

Golf at The Woodlands Resort. 2301 N. Millbend Dr.; (281) 882-3000; woodlandsresort .com. Head to The Woodlands Resort to play golf on 2 of the area's most beautiful 18-hole courses—The Oaks and Panther Trail. The Oaks' rolling greens offer enormous greenside bunkers, large fairways, and challenges from Lake Harrison. Stately oak trees provide golfers on this course with plenty of shade. The Panther caters to both beginning and advanced golfers with 4 tees on each hole.

ditch your wheels

Make your escape from Houston a genuine one by parking your car and traveling by water or trolley. The Woodlands is home to a free water taxi and a trolley, both of which make stops near many of the area's restaurants and shops, The Woodlands Mall, Cynthia Woods Mitchell Pavilion, Town Green Park, and The Woodlands Waterway Marriott Hotel & Convention Center. The Woodlands Waterway Trolley is free; call (281) 363-2447 or visit thewoodlandswaterwaytrolley.com for maps and route information. You can purchase a water taxi day pass on board any of the six wheelchair-accessible water taxis. Call (281) 367-1151 or visit btd.org/waterway .htm to find out where to board the water taxi, which traverses the man-made, 1.4-mile Woodlands Waterway.

Kayak on Lake Woodlands. 2101 Riva Row; (281) 210-3965. Rent a kayak, life jacket, and paddles at the Riva Row Boat House, and take yourself for a kayak ride around The Woodlands Waterway and Lake Woodlands. You'll look out on the wooded scenery that The Woodlands is known for, as well as shops and restaurants along the waterway. Kayak rentals cost $15 for the first hour, plus $5 per each additional hour.

The Spa at The Woodlands Resort. 2301 N. Millbend Dr.; (281) 364-6386; woodlands resort.com. Unwind and rejuvenate at this luxurious spa. Enjoy a couples' massage, a seasonal glow scrub, a manicure and pedicure, an acid-peel facial, a detox footbath, or one of the other many heavenly spa services or packages. Get more for your money with a visit to the Eucalyptus steam room and a sampling of the spa's dried fruits and teas.

Town Green Park. 2099 Lake Robbins Dr.; (281) 363-2447; thewoodlandscvb.com. Forget Manhattan's Central Park. The 4 acres of green space in Town Green Park are every bit as tranquil as those found in New York's most famous refuge. Situated along The Woodlands Waterway, Town Green Park boasts plenty of space for tossing a Frisbee, kicking a ball, sunbathing, and picnicking. There's also lots of room for children to run around in the Children's Garden, a maze of tall hedges that features large storybooks filled with modern takes on *Aesop's Fables.* An entertainment stage at the park is frequently used for community events.

The Woodlands Children's Museum. 4775 W. Panther Creek Dr.; (281) 465-0955; woodlandschildrensmuseum.org. Each year, more than 60,000 people visit The Woodlands Children's Museum to enjoy some hands-on fun. The museum features an array of interactive activities and exhibits that teach children about history, the arts, science, health, nature, and the environment.

where to shop

Charming Charlie. 9595 Six Pines Dr., Ste. 1140; (281) 465-4468; charmingcharlie.com. The fashions and accessories in this boutique are ingeniously arranged by color to make accessorizing a snap. While the apparel and jewelry items are high quality, prices are more reasonable than at other nearby boutiques.

Diva Boutique. 4526 Research Forest Dr., Ste. 125; (281) 364-7467; shopdivaboutique .com. Women shop here to find out what's in style—and to stay in style. Every pair of pants or jeans, blouse, dress, skirt, and accessory here is carefully chosen to create a selection that appeals to both funky and classic tastes.

Francesca's Collection. 9595 Six Pines Dr., Ste. 870; (281) 419-3750; francescas.com. This privately owned retail chain boutique takes pride in presenting unique, one-of-a-kind women's fashions and accessories as well as gift items and fragrances.

Maggies. 9595 Six Pines Dr., Ste. 680; (281) 419-4464; maggies.com. Maggies offers a huge array of specialty items including fragrances, beauty products, gift and home decor accessories, and jewelry by Dogeared and Virgins Saints & Angels.

Market Street. 9595 Six Pines Dr.; (281) 419-4774; marketstreet-thewoodlands.com. The perfect place to get a breath of fresh air, this outdoor shopping district is home to dozens of stores ranging from Sur La Table and Gap Kids to Orvis, Thomas Markle Jewelers, and Ann Taylor. There are also several restaurants and bars. Take a break by sitting under one of the more than 500 trees or frolicking in the lush green grass outside the shops.

The Woodlands Mall. 1201 Lake Woodlands Dr.; (281) 363-3409; thewoodlandsmall .com. More than a hundred stores make their home at The Woodlands Mall, which is anchored by Macy's, JCPenney, and Dillard's. The stores at the mall include a mix of upscale and less expensive shops, with everything from Urban Outfitters, Y'alls Texas Store, and Jos. A. Bank Clothier to Janie and Jack, James Avery Craftsman, and Anthropologie.

where to eat

Amerigo's Grille. 25250 Grogan's Park Dr.; (281) 362-0808; amerigos.com. One of the nicer restaurants in the area, Amerigo's serves classic Italian dishes, as well as more hip, gourmet Italian offerings like the capellini with crawfish and the Bosc pear salad with dried cranberries, Gorgonzola, and blueberry-pomegranate dressing. Unfortunately, the menu isn't very vegetarian-friendly. The service here is good. $$$.

Baker Street Pub and Grill. 25 Waterway Ave., Ste. 100; (281) 362-7431. Between the menu, the darts, and the dark wood paneling, this popular spot will make you feel like you're in the UK. The menu includes fish-and-chips, bangers and mash, shepherd's pie, and beers aplenty. And don't worry if you crave American fare: You can order burgers, sandwiches, soups, and salads, too. The pub often features live music, and there's almost always a game of pool or darts being played. Throughout football season, it's also a popular spot to watch the action. Need to get online? Baker Street Pub and Grill offers free wireless Internet. $$.

Crú. 9595 Six Pines Dr., Ste. 650; (281) 465-9463; cruawinebar.com. This European-inspired wine bar and cafe is best known for its selection of more than 300 wines, but you shouldn't discount the menu here. Those wanting smaller portions may opt for cheese-flight sharing plates such as roasted butternut squash, mussels, stone-fried pizza, or goat cheese beignets. If you want something more substantial, check out the dinner menu, which includes entrees such as pan-seared diver sea scallops or filet mignon with rosemary chianti sauce. Crú is open for lunch and dinner. $$–$$$.

Crush. 20 Waterway Ave., Ste. 200; (281) 362-7874; thecrushbar.com. This upscale restaurant and bar features a chef-inspired menu with flavorful dishes from around the world such as truffled, forest-wild, mushroom flat-bread pizza; Black Forest ham with double-cream brie and arugula panini; and dark chocolate and white, dried cherry truffles with fresh mixed berries. Of course, for many, the main attraction here is the wine, and the options are plentiful. Don't worry if you're not an oenophile, though: The friendly waiters here will help you find the perfect wine. $$–$$$.

Grimaldi's Coal Brick-Oven Pizza. 20 Waterway Ave. at the Town Center; (281) 465-3500; grimaldispizzeria.com. For years, Zagat has been giving high ratings to this small chain, which opened a location at The Woodlands Town Center in the fall of 2009. The hand-tossed, coal oven–baked pizzas and calzones are the main attraction, and you can wash them down with a drink from the extensive beer and wine list. Call ahead if you plan to dine with a party of 5 or more. $$–$$$.

Hubbell & Hudson Market & Bistro. 24 Waterway Ave., Ste. 125; (831) 203-5600; hubbell andhudson.com. This upscale restaurant serves what it calls "progressive new American bistro" food. Among the dishes are pad thai made with house-made noodles, lobster club sandwiches served with frisée and homemade double-cut fries, and a seared sashimi tuna salad topped with spicy mango habañero salsa, though the offerings change frequently to include seasonal produce. The menu includes several specialty drinks, martinis, and fine wines. Call ahead to make reservations, and leave the shorts, jeans, and T-shirts at home. Hubbell & Hudson serves lunch, dinner, and Sunday brunch. Be sure to browse the market before or after your meal to check out the great selection of produce, handmade meats, and sustainably raised fish. $$$.

Jasper's. 9595 Six Pines Dr., Ste. 900; (281) 298-6600; jaspers-restaurant.com. If you're looking for a chic, romantic restaurant, this is a great option. Jasper's serves gourmet southern-inspired dishes like prosciutto wrapped "shrimp 'n' grits," aged Gouda–ham mac 'n' cheese, sweet corn–crusted flounder, and slow-smoked baby back ribs, which

Bon Appetit magazine named some of the country's best ribs. The restaurant is open for brunch, lunch, and dinner. Brunch dishes like crab cake Benedict and vanilla french toast with apple-wood bacon are served until 3 p.m. Dress nicely. $$$.

Masa's Sushi & Robata Bar. 4775 W. Panther Creek Dr., Ste. 430; (281) 298-5688; sushimasahouston.com. From outside, Masa's looks like a hole-in-the-wall, but step inside and you'll discover this is a clean sushi restaurant that serves fresh fish and tasty rolls. The menu includes all of the soups, salads, appetizers, and entrees you'd expect, along with several traditional American sushi rolls. Masa's also has a selection of funky rolls with names like Texas Panther Creek, Cochran Crossing, and Sterling Ridge—all local neighborhoods. $$$.

The Olive Oil Restaurant. 373 Sawdust Rd.; (281) 367-0114; oliveoilgreekrestaurant .com. For more than 30 years, this Greek-American restaurant has been making people say, *"Opa!"* Every dish here is made using imported spices and fresh herbs, meats, fish, and produce. The menu includes the full range of Greek options, including salads, lamb kabobs, vegetarian moussaka, Greek salad, and well-seasoned gyros. Get an extra taste of Greek culture when you dine here on Saturday night. That's when The Olive Oil Restaurant features live music, Greek dancing, belly-dancing shows, and even belly-dancing lessons. $$–$$$.

where to stay

Hyatt Market Street, The Woodlands. 9595 Six Pines Dr.; (281) 203-5005; market streetthewoodlands.hyatt.com. Formerly the AVIA Boutique Hotel, this property located in

satisfy your sweet tooth

*Just 10 minutes up the road from The Woodlands, in the suburb of Shenandoah, you'll find some of the tastiest pies in the Houston area. **Pie Town Cafe & Dessert Shop** serves up a long list of creme pies—topped with meringue, if you like—as well as fruit pies and seasonal favorites like chocolate pumpkin swirl, peppermint pie, and sweet-potato pecan pie. The menu even includes several sugar-free fruit pies in flavors such as pecan, peach, cherry, and apple-cranberry-pecan. The pies range from $14.50 to $16.50. Pie Town recently expanded its menu to include soups and sandwiches. To get to pie heaven, head about 3 miles north on I-45. Pie Town is located in the Venice-inspired Portofino Shopping Center at 19075 I-45 South, No. 111D. For more information call (936) 321-3336 or visit pietown.net.*

the heart of The Woodlands action is now part of the Hyatt family of hotels. It sits right by Market Street, surrounded by some of the area's best restaurants and shops. Guests enjoy personal attention and sleek accommodations, including an outdoor terrace, a pool, and a 24-hour fitness center. $$$.

The Woodlands Resort & Conference Center. 2301 N. Millbend Dr.; (281) 367-1100; woodlandsresort.com. Whether you need to escape for a day, a weekend, or several days, you'll find few options better than this one. The resort's offerings include 2 lush golf courses, a full-service salon and spa, 21 tennis courts (4 indoors), 180 miles of hiking and biking trails, a fitness center, waterslides, 3 restaurants, and a full-service bar and lounge. The Woodlands Resort & Conference Center has 440 rooms and suites. $$.

day trip 02

![north image]

lone star land:
conroe, montgomery, plantersville

conroe

Located in Texas's Piney Woods, Conroe first made its mark in the lumber and oil industries. Today, however, Conroe is best known as the home of Lake Conroe, one of the state's most popular destinations for boating, fishing, and other water sports. Outdoor activities also abound at W. Goodrich Jones State Forest.

While Conroe was once a place that Houstonians visited on the weekends or during holidays, the number of permanent residents has grown as Houston has expanded outward in recent years. Yet Conroe still retains a small-town charm, which is evident when visiting some of the local theaters, shops, restaurants, and the Heritage Museum of Montgomery County.

getting there

Conroe is located about 40 miles north of Houston, off I-45. Take the Conroe/TX 105 exit and follow the signs to get into town.

where to go

The Corner Pub. 302 N. Main St.; (936) 788-2390; thecornerpubinconroe.com. If you're spending an evening in Conroe, head down to The Corner Pub to check out live music,

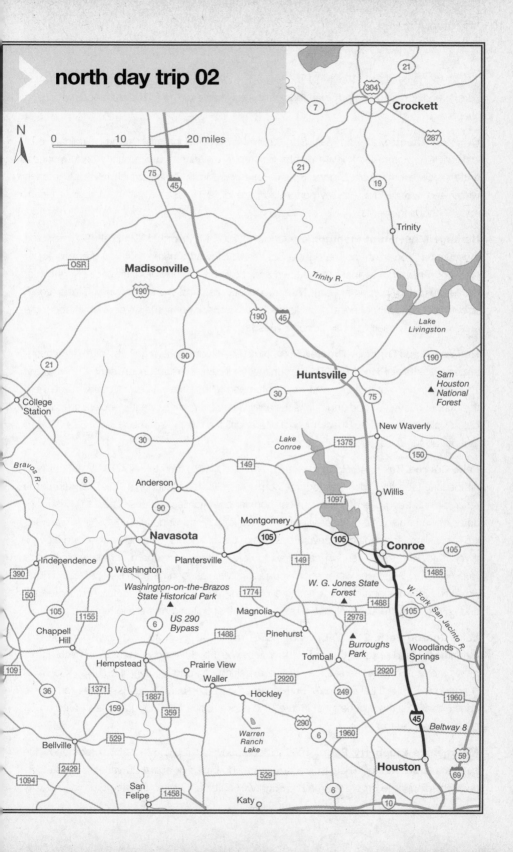

N

0   10   20 miles

21

304

7

Crockett

287

75

45

Trinity

Madisonville

OSR

190

190   45

Trinity R.

19

Lake
Livingston

21

90

190

College
Station

30

Huntsville

30

75

Sam
Houston
National
Forest

New Waverly

Bravos R.

149

Lake
Conroe

1375

150

6

Anderson

1097

Willis

90

Montgomery

Navasota

105   105

Conroe   105

Independence

Washington

Plantersville

149

1485

390

Washington-on-the-Brazos
State Historical Park

1774

W. G. Jones State
Forest

1488

50

105   1155

US 290
Bypass

Magnolia

2978

105

Chappell
Hill

1488

Pinehurst

Burroughs
Park

Woodlands
Springs

Hempstead

Prairie View

Tomball

109

36

1371

Waller

2920

2920

1960

159

1887

Hockley

249

45   Beltway 8

529

359

290   6   1960

59

Bellville

Warren
Ranch
Lake

69

2429

1094

529

Houston

San
Felipe

1458

Katy

6

10

poetry readings, and comedy sketches. Visit the website or call to find out about upcoming events.

Crighton Theatre. 234 N. Main St.; (936) 441-7469; crightontheatre.org. Originally built in 1934, this restored vaudeville theater hosts plays, dance and symphony performances, and musical events, including the Sounds of Texas Music Series, which takes place each winter and spring. Elvis Presley performed here in 1950. Call or visit the website to learn about upcoming events.

Heritage Museum of Montgomery County. 1506 I-45 North; (936) 539-6873; heritage museum.us. You might not recognize Charles B. Stewart's name, but you probably know his work. Stewart, a resident of the town and the first secretary of state for the Republic of Texas, designed the present-day Texas Lone Star flag and the state seal of Texas. Learn about his life and work here and, while you're at it, check out some other exhibits about the area's history. Closed Sunday through Tuesday.

Heritage Place Outdoor Theater. 500 Collins St.; cityofconroe.org/Parks-and-Recreation/ pr-parks/Heritage-Place.html. This amphitheater hosts a free concert series on the first Thursday each month from April to September. Other special events take place here throughout the year. Food and drinks are available for purchase on-site; coolers are allowed but not glass containers. Check the website or call the City of Conroe at (936) 522-3804 to find out about upcoming events.

Lake Conroe. Take I-45 North to exit 87/Conroe/TX 105; then take TX 105 West until you hit the lake (about 8 miles); lakeconroe.com. Since its completion in 1973, this man-made reservoir has been one of Texas's most popular boating destinations. The 21,000 surface acres of water also offer abundant opportunities for sailing, windsurfing, kayaking, waterski-ing, Jet Skiing, and fishing for several species of bass, crappie, channel catfish, and bluegill. If you're looking to windsurf or sail, head to Lake Conroe's southern portion, which tends to be windier. Whatever water sport you prefer, visit lakeconroe.com before heading out. You'll find information about upcoming events, as well as the places to sail, fish, water-ski, and kayak. The site also includes a list of places that sell and rent equipment.

Lake Conroe Park. 210 W. Davis St.; (936) 788-8302. Want to enjoy Lake Conroe with the family? Head to Lake Conroe Park, where you'll find fishing piers, 2 swimming areas, picnic tables and grills, horseshoe pits, volleyball courts, and a playground. Also known as "Park on the Lake," Lake Conroe Park charges a $2-per-person admission fee for guests ages 5 to 65; all other guests get in free. The park is closed on Monday. It is located on TX 105, 7 miles west of I-45.

Moorhead's Blueberry Farm. 19531 Moorhead Rd.; (281) 572-1265; moorheadsblue berryfarm.com. At this 20-acre blueberry farm, you can pick about 20 varieties of blueber-ries, including large crops of Premier, Brightwell, Tifblue, Climax, Garden Blue, and Becky

Blue blueberries. The farm doesn't use pesticides and charges $2 per pound, which includes buckets for holding your berries during picking. Moorhead's is open daily during the season, usually late May through mid-July.

Owen Theatre. 225 Metcalf St.; (936) 539-4090. A staple of the Conroe arts scene, this 1940 downtown theater hosts live performances by the Crighton Players (crightonplayers .org), a volunteer-run theatrical group that puts on plays and musicals each year. Recent shows have included *The Odd Couple, The Sound of Music,* and *Oliver!* With enough seating for just 250 people, the newly renovated theater boasts an intimate, community-oriented atmosphere.

Southern Star Brewing Company. 1207 N. FM 3083 East; (936) 441-2739; southernstar brewery.com. Southern Star Brewing Company opened in 2008 and began producing the Pine Belt Pale Ale. The brewery now produces several other beers, including the Bombshell Blonde, the Por-Am 2012 Double IPA, and the Buried Hatchet Stout. Visit the brewery on Saturday at 1 p.m. for a free tour and tasting. You can also purchase brats, burgers, and other food during the tour. In October, Southern Star hosts its own Oktoberfest, complete with live music, beer, and brats. Visit the website or call for more information.

Tut's. 711 Madeley St.; (713) 539-1500; tutsconroe.com. For more than 25 years, this icehouse has been *the* place to see live music in Conroe. Why? Because Tut's draws some of the area's best Texas Americana, zydeco, rock, and R & B acts. Throughout the year, Tut's also hosts special events such as Halloween costume parties and DJs spinning oldies but goodies. The owner, Charles Tullos, is also one of the founding members of Conroe's annual Cajun Catfish Festival, which takes place each October (see listing in the Festivals & Celebrations appendix). Visit the website or call to find out about upcoming shows.

W. Goodrich Jones State Forest. 1328 FM 1488; (936) 273-2261; texasforestservice .tamu.edu. Named after the "Father of Texas Forestry," W. Goodrich Jones, this 1,722-acre

just like huck finn

During your trip to Lake Conroe, take a small detour to nearby Willis. Located just 8 miles north of Conroe off I-45, Willis is the home base of the paddle wheeler South-ern Empress, a replica of 19th-century stern-wheeler riverboats. Take a relaxing ride along the lake while you enjoy lunch or dinner, watch the sunset, and dance. It's probably best, though, not to try to do all three at once. Call ahead (936-588-3000) to make reservations. The Southern Empress docks at the Sunset Harbor Resort at Seven Coves, 7041 Kingston Cove Ln. Visit southernempress.com for more information.

> ## art on your seat
>
> *As you walk around downtown Conroe, keep your eyes peeled for the painted benches scattered along the sidewalks. Local artists decorated these to highlight Conroe's history, culture, and attractions. If you don't want to go on a treasure hunt in search of these benches, stop into the Conroe Convention & Visitors Bureau (505 W. Davis St.) to pick up a brochure with their locations.*

forest is an excellent place to spot rare birds. To date, more than 150 species have been identified here, including many red-cockaded woodpeckers. You'll also see a variety of plants and other animals as you wander along Sweetleaf Nature Trail amid the pines and hardwoods. Visit the website to download a park map.

where to shop

Barbara's Resale Shop. 1108 N. Loop 336 West, Ste. P; (936) 494-1060; barbarasresale shop.com. This recently expanded resale shop in Conroe's Sunpark Center sells reasonably priced secondhand women's, men's, and teens' clothing, shoes, accessories, and home decor on consignment. Barbara's Resale Shop has a sizeable selection of plus-size apparel. Closed Sunday.

Louis E. Wheeler Art Gallery. 227 N. Main St.; (936) 597-6213 or (936) 648-8097; louis wheeler.com. Local Conroe artist Louis Wheeler has his own art gallery across the street from the Crighton Theatre. Inside, you'll find an extensive collection of fine-art images of land, sea, and flowers from Texas, Greece, Japan, and California's Central Coast.

Outlets at Conroe. 1111 League Line Rd.; (936) 756-0904; outletsatconroe.com. Here you'll find outlet stores from brands such as Carter's, OshKosh B'Gosh, Izod, and Guess. The mall leaves much to be desired, though, since many stores are vacant. Visit during the summer months, and you might find a farmer selling delicious peaches, tomatoes, or other veggies out of the back of a truck.

Wild Birds Unlimited. 27590 I-45 North; (281) 298-7900; conroe.wbu.com. Find a unique birdhouse—and birdseed to fill it—here. Stop in and you're also likely to get plenty of useful birding insight and advice for turning your backyard into a bird habitat.

where to eat

Burger Fresh. 804 Gladstell Rd., Ste. 110; (936) 756-4414; iwantmyburgerfresh.com. Conroe residents aren't the only ones who love the juicy burgers here. In 2009, *Texas*

Monthly ranked Burger Fresh's towering burgers the 13th best in the state. The menu includes burgers made of beef, buffalo, and elk, as well as waffle fries, onion rings, and Tater Tots. Burger Fresh also serves bunless alternatives like the veggie burger, cheesy cheeseburger salad, and grilled chicken salad. Burger Fresh offers daily specials of burgers, fries, and a beverage for $8.99. $–$$.

Carmelitas. 109 W. Davis St.; (936) 539-3323. Reasonably priced, flavorful Tex-Mex is to be expected at Carmelitas, which serves breakfast and lunch. Dishes here are nothing fancy, but customers tend to leave satisfied with everything from handmade tamales to enchiladas. $$.

Conroe Lunch Box. 909 Houston St.; (936) 539-MEAL; conroelunchbox.com. At this Conroe institution, the Canada family has offered their Blue Plate Special and other quick and satisfying meals since 1935. The no-frills diner is a friendly place to grab lunch. $.

Egg Cetera. 3010 W. Davis St.; (936) 539-3447. This Conroe breakfast favorite makes its home in an old Waffle House, but the menu is better than that of the previous tenant. You've got your pick of pancakes, waffles, skillets, and omelets—made largely from fresh organic produce. $.

Joe's Pizza. 1604 N. Frazier St.; (936) 760-9002; joespizzaconroe.com. Joe's creates crowd-pleasing oven-fired New York–style pizza, but that's just the beginning of an extensive Italian menu that includes standbys like chicken cacciatore, veal parmigiana, shrimp fettuccine Alfredo, lasagna, and ravioli. A large wine list complements the selections. Joe's also features daily lunch specials Tuesday through Friday for a measly $6.75. $–$$.

Margarita's Mexican Restaurant. 1027 N. Loop 336 West; (936) 756-8771; margaritas conroe.com. Margarita's serves your basic, greasy Tex-Mex—enchiladas, fajitas, quesadillas, and nachos. You can certainly find better Tex-Mex in Houston, but if you're in Conroe, this is a decent and inexpensive option, especially if you order a margarita. $–$$.

McKenzie's Barbeque. 1501 N. Frazier St.; (936) 539-4300; mckenziesbarbeque.com. This rustic barbecue joint serves up beef, ham, turkey, sausage, and pork by the pound and on sandwiches, along with slaw, corn on the cob, beans, and baked potatoes. Don't let the digs fool you: The food here wins award after award. $–$$.

Vernon's Kuntry Bar-B-Que. 5000 W. Davis St.; (936) 539-3000. Operated by the Bowers family, locally famous for their Kuntry Katfish restaurant down the street, Vernon's offers inexpensive barbecue, ribs, sausage, and chicken served with trusty sides like coleslaw, beans, and fries. Vernon's has an authentic down-home feel with faded photographs on the wall and picnic tables full of local diners at lunchtime. $$.

Vernon's Kuntry Katfish. 5901 W. Davis St.; (936) 760-3386; kuntrykatfish.com. Since its opening in 1984, this family-run restaurant has been known as the place to go in Conroe

for fried catfish. Although Vernon Bowers passed away in 2001, the Bowers family still operates the restaurant, offering catfish, fried pickles, fried scallops, fried oysters, frog legs, and
some Creole dishes. $$.

where to stay

Lake Conroe KOA. 19785 TX 105 West; (936) 582-1200; koa.com. Bring your RV or rent
a cottage at these clean camping accommodations. Guests enjoy free fishing in a stocked
pond, a game room, a pool, and a waterslide—and a location just minutes from the lake. $.

montgomery

Montgomery may comprise just a tiny part of the Lone Star State, but it has a big legacy in
Texas. In 1839, 2 years after Stephen F. Austin established Montgomery as his second col-
ony, the first Republic of Texas flag and the state seal were designed here. Their maker? Dr.
Charles Bellinger Stewart—a Montgomery resident, the Republic of Texas's first secretary
of state, and the first signatory to Texas's Declaration of Independence. Montgomery later
went on to share a name with the county it (along with Conroe) occupied, Montgomery
County. In 1997, then-governor George W. Bush signed a resolution declaring Montgomery
County the "Birthplace of the Lone Star Flag."

Today, Montgomery sits in western Montgomery County on the southwestern edge
of Sam Houston National Forest. You can still see remnants of Montgomery's storied past
while shopping and dining in Montgomery's downtown district, which is composed largely
of restored 19th-century buildings.

getting there

From Conroe, head west on TX 105 for about 15 miles until you reach Montgomery. The
town, which sits on the southwestern edge of Sam Houston National Forest, is located at
the junction of TX 105 and FM 149.

where to go

Cedar Brake Park. On TX 105, a few blocks west of the downtown district. With its play-
ground, picnic areas, grills, and old oaks, this pretty park is a great place to unwind. It's also
one of the few parks in the state that was designed to be fully accessible for wheelchair-
bound and physically challenged visitors.

Cork This! Winery. 21123 Eva St., Ste. 100; (936) 597-4030; corkthiswinery.com. Sip
custom-made wines, or better yet make your own wine and custom labels at this boutique
winery. Eighteen different wines are available for tasting, and most can be purchased to take

montgomery street names, decoded

Inside Montgomery city limits, TX 105 is often referred to as Eva Street.

home. The offerings include a little of everything—Syrah, Cabernet, Chardonnay, Merlot, Pinot Noir, Riesling, and Zinfandel.

Lone Star First Saturday. On the corner of FM 149 and College Street; (936) 597-5004; historicmontgomerytexas.com. On the first Saturday of the month, Montgomery hosts Lone Star First Saturday, an old-fashioned farmers' market coupled with live acoustic music. Stock up on locally grown fruits, veggies, plants, and eggs, as well as homemade pastries, jams, pickles, and salsas. You'll even find a few artisans selling their work. The market runs from about 9 a.m. until 2 p.m., with musicians jamming on store and restaurant stoops starting around 10 a.m. Feel free to join in by bringing your own harmonica, violin, or other instrument of choice. In the event of bad weather, Lone Star First Saturday may be canceled.

N. H. Davis Pioneer Complex & Museum. 308 Liberty St.; (936) 597-4360; historic montgomerytexas.com. In 1831, W. C. Clark built a log house just north of Montgomery. Two decades later, attorney Nat Hart Davis—who had received the cabin from Clark's family as payment for his legal work—moved the house to its current location. Today, you can tour the structure, which was renovated several times during the 1800s. In the process, you'll learn about the history of the area. Closed Sunday through Tuesday.

where to shop

Branding Iron Gifts & Antiques. 212 Liberty St.; (936) 449-5844 or (936) 597-4442; brandingiron-schoolhouse.com. Branding Iron sells antler art, cowboy hats, western cookbooks, Texas flag shirts, stuffed armadillos, spurs, antiques, and authentic Texas flags. The shop's sister store, The Olde School House (see below), is located next door.

The Clover Patch. 14356 Liberty St.; (936) 597-4400. The Clover Patch sells all sorts of unique and antique finds, including collectibles, military memorabilia, furniture, pottery, glassware, and furniture. Closed Monday.

4 Hip Chicks. 15320 Highway 105 West, #116; (936) 588-2525. Located in Montgomery's Waterpointe Center, this trendy shop carries an eclectic mix of designer fashions and casual creations along with stylish accessories, jewelry, local artwork, and gift items suitable for

> ## show yourself around
>
> *While you're visiting the N.H. Davis Pioneer Complex & Museum or shopping in one of Montgomery's many stores, grab a copy of the self-guided City Tour and Shopping Guide, which will show you around and give you the backstory on some of the area's historical buildings. The museum serves as a branch of the Conroe Convention & Visitors Bureau (936-522-3500; conroecvb.net).*

all ages. Owner Deanna Holik, who opened the boutique in 2009, named it for herself, her mother, and her two daughters. Open daily.

Front Porch Friends. 202A McCown St.; (936) 597-8636. Home and garden decor will greet you from the porch of this cute shop. Inside, you'll find books, gourmet foods, gifts, cards, Tyler Candles, some Texas decor, and goodies for women and babies. Closed Sunday and Monday.

Garrett House Antiques and Doll Hospital. 315 Caroline St.; (936) 597-5400; garrett houseantiques.com. Antiquers, take note: You'll find a great selection of old toys and dolls here, along with furniture dating back to the 1800s, art glass, coins, and Roseville pottery.

Kerr's Western Interiors. 21499 Eva St.; (936) 597-4000; kerrswest.com. Here you'll find upholstered furniture, as well as home decor, cowhide accessories, and plenty of Texas decor and gifts. If you have your heart set on a cowhide purse, tooled-leather briefcase, or a wrought-iron chandelier, you'll find it here. The shop is open Monday through Saturday, 10 a.m. to 5 p.m. or by appointment.

Liberty Bell Antiques. 14363 Liberty St.; (936) 597-4606; libertybellantiques.com. Arguably the best antiques shop in town, this well-organized store sells beautiful jewelry, Depression glass, silver, collectibles, yard art, and more. They also offer appraisals. Closed Monday.

The Olde School House. 306 E. Eva St.; (936) 597-4442; brandingiron-schoolhouse.com. For forty years, black children in the area attended school in this building, which was previously located in nearby Dobbin. In 1995, the old schoolhouse was moved to Montgomery, where it was restored and reopened as a popular gift shop. Inside you'll find a hodgepodge of kitschy home decor, antiques, Texas decor, collectibles, jewelry, wrought-iron Texas longhorns, gourmet food, and clothes for women and children. Visit the website to print out a coupon for 10 percent off your purchase. The shop's sister store, Branding Iron Gifts & Antiques, is located next door.

The Rancher's Daughter. 14387 Liberty St.; (936) 449-4100; ranchersdaughter.net. Mother and daughter owners Rendy and Taylor Kerr are indeed both ranch-raised Texans and delight in showcasing "all things fine and funky" in their shop. Their collection includes wine and wine items, home decor, and western-themed apparel. Closed Sunday and Monday.

where to eat

Commodore Dining Room. 13301 Walden Rd.; (936) 582-4222; waldenonlakeconroe .com. If you're in the mood for a nice lunch or dinner overlooking Lake Conroe, this restaurant at the Yacht Club in the planned lakeside community of Walden has a lot to recommend it. You don't have to be a member of the club to dine here; just come hungry and leave the flip-flops and T-shirts behind ("appropriate club dining attire" is requested). Closed Monday and Tuesday. $$–$$$.

Kaiserhof European Restaurant. 10630 Commerce Row; (936) 448-4111; kaiserhofusa .com. Serving German and continental menu favorites, Kaiserhof brings an old-world menu to Montgomery. Favorites here include various schnitzels, bratwursts, potato dumplings, and spaetzle (German noodles), as well as other European dishes. If the weather is good, dine in the beer garden for a real German experience. $$–$$$.

Magnolia Diner. 19784 TX 105 West; (936) 582-1788; magnoliadiner.com. This Hollywood-themed diner serves up big portions of American favorites, including burgers, sandwiches, and salads. Food off the breakfast menu—think skillets, breakfast tacos, french toast, eggs, and ham—is also served all day. $.

Papa's on the Lake. 14632 TX 105 West; (936) 447-2500; papasonthelake.com. Dine at Papa's on the Lake and enjoy a side of entertainment with your meal. This popular destination sits right on the south shore of Lake Conroe and features live music, boat docks, sand volleyball, billiards and video games, volleyball, and a menu of sandwiches, burgers, and greasy appetizers. Some diners arrive here by boat. $–$$.

The Pizza Shack. 20873 Eva St., Ste. G; (936) 597-9488; pizzashack.net. Get your fill of some of the best specialty pizzas and calzones in the area at this family-run Italian restaurant. Or if you prefer, choose from one of the many other entrees—veal, pasta, subs, chicken, seafood, and steak. The menu also includes some "Healthier Choice" selections. $$.

Sam's Boat. 15250 TX 105, No. 150; (936) 588-1212; samsboat.com. Visit Sam's Boat and stay to enjoy live music, view sporting events on TV, or gaze at the Lake Conroe view. The extensive menu includes a mix of burgers, sandwiches, fresh seafood (some Cajun-style), Tex-Mex, and specialty drinks. $$.

The Vintage Garden Tea House. 304 Caroline St.; (936) 597-4004; vintagegardentea .com. Visit this quaint teahouse and garden for lunch or afternoon tea, and enjoy a taste of

> ## tee country

Montgomery and the surrounding areas are home to several beautiful golf courses. If you want to wrap up—or start—your visit with some time on the greens, check out the list of Montgomery golf courses at conroecvb.net.

small-town life. Rated one of the best teahouses in Texas, The Vintage Garden Tea House serves great salads, sandwiches, quiches, loose leaf tea, wine and cheese, and homemade desserts worth breaking your diet for. You can even eat in the garden. Traditional high tea is available with advance reservations. Stop in the gift shop after your meal. $–$$.

Wolfies. 14954 TX 105 West; (936) 588-8200; wolfiesusa.com. This restaurant and sports bar bills itself as the Crawfish Capital of the World, but the menu is filled with plenty of other seafood, salads, steaks, sandwiches, quesadillas, and, of course, wings. Outdoor seating is available for those who want a good view of the lake. $$–$$$.

where to stay

The Caroline House Bed and Breakfast. 811 Caroline St.; (936) 524-0406; thecaroline housebb.com. Guests here stay in one of 5 rooms decked out in country decor; each room has its own private bathroom. Breakfast is served in the main dining room—or if you prefer, the Garden Cottage—each morning. Wine and cheese are served daily, and guests have their choice of indoor and outdoor chairs for lounging and daydreaming. Innkeeper Mary Eckhart allows guests to bring small pets and children. $$ (private rooms), $$$ (Garden Cottage).

La Torretta Del Lago Resort and Spa. 600 La Torretta Blvd., just off TX 105; (936) 448-4400; latorrettalakeresort.com. Pamper yourself with a visit to La Torretta Del Lago, which sits on 300 acres of the Lake Conroe shore. Guests staying in the 445 lavish suites at this contemporary resort enjoy access to an 18-hole golf course, spa, tennis courts, a fitness center, a miniature golf course, a beach, kayaking, and several fine restaurants and lounges. $$.

plantersville

Plantersville was founded around 1885 along the Gulf, Colorado & Santa Fe Railway, giving it a big role in the regional agriculture scene. In those early days, Plantersville was also home to wagon-making efforts.

Today, the town has a population of just over 200, but its best-known resident isn't a person. It's the Texas Renaissance Festival, an elaborate theme park–like celebration that introduces thousands of 21st-century Texans to the sights, sounds, smells, and flavors of 16th-century England over 8 weekends each October and November. (See listing in the Festivals & Celebrations appendix to learn more about the Texas Renaissance Festival.)

Of course, while the Renaissance Festival may have put—or rather, kept—Plantersville on the map, it's certainly not the only reason to visit this town. A winery, orchard, and B&B—not to mention some small-town hospitality—make this agricultural town the perfect spot to wrap up your visit to the Conroe/Montgomery area.

Hungry travelers, take note: There aren't many places to eat in Plantersville, so you may want to consider grabbing something in Montgomery or dining at the Bernhardt Winery.

getting there

From Montgomery, take TX 105 West/Eva Street west about 11 miles and then take a left at FM 1774 South. Keep your eyes peeled for the Plantersville signs. The town is so small that you're likely to miss it if you don't pay close attention.

where to go

Bernhardt Winery. 9043 CR 204; (936) 894-9829 or (936) 520-8684; bernhardtwinery .com. Wind down your day trip with a visit to this local winery, where you can participate in a group or private tasting, and nibble on some lunch, dinner, or dessert. You can even sip your wine while atop the hill or under the winery's old pecan trees. On Sunday evenings from April through November, Bernhardt Winery hosts the Lawn Concert Series, which features top entertainers from across the state. The winery also has its own B&B, which is listed in the Where to Stay section below.

St. Mary Catholic Church. 8227 CR 205; (936) 894-2223; smsj.org. This wooden country-Gothic structure dates back to 1917 when the original church building was struck by lightning and burned. The church features a colorful interior covered with hand-stenciled designs on the arched ceiling, walls, and columns and with the original wooden pews. Another notable feature is an original painting of the Lamb with Adoring Angels, which adorns the ceiling above the altar. The church is available for viewing by appointment.

where to eat

Allphin Barbeque & Smokehouse. 15172 TX 105; (936) 894-3444. This Plantersville joint is nothing fancy, but the barbecue, ribs, chicken, and burgers keep locals coming back for more. If you're really hungry, opt for the Special Dinner, which includes barbecued beef, hot links, and ribs plus two sides and bread. Sides include potato salad, cole slaw, green beans, and pinto beans. Closed Sunday. $.

Relay Station Restaurant. 15680 TX 105 East; (936) 894-3111. If you're insanely hungry, this rustic restaurant will almost surely satiate. Portions are huge, and the menu includes plenty of burgers and fried dishes, such as fried mushrooms and chicken-fried steak. If you can eat a 5-pound, 5-ounce steak in 75 minutes here, it's free (call ahead if you plan to take this challenge). $–$$.

where to stay

The Loft. 9043 CR 204; (936) 894-9829 or (936) 520-8684; bernhardtwinery.com. Turn your day trip into a romantic getaway by spending a night or two above Bernhardt Winery in a beautiful Tuscan-style guest room. Guests enjoy a complimentary bottle of wine, hors d'oeuvres at sunset, continental breakfast, wireless Internet, a striking hilltop view, and first-class service. $$.

day trip 03

north

sam's town:
huntsville

huntsville

To many people, Huntsville is best known as the headquarters of the Texas prison system and the state's execution chamber. While the Texas Prison Museum—and the chance to gaze at the state's oldest prison—is certainly worth a visit, Texas history buffs will find many more reasons to visit this hospitable town. Founded in 1835—a year before Texas declared its independence—Huntsville's story is, in essence, Texas's story. Huntsville was also the adopted home of General Sam Houston and many settlers from Alabama, Tennessee, and Virginia. Today, Huntsville continues to honor its most famous resident at the Sam Houston Memorial Museum Complex and the late general's educational namesake, Sam Houston State University, giving the town a vibe that is both youthful and historic.

getting there

Located just off I-45 North, Huntsville is about 70 miles north of Houston and 30 miles north of Conroe. In fact you can shift from I-45 to US 75 at Conroe. The city itself sits on the northwestern boundary of Sam Houston National Forest, which makes for some beautiful wooded scenery. Don't worry if you accidentally stop reading the signs: You'll know it's time to exit when you see the gigantic statue of Sam Houston off the highway.

When you reach downtown, be aware that the name of US 75 (aka Highway 75) changes to "Sam Houston Avenue."

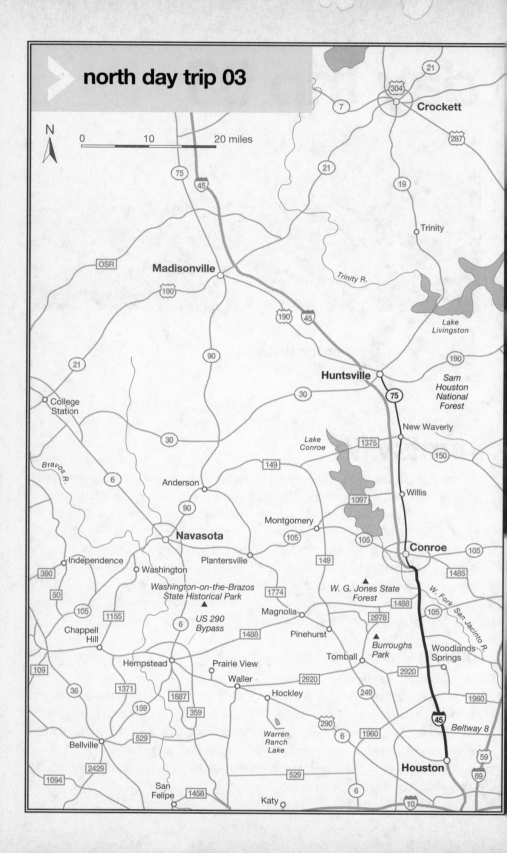

north day trip 03

N

0   10   20 miles

Crockett

21
304
7
287

19

Trinity

75
45

Trinity R.

Madisonville

190

190 45

Lake
Livingston

21

90

Huntsville

190

30

75

Sam
Houston
National
Forest

College
Station

30

New Waverly

150

Lake
Conroe

1375

Bravos R.

6

Anderson

149

1097

Willis

90

Montgomery

Navasota

105

105

Conroe

105

Independence

390

Washington

Plantersville

149

1485

50

Washington-on-the-Brazos
State Historical Park

1774

W. G. Jones State
Forest

W. Fork San Jacinto R.

105

1155

US 290
Bypass

Magnolia

1488

105

Chappell
Hill

6

Pinehurst

2978

Burroughs
Park

Woodlands
Springs

1488

Hempstead

Prairie View

Tomball

109

Waller

2920

2920

1960

36

1371

Hockley

249

45

Beltway 8

159

1887

290

6

1960

59

529

Bellville

Warren
Ranch
Lake

Houston

69

2429

San
Felipe

1094

1458

529

6

Katy

10

where to go

Blue Lagoon. 649 Pinedale Rd. (take exit 123 from I-45 and head 4 miles east); (936) 438-8888; bluelagoonscuba.net. Hey, scuba divers: This artesian spring–fed rock quarry offers clear blue water and sunken boats and planes for your diving pleasure. The beaches have just a mild slope, so it's easy to walk into the water for your dive. Certification is required to dive here. Gear is available for rental on-site; there's also an air station and concession stand.

Cabin on the Square. 1105 University Ave.; (936) 435-1091; huntsvilletx.gov. This simple log cabin was originally called Roberts-Farris Cabin when Allen Roberts had it built for his stepfather, Hezekiah Farris, after they moved to Texas in the mid-1840s. Local lore suggests that a roving builder may have constructed the cabin, which shares the same square-hewn logs and half-dovetail notches of other cabins and buildings around town. The cabin belonged to the Farris family for six generations and was moved to different locations over the years. In 2001, after spending 60 years as a storage shed, the cabin was donated to the City of Huntsville, which moved it to the town square with the help of Sam Houston State University students. The cabin is open to visitors Thursday through Saturday from 10 a.m. to 2 p.m. During that time, local artisans sell quilts and other handmade items here.

Gibbs-Powell Home & Museum. 1228 11th St. at Avenue M; (936) 295-2914; walker countyhistory.org/wc-museum.php. Early Huntsville businessman Thomas Gibbs built this Greek Revival–style house in 1862 and often welcomed his friend Sam Houston for visits. Now a registered Texas landmark, the house has also been named an archaeological landmark by the Texas Antiquities Committee. The house is open to visitors from noon to 4 p.m. Friday and Saturday and by appointment. For more information contact the Walker County Historical Museum, which maintains the house, at (936) 291-3581.

HEARTS, The Veterans Museum of Texas. 463 TX 75 North; (936) 295-5959; hearts museum.com. HEARTS, short for Helping Every American Remember Through Serving, seeks to commemorate military veterans with an interactive museum. To this end, the 5,000-square-foot space houses an extensive collection of war memorabilia and correspondence. Oral presentations teach younger generations about previous wars and the men and women who fought in them. Closed Sunday.

Huntsville Community Theatre. 1023 12th St.; (936) 291-7933; huntsvillecommunity theatre.org. This theater is a local labor of love, with Huntsville residents doing everything from acting and designing costumes to creating props and running the box office. Each year, the group produces about 4 shows—a mix of musicals and plays. Call or visit the website to learn about upcoming shows. Both matinee and evening performances are offered.

Huntsville State Park. State Park Road 40; (936) 295-5644; tpwd.state.tx.us. Located 6 miles southwest of Huntsville, this 2,000-plus-acre park offers plenty of opportunities for hiking, camping, biking, studying plants and animals native to the East Texas Piney Woods, and fishing in Lake Raven. To reach Huntsville State Park, take I-45 North to exit 109; then drive west along State Park Road 40 until you reach the park.

Oakwood Cemetery. 9th Street at Avenue I; (936) 295-8113. This cemetery is the final resting place of General Sam Houston, as well as Texas pioneers and Union and Confederate soldiers. Visit the *Sam Houston Statue* and Visitors Center (listed below) to get a map for a self-guided tour, or download a self-guided walking tour map from the chamber of commerce's website (huntsvilletexas.com) so that you can spot the headstones of the cemetery's most famous residents.

Sam Houston Memorial Museum and Park Complex. 1402 19th St.; (936) 294-1832; samhoustonmemorialmuseum.com. Honor the memory of General Sam Houston with a visit to this museum and park. The complex sits on 15 acres that once belonged to General Sam Houston, Texas's first president, who defeated General Santa Anna's Mexican troops in 1836 to win Texas its independence. The 8 buildings occupying the land include General Houston's law office, a replica of the Woodland Home kitchen, and 2 period-furnished homes in which Houston lived (the Woodland Home and the Steamboat House, where Houston died). Blacksmithing, pottery making, weaving, and spinning demonstrations often take place on the weekends. In late April or early May, the museum hosts the General Sam Houston Folk Fest. Closed Monday.

Sam Houston Statue **and Visitors Center.** 7600 TX 75 South; (936) 291-9726; sam houstonstatue.org. General Sam Houston, who led Texas revolutionaries to defeat the Mexican army and win Texas's independence in 1836, may *seem* larger than life when you hear or read about him, but this 67-foot statue version of him actually *is* larger—much larger—than life. Built by Huntsville native David Adickes using 67,000 pounds of concrete,

take a hike

Huntsville sits near the edge of Sam Houston National Forest, where wooded beauty abounds. Check out this scenic area by hiking along the park's Lone Star Hiking Trail, where you can fish, swim, or have a picnic. If you prefer to stay in the car, take a scenic drive along one of several Forest Service roads that offer a close-up look at the untouched Big Thicket. It can be difficult to navigate your way into the park, especially since some of the roads that lead to it don't appear on most maps. Your best bet is to call (936) 344-6205 or visit fs.fed.us to get a forest map and detailed directions.

this is the world's tallest statue of an American hero. To reach the statue, take exit 116 from I-45 North and travel east 1 mile to downtown Huntsville. The Huntsville Visitors Center is at the statue location, as is the Huntsville gift shop, where you'll find all things Huntsville and Texas—videos, maps, brochures, gifts, collectibles, and more.

Samuel Walker Houston Museum and Cultural Center. 1604 10th St.; (936) 295-2119. This cultural center is dedicated to the life and educational legacy of Samuel Walker Houston, a prominent African-American Walker County educator and the son of General Sam Houston's former slave Joshua Houston. Located on the campus of Sam Houston State University, it features a variety of exhibits and artifacts that depict African-American life in Huntsville after the Civil War. It's also home to *The Dreamers* sculpture, which highlights the faces of 69 people and depicts three generations of African-American Huntsville residents. Admission is free.

Texas Department of Criminal Justice Institutional Division. 39 FM 247 Rd. See the Texas prison system up close by taking a driving tour of the Texas Department of Criminal Justice, which has its headquarters right here in Huntsville. Visit the *Sam Houston Statue and Visitors Center* to get a map for a self-guided tour, or download a self-guided driving tour map from the chamber of commerce at huntsvilletexas.com. Among the dozen-plus stops on the tour are the Texas Prison Museum, some of the prisons in the area, and Peckerwood Hill Cemetery, where more than 1,700 unclaimed or unwanted prisoners have been buried.

Texas Prison Museum. 491 TX 75 North; (936) 295-2155; txprisonmuseum.org. Visit the Texas Prison Museum to learn the history of the Texas prison system, which makes its home right here in Huntsville. You can check out some haunting prison technologies such as an old electric chair, balls and chains, and a replica of a 9-foot-by-6-foot cell. The museum sells arts and crafts made by the inmates.

where to shop

Whether you're craving a little retail therapy or just want to see what the local stores have to offer, visit the Downtown Courthouse Square area along Sam Houston Avenue at 11th Street. Here you'll find more than 40 retail stores and restaurants, murals by Richard Haas, as well as a restored log cabin visitor center and 20 registered historic sites. A small sampling of the stores in historic downtown Huntsville can be found here. Stroll the area or visit huntsvilletx.gov to discover even more.

Bluebonnet Square Antiques. 1110 11th St.; (936) 291-2800. More than 15 dealers sell a wide selection of antiques and collectibles here, including furniture, vintage clothes, toys, books, records, linens, sports paraphernalia, jewelry, ceramics, and glassware.

Inscriptions of the Heart Gift Shop. 1117 12th St.; (936) 295-5654; inscriptionsofthe heart.com. Find unique and personalized gifts here, including laser-engraved frames, mirrors, and tiles. This Christian business also carries an extensive collection of crosses and other Christian gifts.

Lisa's Gift Box. 1103 12th St.; (936) 295-0892; facebook.com/lisas.g.box. This brightly decorated store sells cards and gifts such as Colonial Candles, Jim Shore figurines, and Lah-Tee-Dah lamps and scents. Closed Sunday.

Mt. Vernon Gift Shop and the Children's Room. 1107 12th St.; (936) 295-6633. For more than a century, this family-run business has been a popular spot to find gifts such as home decor, jewelry, children's clothes and toys, and bath products.

A Nitsch in Time. 1108 11th St.; (936) 436-0265; anitschintime.com. More than 20 dealers sell vintage glasses and jewelry, pottery, home decor, and other antiques in this 4,000-square-foot space.

Sam Houston Antique Mall. 1210 Sam Houston Ave.; (936) 295-7716; facebook.com/pages/Sam-Houston-Antique-Mall/163756180319220. Some 30 dealers fill the 3 floors of this antiques mall with old furniture, coins, glassware, gifts, metal masterpieces, paintings, and more.

where to eat

City Hall Cafe & Pie Bar. 1399 FM 1791; (936) 436-0449. Although it was recently awarded a Readers' Choice award by Huntsville residents for its chicken-fried steak and offers plenty of traditional American options like catfish and burgers, this casual eatery also makes a mean pie. The list is extensive: coconut cream, coconut meringue, chocolate meringue, sweet potato and pecan pies, and more, all made from scratch. Closed Sunday and Monday. $–$$.

Farmhouse Cafe. 1004 14th St.; (936) 435-1250; farmhousecafe.net. Hiding behind an unassuming exterior, this is the spot for down-home Texas country favorites such as chicken-fried steak, fried shrimp, sandwiches, and burgers. Daily blue plate specials, including such options as poppyseed chicken, meat loaf, chicken and dumplings, and Salisbury steak, inspire a busy lunch crowd. Closed Sunday. $$.

Farmhouse Sweets & Eats. 1112 11th St.; (936) 291-6988; farmhousesweetsneats.com. Take a trip back to the mid-1900s at this charming old ice-cream shop, where you'll sit in metal drugstore chairs and tables and can order drinks from an authentic 1936 soda machine. You can also select candy from the old glass jars lined up on the counter or order a sandwich off the menu. $.

"jerky capital of the world"

If you're a true jerky aficionado, schedule in some extra time to visit **Woody's**
Smokehouse, *located about 45 miles north of Huntsville in Centerville. Many Tex-*
ans insist upon stopping here to choose from almost every kind of jerky imaginable,
buffalo and elk included. They're not alone: On any given day, hundreds of truckers,
travelers, and locals stop into the store's two locations off I-45 to buy jerky and sau-
sage, cheese, made-to-order sandwiches, and homemade bread, pies, jellies, and
dressings. Even more order jerky and other treats online and by mail. No wonder
Woody's bills itself as the "Jerky Capital of the World." Woody's has two locations
off I-45 at TX 7 West (exit 164)—for south- and northbound drivers. Visit the web-
site (woodys-smokehouse.com) or call (903) 536-9663 (Northbound Woody's) or
(903) 536-2434 (Southbound Woody's) for more information.

The Homestead on 19th Street. 1215 19th St.; (936) 291-7366; homesteadon19th
.com. Part of The Homestead's allure is the place it calls home: The restaurant is made up
of a log cabin dating back to around 1835, as well as 2 other historic buildings that were
moved to the current location during the 1980s. The menu includes more modern culinary
creations such as smoked trout and apple salad and Cajun chicken scallopini, as well as
fresh seafood from the Gulf of Mexico and steak. Dinner only Tuesday through Saturday,
and Sunday brunch. $$–$$$.

McKenzie's Barbeque. 1548 11th St.; (936) 291-7347; mckenziesbarbeque.com. For 14
consecutive years, locals have rated McKenzie's the best barbecue in Montgomery County.
If that's not enough of a selling point, the prices should be: A sandwich with beef (sliced
or chopped), turkey, ham, pork, chicken breast, or sausage will cost you just $4.99. Other
options include ham, sloppy joes, ribs, baked potatoes, potato salad, and slaw. Wash your
meal down with a slice of McKenzie's apple cobbler. $–$$.

New Zion Missionary Baptist Church B-B-Q. 2601 Montgomery Rd.; (936) 294-0884.
If you want some great barbecue, try this joint run by New Zion Missionary Baptist Church.
The digs are essentially a shack and the service doesn't always come with a smile, but
people come from across Texas and Louisiana for the ribs, brisket, and sausage. It's no
wonder why: *Texas Monthly* named this one of the state's best barbecue joints. Call ahead
to make sure New Zion B-B-Q is open before you head out here. $–$$.

where to stay

Oakview Manor Bed & Breakfast. 7137 TX 75 South; (936) 295-3352; oakviewmanorbnb .com. This 1925 home is set on 3 wooded acres. There are 3 bedrooms and 2 bathrooms. Sit out on the deck or in the sunroom to relax or use the free wireless Internet. Continental breakfast is served every morning. $.

Sam Houston State University Hotel. 1610 Bobby K. Marks Dr.; (936) 291-2151; shsuhotel.org. This hotel is nothing fancy, but it offers easy access to Sam Houston State University. Wireless Internet service is available, and there's a small exercise room on-site. $.

The Whistler Bed & Breakfast Inn. 906 Ave. M; (936) 295-2834; thewhistlerbnb.com. Also known as the Eastham/Thomason Home, this majestic Victorian house dates back to 1859 and still includes some of the original furniture and accents. Guests enjoy private bathrooms, beautiful antiques, a full breakfast every morning, and a lovely refuge on 3 acres of the East Texas Piney Woods. The Whistler is located just 2 blocks from the center of town. Unfortunately, the owners don't allow young kids or pets. $$.

northeast

day trip 01

northeast

into the piney woods:
humble, cleveland, coldspring

humble

Thanks to the recent expansion of US 59, Humble is quickly becoming a popular Houston suburb, with many people moving here to take advantage of the area's natural beauty and recreational opportunities on Lake Houston and the San Jacinto River—and new commercial developments.

While you've probably seen enough strip malls in your own neck of the woods, the Humble hidden behind the commercial development is worth a visit. Stop off here on your journey along US 59 to enjoy a hike through the Jesse H. Jones Park & Nature Center and smell the flowers at the Mercer Arboretum and Botanical Gardens.

You might also want to stop into the Humble Historical Museum to learn more about this little town that postmaster and justice of the peace P. S. Humble founded and named after himself in 1886. As you'll discover, oil and water have played a big part in this city's history: Oil was discovered here in 1904, leading to the founding of Humble Oil & Refining Company—now known as Exxon Mobil—5 years later. While drilling for oil in 1912, workers discovered artesian water. Oil field workers used this water in their bathhouses; it was also supplied to nearby houses through pipes.

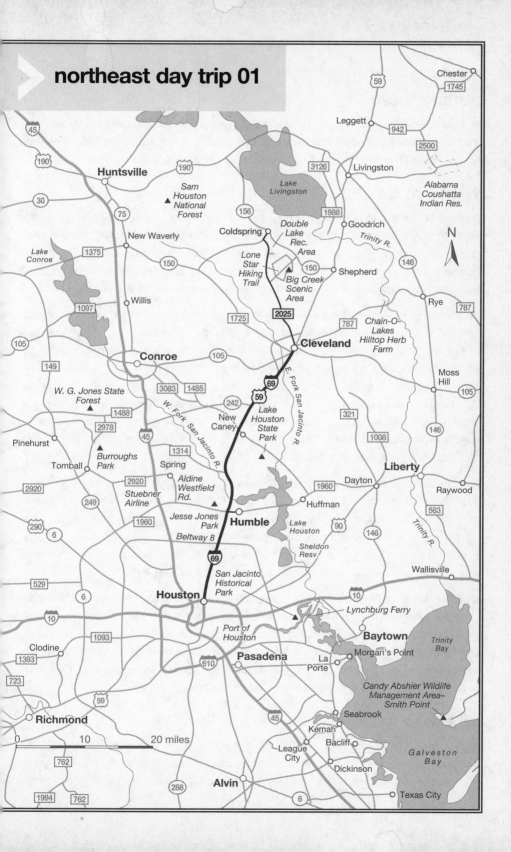

getting there

Humble is about 21 miles northeast of downtown Houston. To get there, take US 59 North for 21 miles to the FM 1960 Business/FM 1960/Humble exit and merge onto the Eastex Freeway Service Road. Then turn right or left on one of the side streets, depending on your destination.

where to go

Humble Historical Museum. 219 Main St.; (281) 446-2130; humblemuseum.com. Learn about this town's roots by checking out old oil field equipment and farming tools, photographs and memorabilia, and clothes and furniture from some of Humble's first residents. Special exhibits are held throughout the year. One recent exhibit showcased vintage cameras. Closed Sunday and Monday. Admission is free, but donations are encouraged.

Jesse H. Jones Park & Nature Center. 20634 Kenswick Dr.; (281) 446-8588; hcp4.net/jones. Walk along the 5-mile hiking trail at this 300-acre nature park, and you'll see a little of everything—unusual animals, meadows filled with colorful wildflowers, old cypress bogs, and Spring Creek's white-sand beach. Be sure to stop into the Nature Center to learn how some of the area's earliest settlers made their home in the area in the 1700s and 1800s. While you're there, you can also learn about the park's many ecosystems. The park is a great place to take kids. Not only can they learn about different animals and plants through special exhibits and programs throughout the year; the frontier fort–inspired playground here lets young imaginations run wild.

Mercer Arboretum and Botanical Gardens. 22306 Aldine Westfield Rd.; (281) 443-8731; hcp4.net/mercer. Forget the spa day. You'll find plenty of fresh air and peace of mind at the tranquil gardens and nature trails here. The Mercer Arboretum and Botanical Gardens are home to the Gulf Coast's largest collection of native and cultivated plants—and plenty of animals, to boot—so you're also sure to discover more than a few blooms and creatures you've never seen before. Bring a picnic and feast in the arboretum.

Old MacDonald's Farm. 3203 FM 1960 Rd. East; (281) 446-4001; oldmacdonaldshumble .com. If you've got little ones, put smiles on their faces with a trip to this 15-acre park. Here they can pet some goats in the petting zoo, ride ponies, take a swim, ride a little red train, play on the playground, enjoy games of volleyball and tetherball, and go crawfishing. During the fall, visitors can pick out pumpkins in the pumpkin patch. The farm is open daily from March through October and on weekends November through February.

where to eat

Bill's Cafe. 22845 Loop 494; (281) 358-6198. If you want chicken-fried steak or non-fried veggies, go elsewhere. For 40 years, locals have been coming here for the big, juicy burgers, thick onion rings, fried okra, and fries. Before you visit, take note: Some maps identify

Bill's location as Kingwood, others Humble, and a few others (including Google Maps) as Houston. It's all the same location. $–$$.

Chelsea Deli & Cafe. 1538 Kingwood Dr.; (281) 359-2972. Why go all the way to New York City when there's a great little deli in the Kingwood neighborhood? You'll find the usual deli selections, including salami po'boys and a tasty tuna salad sandwich. All the sandwiches are served on fresh baked bread. Visit during lunchtime and you may have to stand in line because everyone in the area knows this is the place to go. $–$$.

Magnolia Gardens Restaurant & Tea Room. 601 1st St.; (281) 540-3083. Located inside a cute little house, Magnolia Gardens serves soups, salads, sandwiches, and 2 rotating lunch-plate choices that come with 2 side dishes, corn bread, dessert, and a drink. This is also one of the largest teahouses in the area, giving tea aficionados their choice of over a hundred specialty teas. Closed Sunday and Monday. $–$$.

Railroad Cafe. 105 N. Railroad Ave.; (281) 319-6244. With just 8 tables, this railroad car–turned–Italian restaurant offers an intimate dining experience, complete with good food, wine, and service. Want something that's not on the menu? The chef just might make it for you. Want advice on which wine to pair with your dinner? Your waiter has you covered. Want a place to woo your sweetie? The Railroad Cafe has you covered in that department, too. $$–$$$.

Tin Roof BBQ & Steaks. 18918 Town Center Blvd.; (281) 852-5577; tinroofbbqandsteaks .com. Tin Roof isn't a big or particularly clean barbecue joint, but it wins over diners with its laid-back atmosphere, big portions, and low prices. The menu features burgers, steaks, grilled salmon, and baked potatoes stuffed with brisket, with potato salad, corn on the cob, or green beans available as sides. This family-friendly spot has room for the kids to run around outside and offers karaoke on Thursday evenings and live music on Friday and Saturday nights. Closed Monday. $–$$.

cleveland

Unofficially, Cleveland is as old as Texas: The General Land Office began offering land here in exchange for military service in 1836. But the community didn't form until after 1878, when Charles Lander Cleveland sold nearly 64 acres of land here to the Houston, East and West Texas Railway and requested that the railroad station bear his name. Not only did the town get a name in the process; it became a timber, lumber, and lumber by-product shipping point.

Today, Cleveland's economy depends on oil and gas, lumber, cattle, and farm products—a fact that's evident in the main attractions here: a cheese plant and a hiking trail in the Sam Houston National Forest.

getting there

From Humble, get back onto US 59 North and drive for about 23 miles until you reach the TX 573 Loop/Washington Avenue exit. Which street you turn onto and whether you turn right or left depends on which Cleveland spot you choose to visit.

where to go

Cheesemakers, Inc. 2266 S. Walker Rd.; (866) 593-1319 or (281) 593-1319; cheese makers.com. Take a tour of this Texas cheese plant, and watch as the artisans make goat cheese, fresh mozzarella, and braided Mexican cheeses. Afterward, visit the gift shop and pick up some cheese—and some Cheesemakers, Inc. paraphernalia—for the road. Tours are offered Monday through Friday (call 936-537-3570 for tours).

Lone Star Hiking Trail. (936) 537-3570; fs.fed.us. This National Recreation Trail winds about 129 miles from the Cleveland area to Richards, offering opportunities to bird-watch and picnic among the towering pine trees for which the area is known. Sections of the trail run along old railroad paths, others over creeks. Be sure to read the signage: Some areas lack drinking water and are accessible by foot only; others have camping grounds. There are several entrances to the trail: The Winters Bayou/Tarkington Creek section begins northwest of Cleveland on FM 1725; another entrance can be found about 4 miles northwest of Magnolia on FM 945.

where to eat

Hilltop Herb Farm & Restaurant. 235 Chain-O-Lakes Resort (16 miles east on FM 787); (832) 397-4008; artesianlakes.com. Partake in all things herb—and nature—here. Home to more than 2,000 different herbs, Hilltop Herb Farm offers workshops and lectures about growing and cooking with herbs. Dine at the restaurant and you'll enjoy fresh Hilltop herbs in dishes such as the roasted red pepper and corn chowder and the grilled beef and chicken fajitas. The restaurant is part of the Retreat at Artesian Lakes, where visitors can hike, picnic, and even spend the night in log cabins on the Big Thicket National Preserve's western edge. Reservations are required. $$$.

Pueblo Viejo Restaurant. 146A Truly Plaza; (281) 432-2616; mypuebloviejo.com. The food at this Tex-Mex restaurant is prepared with fresh veggies, which makes for some good options. Try the taco salad or fajitas poblanos (meat, poblano peppers, bell peppers, onions, and bacon). The service here is usually pretty decent. $$.

Ranch Hand Cafe. 24626 TX 321; (281) 592-2545. Don't judge Ranch Hand by its exterior. It may look like a dive, but step inside, and you'll find a surprisingly clean burger joint that's perfect for a family meal. Even better: the homemade burgers here are cheap—and Texas-size. $–$$.

Red Rooster. 301 Birch St.; (281) 659-1172. Craving something utterly unhealthy? This is the place to go. This popular restaurant serves up all things fried—chicken-fried steak, fried pickles, fried mushrooms, fried zucchini, and egg rolls. Those who want to skip the fried food have their pick of sandwiches, burgers, baked potatoes, and steaks. The service here can be pretty slow, so be sure to stock up on patience and spare time before stopping in for a meal. $–$$.

where to stay

The Retreat at Artesian Lakes. 235 Chain-O-Lakes Resort; (832) 397-4008; artesian lakes.com. Guests may stay in one of 30 log cabins or 5 log suites, or rent a privately owned home here. Wherever you stay, you'll enjoy exquisite decor and picture-worthy natural surroundings. If you're a foodie, be sure to reserve a table at the resort's Hilltop Restaurant, listed in the Where to Eat section of this trip. $$.

coldspring

This little town has had a few names over the years: When it was founded in 1847, it was known as Coonskin before later being renamed Firemen's Hill, Cold Springs, and eventually Coldspring. The San Jacinto River runs through Coldspring, so it seems somehow fitting that this town is the county seat of San Jacinto County.

Coldspring lacks glitzy modern-day attractions, but it makes up for it in history. Both General Sam Houston and George Tyler Wood, the second governor of Texas, lived here, and their old homes are among the three-dozen-plus buildings here identified with historical markers.

History isn't the only thing keeping Coldspring on the map, though. This lumber and livestock town also has some lovely park and forest areas, perfect for hiking, birding, and checking out the wildlife and flora.

Coldspring is about 64 miles north of downtown Houston.

getting there

To get to Coldspring, you have a couple options: If you prefer the scenic route (which takes you through part of the Sam Houston National Forest), head north on FM 2025 for 17 miles; then turn east on TX 150 and stay on there for 2 more miles. The other alternative (which takes a little longer) is to take US 59 North for about 8 miles to Shepherd and then take TX 150 West 11 miles to Coldspring.

where to go

Big Creek Scenic Area. Six miles west of Shepherd off FS 217. Established as a special interest area in 1962, this 1,420-acre section of the Sam Houston National Forest is home

> ## the old church
>
> *One of the oldest—if not the oldest—continually active United Methodist churches in the Lone Star State can be found here. Coldspring United Methodist Church has been around and in use since 1858, when the sanctuary and bell were built. The church has added a Sunday School Annex (1939) and a modernized pulpit. The church is located on TX 150 and Cemetery Road. To learn more call (936) 653-2287 or visit coldspringmethodist.org.*

to an array of plants and wildlife. The Lone Star Hiking Trail runs through here, creating 4 different loop trails. Although Big Creek Scenic Area was established primarily for recreation, camping is prohibited. For more information contact the Sam Houston Ranger District (394 FM 1375 West, New Waverly; 936-344-6205; fs.fed.us).

Double Lake Recreation Area. 301 FM 2025; (936) 653-3448; camprrm.com/2009/09/double-lake-campground. Between the 24-acre Double Lake and the acres upon acres of pines and hardwoods, this is a great place to camp, picnic, swim with the family, and fish for bass, catfish, and bream. You can rent a canoe or paddleboat at the concession stand, which also sells groceries for those who want to camp out. The family and group camping units here have tables, fireplaces, tent pads, parking spurs, and posts to hold a lantern. Some units also have water, electrical, and sewer hookups.

George Tyler Wood Monument. Near the intersection of US 190 and TX 156 in Point Blank, close to the entrance to Robinson Cemetery (follow signs to Gov. Wood monument); sanjacintocountytourism.org. Texas's second governor, George Tyler Wood, lived in nearby Point Blank up until his death. Today, a historical marker identifies the home where the governor and his family lived—and near which he was buried—after he failed to get reelected.

Old Town Coldspring. Slade Street near East Pine; (936) 653-2009; sanjacintocounty tourism.org. Several buildings dating back to the late 1800s and early 1900s can be found in Old Town Coldspring, the area where the town was initially built. The most notable of these is the old jail, which was built in 1881 and was restored and turned into a museum (known as Old Jail Museum) in 1983. Inside, you'll find artifacts from the town's early days, including old photos and farming tools. The museum is open Thursday through Saturday. Around the museum are other relics of old Coldspring, including the Urbana Train Depot, Old Camilla Post Office (1927), Ellison Corn Crib (1840), and the 1926 Waverly School-house. Call for additional information.

Wolf Creek Park. FM 224 at Park Rd. 60, about 5 miles off TX 156; (936) 653-4312; trinity ra.org. Get your fill of fishing, boating, swimming, hiking, waterskiing, and camping right on Lake Livingston. The Trinity River Authority of Texas operates this park, which also has a fish-cleaning station, a grocery, and washers and dryers.

where to eat

The Hop. 14801 TX 150 West; (936) 653-4889. Like its name suggests, The Hop epitomizes 1950s kitsch from the decor to the servers' outfits to the lack of healthy options on the menu. But if you're up for onion rings, burgers, chicken strips, and fries, this is a palatable option in an area lined with fast-food chains. $–$$.

where to stay

Coldspring Sunday Houses. 61 Slade St.; (936) 653-2525; coldspringsundayhouses .com. Enjoy the amenities and space of home in one of these little cottages. Fully furnished and decorated, each cottage includes DirecTV and a kitchenette with all the utensils you might need. $.

day trip 02

northeast

lumber land:
livingston, woodville

livingston

Moses L. Choate founded Livingston in 1846 and named it for his Alabama hometown. Unfortunately for history buffs, there's little here that dates back that far. In 1902, a fire—rumored to have been set to protest Livingston's prohibition on alcohol—destroyed much of the city.

As a result, the historical offerings here aren't yet 100 years old. In Heritage Park, for instance, you can see a 1933 log cabin and a 1911 W. T. Carter Steam Locomotive. These, however, are just about the only historical options worth visiting here.

Some of the biggest draws are natural attractions, making this an appealing town for outdoor enthusiasts. It's easy to see why: Livingston is home to the tree-lined Lake Livingston and is located in the rather fertile Trinity River Valley. This makes for good fishing, swimming, horseback riding, picnicking, and camping. The town has also produced some great local farms where you can pick berries and find your own Christmas tree.

Livingston is the county seat of Polk County, the namesake of US president James K. Polk.

getting there

Livingston is about 74 miles northeast of downtown Houston, just off US 59.

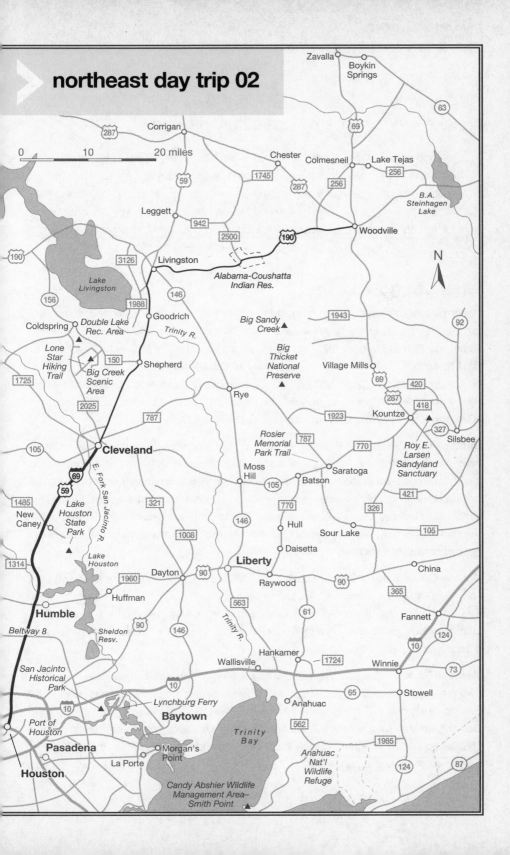

Zavalla

Boykin Springs

63

Corrigan

287

69

0   10   20 miles

Chester

Colmesneil

Lake Tejas

1745

256

256

B.A. Steinhagen Lake

59

287

Leggett

942

190

Woodville

2500

190

3126

Livingston

Alabama-Coushatta Indian Res.

156

146

1943

92

Lake Livingston

1988

Goodrich

Big Sandy Creek

Coldspring

Double Lake Rec. Area

Trinity R.

Big Thicket National Preserve

Village Mills

69

420

Lone Star Hiking Trail

150

Shepherd

287

418

1725

Big Creek Scenic Area

Rye

Kountze

327

Silsbee

2025

Roy E. Larsen Sandyland Sanctuary

787

Rosier Memorial Park Trail

787

105

Cleveland

Moss Hill

770

Saratoga

421

E. Fork San Jacinto R.

105

Batson

326

105

69

321

1485

59

Lake Houston State Park

770

New Caney

146

Hull

1008

Daisetta

Liberty

Sour Lake

China

1314

Lake Houston

Dayton

90

Raywood

90

365

1960

Huffman

563

61

Fannett

Humble

90

146

124

Beltway 8

Sheldon Resv.

Hankamer

1724

Winnie

10

73

San Jacinto Historical Park

Wallisville

Stowell

10

65

Lynchburg Ferry

Anahuac

Port of Houston

10

Baytown

562

Pasadena

Morgan's Point

Trinity Bay

1985

La Porte

Anahuac Nat'l Wildlife Refuge

124

87

Houston

Candy Abshier Wildlife Management Area– Smith Point

N

lake livingston dam observatory gazebo

Visit the Observatory Gazebo on Recreational Road 5, just off FM 1988, for the best view of the Lake Livingston Dam. From there, you can see plenty of boats, people fishing, and if you're lucky, some great egrets and great blue herons flying by. Don't come here in search of the perfect proposal spot, though: The chain-link fence between the gazebo and the dam doesn't exactly scream romance.

where to go

Berry picking. If you're in the Livingston area in the late spring or early summer, you can pick berries at several farms within a few miles of town. For blueberries, try **Baxter's Blueberry Farm** (936-685-7927), about 15 miles south of town, or **Sandy Foot Farm on Bird Road** (936-327-2744). For blackberries, try **D&D Fruit Farm** in June and July (157 Lambright Rd. in Livingston, 936-563-4880) or **Jackson Fruit Farm** (Holly Grove Road; 936-685-4658) from mid-May through July. For both blueberries and blackberries, visit **Hamilton Berry Farm** on Camp Ruby Road (936-563-4910).

Birding. The Livingston–Polk County Chamber of Commerce (lpcchamber.com) offers a free downloadable brochure of local and migrant birds as well as birding sites in the region. The 1,110 square miles that make up the county (the state's fourth largest) include numerous excellent birding sites thanks to its location on the Central and Mississippi Flyways, two of the four migratory routes in North America. Commonly seen birds include the red-bellied woodpecker, osprey, blue-winged teal, Inca dove, black-bellied whistling duck, blue heron, painted bunting, great egret, and more.

Double Creek Farm. 1288 Oak Dale Loop; (936) 967-3912; doublecreektreefarm.com. From Thanksgiving to Christmas, you can choose and cut your own locally grown Christmas tree at Double Creek Farm. Bring the family along and take a hayride, have a picnic, play in the sandbox, or do some holiday shopping in the gift shop. In October, the farm offers pumpkin picking and other fun fall activities.

Heritage Park. On Church Street, 3 blocks past the courthouse square; (936) 327-4929. Two pieces of the area's days of old can be found here: One of the last members of the Pakana Muskogee Indian tribe to live in the area built the Jonas Davis log cabin in 1833. Originally erected on a reservation near modern-day Onalaska, the log cabin was restored and moved to 530 W. Church St. by the Polk County Heritage Society in the 1980s. Also making its home at the park is the W. T. Carter Steam Locomotive No. 5, which was put together in 1911 and used to carry timber to the mills for 30 years. Guided tours are typically offered only during special events, but it doesn't hurt to call ahead and ask.

Lake Livingston State Park. 300 State Park Rd. 65, off US 59; (936) 365-2201; tpwd .state.tx.us. Located about a mile southwest of Livingston, this park offers 635 acres of recreational opportunities along Lake Livingston. It's a great place to camp, swim, picnic, boat, and fish for crappie, catfish, perch, and bass. There are also trails through the forests for hiking, horseback riding, and mountain biking. To see the many plants and animals that make their homes here from another vantage point, take a free guided trail ride through 2.5 miles of the park.

Livingston Farmers Market. 111 US 59 Loop North; (936) 685-7508. This farmers' market is held in an open-air shed on Tuesday, Thursday, and Saturday during produce season (primarily the spring, summer, and fall).

Miss Effie's Cottage. 204 W. Mill St.; (936) 327-7790. If you're a gardener or a nature fan, this historical landmark is worth a visit. The Polk County Garden Club maintains the grounds at this 19th-century cottage. Surrounding the house are beautiful antique roses, pear trees, butterflies, and other plants and creatures. Stop into the gift shop to get some goodies for your garden, as well as homemade edibles. Call ahead to schedule a tour.

Polk County Memorial Museum. 514 W. Mill St.; (936) 327-8192; users.livingston .net/~museum. This local history museum educates residents and visitors about the area's past. The 4 exhibit rooms in the small museum display relics from Indians and early settlers, weapons from the Civil War, and photos of the town's early logging and sawmill days. Closed Saturday and Sunday. Admission is free, but donations are encouraged.

where to shop

Antiques Old and New. 323 W. Church St.; (936) 327-6464; antiquesoldandnew.com/ about.php. Jewelry, animal hides, handbags, glassware, rugs, furniture, and homemade desserts are among the items you'll find here. As the shop's name suggests, the inventory is a mix of antiques and newer items, some of them antique-inspired replicas.

The Bookstore. 310 S. Washington Ave. (US 59 Business); (936) 327-8732. For 3 decades, Livingston residents have been coming here in search of new and used books. The books are arranged and categorized, but it's also fun to poke around in search of unexpected finds. The Bookstore is located inside a big blue house that dates back to the 1920s. Closed Sunday.

Downtown Treasures. 400 N. Washington Ave.; (936) 327-7740; downtown-treasures .com. This downtown gift shop sells a little bit of everything—art glass, figurines, home and holiday decor, candles, and other gifts.

trade days

Year-round, Livingston hosts "Trade Days." On the Friday and Saturday before the third Monday of each month, more than 350 vendors set up shop in Pedigo Park to sell arts and crafts, antiques and collectibles, local honey products, handmade jewelry and candles, gifts, and food. Admission is free. Pedigo Park is located just off US 59 North, 0.75 mile north of US 190. Learn more by visiting ubhookd.com or calling (877) UBHOOKD or (936) 327-3656.

Marilyn's Lawn Furniture & Yard Art. 3959 US 59 South; (936) 328-8640; eastex.net/maripete. Located about 3 miles south of town, this unique shop sells funky (and in many cases, kitschy) lawn furniture and yard art. You'll also find Texas items, porch swings, wind chimes, jewelry, birdhouses, and other gift items here. Call ahead for hours.

Raindance Designs. 8536 FM 3126; (936) 566-5312. This pottery studio and gift shop sells attractive, functional kitchenware such as bowls, mugs, and platters that can go in the microwave and dishwasher. You can also find crosses and other gifts here. Open Friday and Saturday only.

The Unique Mall. 312 N. Washington Ave.; (936) 329-8181. You'll find more than 30 antique, collectible, and gift merchants under one roof here. There's also an old-timey cafe. You might call The Unique Mall one of those "one-stop shopping" kind of places, especially when it comes to gifts and antiques. A clock lover's dream, this mall is also filled with furniture, home decor, antiques, collectibles, and more for a diverse collection of vendors.

where to eat

The Courthouse Whistle Stop Cafe. 318 N. Washington Ave.; (936) 327-3222; courthousewhistlestop.com. Located downtown, just across the street from the Polk County Courthouse, this local favorite serves southern fare like chicken-fried steak burgers, as well as Cajun dishes and a few Italian dishes. Whistle Stop Cafe is open for breakfast and lunch and also sells antiques and gifts. Visit on Friday for acoustic night. $–$$.

Florida's Kitchen. 796 FM 350 South; (936) 967-4216; floridaskitchen.com. The service here can be kind of slow, but that's largely because word's gotten out that this is one of the best restaurants around. The biggest draws? The barbecue, burgers, and salads. Closed Monday and Tuesday. $–$$.

Jalisco Texas Pepper. 930 US 59 Loop North; (936) 327-2794. This family restaurant offers a little bit of everything, making it a good option for groups that can't agree on what kind of food to eat. Whether you order Tex-Mex, seafood, pasta, chicken, burgers, steak, or the popular chicken-fried steak, you'll get a large portion. Closed Monday. $–$$.

Shrimp Boat Manny's. 1324 W. Church St.; (936) 327-0100; shrimpboatmannys.com. For more than 20 years, locals have been coming here for down-home Cajun cookin'. The menu includes oysters, catfish, gumbo, shrimp, crawfish étouffée, po'boys, steaks, salads, and red beans and rice with sausage. $–$$.

where to stay

Lake Tombigbee Campgrounds. 571 State Park Rd. 56; (936) 563-1221 or (800) 926-9023; alabama-coushatta.com. Stay at the campgrounds of the Alabama-Coushatta Indian reservation, located about 17 miles east of Livingston. There are several different campsite options, including RV sites with full hookups, cabins, and tents. Everything is located around Lake Tombigbee. Quiet time starts at 10 p.m., and rates range from $12 to $100 a night. $–$$$.

McCardell Cottage. 705 N. Beatty St.; (936) 327-3537 or (936) 433-1614; mccardell cottage.com. In the 1800s, this bright-colored Victorian cottage served as a medical facility and as the hub of Livingston cultural and social activity. Today, this historic house is considered one of the area's best bed-and-breakfasts. With old-fashioned decor and antique adornments and linens, McCardell Cottage gives visitors a good taste of the area's past. $$.

Milam Home Bed & Breakfast. 412 W. Milam St.; (936) 327-1173. Enjoy a little southern hospitality when you stay in one of the guest rooms or the 2-bedroom suite at this restored old house. The antiques and fresh flowers decorating the guest rooms and common rooms give this B&B a homey feel, with the perks of staying in a hotel. A continental breakfast is included in your stay. $$.

woodville

Visiting Woodville, you might think there was never a town with a more appropriate name. After all, more than 90 percent of the town is forest, making lumber production and forestry the heart and soul of Woodville's economy.

Peculiarly, though, the town was actually named after the Lone Star State's second governor, George Tyler Wood, who took office in 1847, right around the time Woodville was founded and became the county seat of Tyler County.

Visitors will find a few relics of the town's early years at the Heritage Village Museum, which houses an 1866 log cabin. And memorabilia from Texas's 37th governor, Allan Shivers, can be found at the Allan Shivers Library & Museum. But as is the case with Livingston,

the first residents

Texas's oldest Indian reservation is located right here in Polk County. Since the 1780s, the Alabama-Coushatta Indian tribe has made its home on more than 4,600 acres of the heavily wooded area known as the Big Thicket. Originally separate groups—the Alabama and the Coushatta—they migrated from Alabama and Mississippi and eventually merged. Today, they belong to the Muskogean Nation and speak languages similar to the Muskogean dialect.

While the Alabama-Coushatta have ceased offering tours and a museum to the public, you can still fish, canoe, paddleboat, and swim in the reservation's Lake Tombigbee and spend the night at the Lake Tombigbee Campgrounds, which offers cabins, full hookup sites, and even tepees. If you're in the area during the first weekend of June, stop by the reservation for the annual powwow, which celebrates the tribe's long heritage. On July 4 the tribe also welcomes visitors for fireworks and a music festival. To learn more about the Alabama-Coushatta and upcoming events, call (936) 563-1100 or visit alabama-coushatta .com. The tribe's offices are located at 571 State Park Rd. 56 in Livingston.

some of the biggest reasons to come here are found outdoors. Among the offerings are a 1.5-mile dogwood trail, one of just five Texas state forests, Lake Tejas, Martin Dies Jr. State Park, and easy access to the Big Thicket National Preserve, which is located just south of town.

getting there

In Livingston, head east on West Church Street/US 190 toward North Washington Avenue and follow US 190 East about 32 miles until you reach Woodville.

where to go

Allan Shivers Library & Museum. 302 N. Charlton St.; (409) 283-3709; allanshiverslibrary .com. This museum and library were gifted to Woodville and its residents by Texas's 37th governor, Allan Shivers, who served during the mid-1900s. The restored Victorian manse houses memorabilia from the former governor's administration as well as a fully equipped library that can be used for reading, research, and studying. Closed Sunday. There is a small fee for tours of the museum.

Dogwood Trail. On US 190, 3 miles east of Woodville. Stretch your legs and take a walk on this 1.5-mile trail, which runs along Theuvenin Creek and is home to dogwood trees and other flora. The trail gets quite a bit of rain, especially in May, so take note of the weather beforehand or bring a poncho or umbrella along, just in case. The dogwood blooms peak in early spring.

Heritage Village Museum. On US 190, 1 mile west of Woodville (and US 69); (409) 283-2272 or (800) 323-0389; heritage-village.org. Take a trip back to Texas's early days with a visit to this living museum of pioneer history. Ceramist Clyde E. Gray created the open-air museum, which boasts a restored log cabin built in 1866, old shops and other buildings, photos, vehicles, maps, and more. During your visit, dine at the Pickett House Restaurant, which is housed in an old schoolhouse. The menu includes country favorites such as fried chicken, cobbler, biscuits, and corn bread. Special events are held at the Heritage Village Museum almost every month, so call ahead or visit the website to see if you can time your visit to take place during one of these.

Kirby State Forest. Off US 287, 14 miles south of Woodville; (409) 283-3785; texasforest service.tamu.edu. One of just five Texas state forests, Kirby State Forest was donated to the state in 1929 by lumberman John Henry Kirby and is managed by the Texas Forest Service. The 600-plus-acre forest is primarily used for research, but the park is open to the public for picnicking, hiking, and birding.

Lake Tejas. Eleven miles north of Woodville on US 69 and 1 mile east on FM 256 in Colmesneil; (409) 837-2063; laketejas.net. Essentially a big swimming hole with a sand bottom, Lake Tejas features clear, spring-fed waters and 80 yards of sandy beach. Throughout the summer, the lake is open for swimming. It attracts tons of regulars who come to float in tubes, sunbathe, and ride in paddleboats. There are lifeguards on duty during the summer, and visitors can picnic or camp here throughout the year. All visitors age 3 and older are charged $6 to swim; additional fees apply for renting inner tubes, boats, tables, life jackets, and camping here.

Martin Dies Jr. State Park. 634 Park Rd. 48 South, off US 190, 14 miles east of Woodville; (409) 384-5231; tpwd.state.tx.us. Situated on the eastern side of B. A. Steinhagen Lake and on the edge of the Big Thicket National Preserve, this 705-acre park is sure to satisfy almost any outdoorsy type. Recreational opportunities here include hiking, swimming, camping, canoeing, fishing, bird watching, and mountain biking. The heavily forested area also offers many opportunities to study a variety of plants and wildlife, including the occasional alligator in the water. Canoes, bicycles, volleyballs, horseshoes, and a flat-bottom boat are all available for rental. On the weekends, the park offers special naturalist programs, and on the third Saturday of the month (August excluded), the park offers group canoe trips down the Angelina or Neches Rivers. Call ahead to reserve your spot.

Tyler County Fine Art Centre & Gallery. 210 W. Bluff St.; (409) 283-2788; tylercounty artleague.org. Located in the historic Warfield Building (1918), this gallery highlights the work of local artists. The Warfield Building also houses the Tyler County Art League, which

a haunted town?

For the most part, Woodville seems like a normal little town. But some residents and visitors speculate that Woodville is haunted. Reported spooky sightings include a flight attendant's ghost in a trailer and a black snake that shifted into a female shape and was seen smoking a pipe. To learn about other incidents—or to report a ghost sighting of your own—visit ghostsofamerica.com.

hosts special arts events throughout the year. To find out about upcoming events, visit the website.

where to eat

Pickett House Restaurant. US 190 West; (409) 283-3371; heritage-village.org. Located in an old schoolhouse at the Heritage Village Museum, this restaurant is considered *the* place to eat in Woodville, though some diners think the quality of the food has declined recently. The all-you-can-eat country restaurant is known for its fried chicken and its chicken and dumplings. Vegetarians won't find much to eat here since even the vegetables are cooked in ham. $–$$.

The Tree Restaurant Bar & Grill. 209 S. Magnolia; (409) 283-8040; thetreerestaurant .com. Recently relocated from the nearby village of Hillster, the Tree still offers some of the best comfort food in East Texas. Along with the ribs and steaks cooked on an open grill, the restaurant's expanded menu now includes seafood and pasta dishes and daily lunch specials. The place is bigger now, too, and encompasses a bar serving beer and offering some tasty bar menu items like wings, crab-stuffed jalapeños, and cheesesticks. $–$$$.

day trip 03

northeast

nature's finest:
liberty & dayton, big thicket national
preserve, kountze, silsbee

liberty & dayton

Located about 47 miles northeast of Houston off US 90 East, Liberty is rich with history. The first pioneers began arriving here around 1818, hoping to be part of Stephen F. Austin's colony. When their petition was denied, the Mexican land commissioner created a new municipality called Villa de la Santísima Trinidad de la Libertad. That name was a bit long by American standards, so the new residents renamed their town Liberty—the same name of the Mississippi town from which some of the pioneers had come.

Dayton, located 6 miles west of Liberty, was originally called West Liberty and was considered part of Liberty when it was founded. Though the two parts of town were divided by the Trinity River, they were connected via a road and ferry.

In 1836, Liberty really put itself on the map. That year, the town opened a post office and held captured Mexican army officers after their defeat by the Texas revolutionaries at the Battle of San Jacinto. Just a year later, the town was incorporated and named the county seat. Over the next few years, Liberty became an important access point in Texas. In addition to providing steamship connections to Galveston, it gave passers-through access to routes across the Trinity River. It also had a railroad stop as early as 1858. Liberty's most famous resident during its early years was General Sam Houston, who owned two plantation homes in Liberty County and practiced law in Liberty.

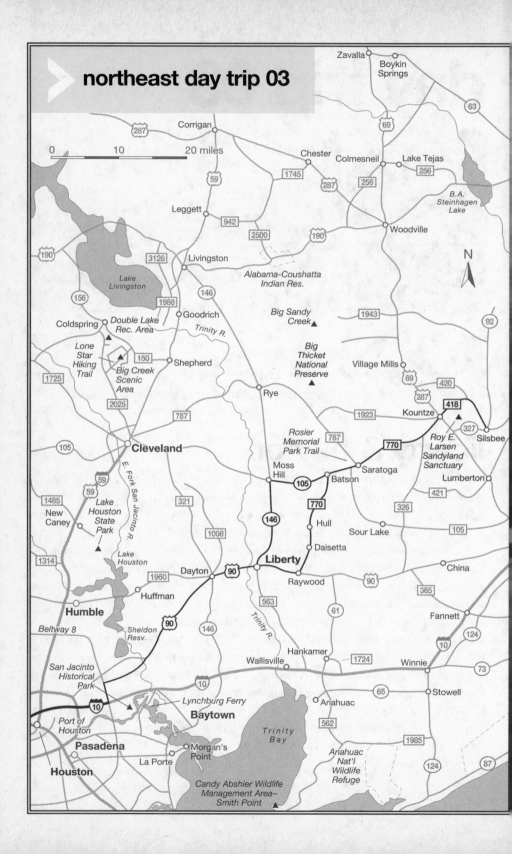

northeast day trip 03

Sometime after 1854, West Liberty became known as Day's Town, and the name Dayton appeared on the local post office in 1877, though the town's name did not officially change for close to a decade.

Today, visitors can get a taste of the area's early history by visiting several historic houses as well as a haunted hotel and a restored 1900 schoolhouse.

getting there

To get to Dayton from Houston, follow I-10 East toward Beaumont; then take exit 781B and merge onto the East Sam Houston Parkway North/Sam Houston Tollway North/TX 8 Beltway North for 4.9 miles. When you reach Crosby Freeway/US 90 East, take a right and follow US 90 East for 23.4 miles. To reach Liberty, follow US 90 from Dayton for about 5.5 miles.

where to go

Birding. As part of the Great Texas Coastal Birding Trail, the Liberty-Dayton area is well known for its birding, especially for sightings of the swallow-tailed kite. This black-and-white bird, with a wingspan of over 4 feet, is most often seen along US 90 between Liberty and Dayton. For maps, field guides, and more information on birding opportunities in the region along the Trinity Loop, part of the Upper Texas Coast Wildlife Trail (UTC), visit tpwd.state .tx.us.

Champion Lake. At the end of CR 417, 2 miles east of FM 1409, about 10 miles south of Dayton; (936) 336-9786; fws.gov. Buttonbush and cypress trees surround this 800-acre lake, which is part of the Trinity River National Wildlife Refuge. It is the largest and most easily accessible of the 3 fishing tracts in the refuge, with 150-foot piers, a 3,000-foot levee, and easy boat access. Throw a line in the water, and you're likely to land a bass, crappie, or catfish. The area also offers opportunities to hunt and explore nature.

Dayton Old School Museum. 111 W. Houston St., Dayton; (936) 258-3443; daytonold schoolmuseum.com. From 1900 to 1910, first- through seventh-grade students attended this 2-room school. The Dayton Historical Society has since restored the old schoolhouse so that visitors can see how the school was laid out and look at old photos, student and teacher desks, an old phone, and other memorabilia. Today, the building doubles as a museum and meeting space for the Dayton Historical Society and other nonprofit organizations. The museum is open to the public Thursday through Saturday from 10 a.m. to 2 p.m.; special tours are also available if you call ahead to schedule them.

Geraldine D. Humphreys Cultural Center. 1710 Sam Houston Ave., Liberty; (936) 336-8901; libertydaytonchamber.com. Built in 1970, Geraldine D. Humphreys Cultural Center is the hub of cultural and literary activity in the area. Part of the center houses the Liberty Municipal Library and its 43,000 books, and offers special literacy events for children, teens, and adults. Another section of the center houses the Humphreys-Burson Theatre, where

> ## private homes

Liberty and Dayton are home to several historic houses, but many of these are owned by residents. Though these homes are closed to the public, you can drive by for a look. This will give you a glimpse of architecture dating from the 1840s through the early part of the early 1900s. In Liberty, historic private residences include the Abbott-Parker home (1841) at the corner of Grand and Fannin Streets; the Bailey-Chambers home (1880) at 1821 Trinity St.; the Cameron-Norman home at 2023 Cos St.; the Lovett-Sampson home (1902) at 1723 Webster St.; the Cameron-Norman home (1880) at 310 Fannin St.; the T. J. Chambers Home (1861) at 624 Milam St.; and the E. W. Pickett home (1911) at 405 Bowie St. An additional Liberty house, the G.W. Pounds home (1890), is temporarily closed to the public while it undergoes renovations. You can still drive by and see it south of Daisetta on FM 770.

In Dayton, consider driving by the Judge Neel home (1923) at 1204 Main St.

the Valley Players—a local theater group—perform 3 shows a year, including a spring musical, a fall comedy or drama, and a third show during the Christmas season. Call to find out about upcoming performances.

Gillard-Duncan House and Norman House. 650 FM 1011, Liberty; (936) 336-8821; tsl .state.tx.us/shc/gdhouse.html. Dr. Edward J. Gillard and his wife, Emma DeBlanc Gillard, built the Gillard-Duncan House in 1848, and it is now one of Southeast Texas's oldest homes. Their descendants kept the house in the family until 1976, when Elizabeth Gay Bennett donated it to the Texas State Library and Archives Commission.

With its Greek Revival architecture, the 1883 Norman House is typical of houses built during that era. Miss Edna Norman donated the house to the Atascosito Historical Society in 1988.

Both the Gillard-Duncan House and the Norman House have been fully restored and feature much of the original furniture and accents. They are located on the grounds of Sam Houston Regional Library & Research Center and are open to the public for tours. However, tours should be scheduled 2 weeks in advance.

The Haunted Historic Ott Hotel. 305 Travis St., Liberty; (936) 336-3832; hauntedotthotel .com. With the Liberty area playing a large role in the oil boom and the timber industry, a growing number of people began riding the T.N. & O. Railroad into town and needed a place to stay. So in 1928, this historic hotel opened to accommodate passengers who needed a place to rest their weary heads. Today, it is the last original functioning train depot hotel.

Almost since opening, the Ott Hotel has been associated with paranormal activity. Paranormal groups often visit the reportedly haunted hotel to see if they can get in on the ghostly action. The hotel, which looks virtually the same as it did in 1928, plays up its haunted appeal and invites guests to bring their cameras and document any unusual sightings. Tours are available by appointment.

Huffman Horse Auction. 9903 FM 1960 East, Dayton; (936) 257-8233; daytonhuffman horsecenter.com. If you're seeking a true Texas country experience, you'll find it here on Saturday. That's when visitors are welcome to check out the livestock in the big red barn. If you're interested in taking an animal (or saddle) home, stick around for the auctions, which start at 7 p.m. Anyone can bid on used saddles, mules, horses, and ponies.

Liberty County Courthouse. 400 Travis St. (Courthouse Square), Liberty; co.liberty.tx.us. Now listed in the National Register of Historic Places, this courthouse was built in the early 1930s, making it the last of 7 courthouses built at this location. The Texas Historical Commission describes it as one of the state's "most well-kept historic courthouses."

Liberty Opry on the Square. 1816 Sam Houston Ave., Liberty; (936) 336-5830 or (877) 729-9103; libertyopry.com. If you're visiting Liberty on Saturday, stick around for the evening. At 7 p.m. each Saturday, the Liberty Opry Band and other musicians deliver family fun and a rockin' good time at Liberty's Old Park Theater. Each show has its own theme. Recent shows have featured 1950s and '60s tunes, country western, gospel music, and Christmas songs.

Sam Houston Regional Library & Research Center. 650 FM 1011, Liberty; (936) 336-8821; tsl.state.tx.us/shc/index.html. Giant oak trees dot the outside of this state-owned library and research center, which holds special exhibits highlighting historical objects and documents related to the area's history. The center is also a repository for historical photos, documents, public records, microfilm, and other artifacts. The center's website includes a list of its holdings, some of which you must make a special request to see. None of the holdings can be borrowed or taken off the premises. Admission is free. To reach the Sam Houston Regional Library & Research Center, take TX 146 about 4 miles north of Liberty and then turn left on FM 1011. Closed Sunday and Monday.

Trinity Valley Exposition (TVE Fairgrounds). 321 Wallisville Rd. (FM 563), Liberty; (936) 336-7455; tvefair.com. For the past 100 years, these 60-acre grounds have hosted dozens of rodeos, carnivals, and other special events. TVE Fairgrounds is a charitable corporation, so proceeds go toward scholarships for local students. Call or visit the website to find out what's happening during your visit.

where to eat

Cedar Landing Marina. 10614 FM 1960 East, Huffman (head east on FM 1960 West from Dayton); (281) 324-1113; cedarlanding.com. Take in a sunset or watch boaters sail past

wine land

Love a fruity vino? On your way to the Big Thicket, make a pit stop at **Bruno and George Winery** *in nearby Sour Lake (400 Messina Rd., Sour Lake; 409-287-1212 or 409-963-8235; brunoandgeorge.com). This boutique winery blends wines using the same recipes that the owner's great-grandfather used in Sicily in the late 1800s. When the winery produced its first wines in 2001, it sold only raisin wine—a vino made from dried grapes that were popular in old Sicily. Today, Bruno and George is also known for its fruit offerings, including Yellow Jacket Raspberry Wine, the winner of the 2008 Houston Livestock Show & Rodeo wine competition. The winery offers tours and tastings by appointment. To reach Bruno and George Winery from Liberty, follow TX 146 North/US 90 East for about 20 miles and then take a left at Old US 90 East/TX 326 North. Take a right at Old Beaumont Road and then take the second right onto Nevada Street. Continue onto Messina Road until you reach the winery.*

as you dine right on the edge of Lake Houston. The menu includes grilled, blackened, and fried seafood, as well as steaks, salads, burgers, wraps, and sandwiches. Cedar Landing also makes its own potato chips. Closed Monday. $$–$$$.

Gankye's Cook Shack. 1202 Hwy. 90, Liberty; (409) 267-7426; gankyescookshack .vpweb.com. If you need more protein in your life, Gankye's Cook Shack will fit the bill. Specializing in oak-smoked barbecued beef, pork, sausage, pork spareribs, and chicken smeared with their original Papaw's Boss Sauce BBQ Sauce, the restaurant also serves up some pretty good Cajun-inspired dishes. Closed Sunday. $$.

Jose's Mexican Restaurant. 901 W. Clayton St. (FM 1960 E), Dayton; (936) 258-5887. You probably won't eat the best Tex-Mex you've ever had here, but Jose's is a decent option if you're in the area and need to satisfy a hungry crew on a budget. In addition to Tex-Mex favorites, Jose's serves salads, chicken, and burgers. $–$$.

big thicket national preserve

When a place has nicknames like "an American ark" and "the biological crossroads of North America," it should be on your "must-see" list. Such is the case with the Big Thicket, a biological wonder with a name that doesn't really fit. The Big Thicket National Preserve's more than 105,600 acres are not, as the word "thicket" suggests, a bunch of tangled little trees or bushes. The area actually encompasses virgin pine and cypress forest, meadow, hardwood forest, blackwater swamp, plains, and sand hills. It is home to more than 85 species of trees, 60 species of shrubs, and close to 1,000 other plant species, including orchids, ferns, allies, and four of the five insect-eating plants found in North America. And that's just the plant life!

More than 180 bird species make their homes here or pass through on their way to warmer spots, making this an important stop along the Great Texas Coastal Birding Trail.

There are also about 50 reptile species that reside in the Big Thicket, including frogs, toads, and even the occasional gator.

Though Native Americans—specifically, the Caddos, the Alabama-Coushattas, and the Atakapas—hunted the area prior to and during the 1800s, they didn't go too deep into the Big Thicket. In the 1830s, Texas settlers began inhabiting the area, but only to a limited degree. The ground, despite being unusually fertile, wasn't used for plantation farming and was instead used only for some smaller-scale subsistence farming.

Only beginning in the 1880s did the Big Thicket start to face the onslaught of human activity. During that time, the lumber industry began cutting down the virgin pines here so there'd be more ground for farming and grazing. And in 1901, oil fields were discovered in the area. Nearly a quarter century later, in 1927, conservationists established the East Texas Big Thicket Association and initiated work to protect the Big Thicket from the oil and lumber industries, hoping to get the area designated as a national forest.

Though those efforts failed, a new movement began in 1966 to win the area a national park designation. Eight years later, conservationists' dream finally became a reality when President Gerald Ford signed a bill to establish the 84,550-acre Big Thicket National Preserve. This status prohibits the cutting down of trees for commercial purposes, but it allows hunting, trapping, and oil exploration.

The preserve also offers recreational opportunities aplenty. Hiking and birding, of course, are possible throughout the preserve. Those with a fishing license can throw a line in any part of the water here, and though there are no swimming areas, you'll see many people frolicking in the water in parts of the preserve. Hunters and trappers can catch their prey with a permit in certain areas; call (409) 951-6701 for more information. You can also camp in many sections of the preserve with a free permit; call (409) 951-6700 for more information. The preserve does not include any restaurants or hotel accommodations, so it's a good idea to bring a picnic to enjoy at one of the many picnic sites around the park. Bring your own water, too.

getting there

The Big Thicket has about a dozen different entry points in several towns in the region. The easiest way to get to the Big Thicket is through Saratoga. One option is to follow US 90 East and then take a left turn at FM 770 North at Raywood and continue on to Saratoga. Or, if you're skipping the first parts of this day trip and driving directly from Houston, you could take I-10 East to Hankamer and then head north on TX 61 to US 90, where you should head west and travel 4 miles to FM 770 before driving north to Saratoga. Alternatively, you can reach the Big Thicket National Preserve through Kountze (at the Big Thicket National Preserve and Big Thicket Information Station, listed in the next part of this trip), Beaumont (East Day Trip 02), Woodville (Northeast Day Trip 02), or Cleveland (Northeast Day Trip 01).

Having said this, you shouldn't rely on these directions alone to get to the Big Thicket. There are a lot of small roads involved, and you kind of have to know what you're looking for, no matter which section of the preserve you're visiting. For this reason, we strongly recommend that you get your hands on a good map of Texas—or even better, just Southeast Texas—as well as some of the guides from the Big Thicket National Preserve and Big Thicket Information Station (6044 FM 420; 409-951-6700; nps.gov/bith), located 7 miles north of Kountze and listed below.

where to go

Because the preserve is so vast, the US National Park Service has divided it into 9 land units and 6 water corridor units. These units are located primarily in parts of Liberty, Polk, Hardin, Jasper, and Tyler Counties. The land units include Beech Creek, Hickory Creek Savannah, Turkey Creek, Lance Rosier, Beaumont, Big Sandy Creek, Neches River Bottom/Jack Gore Baygall, Canyonlands, and Lobolly; the water corridor units are Upper Neches River, Lower Neches Rivers, Little Pine Island/Pine Island Bayou, Big Sandy Creek, Village Creek, and Menard Creek.

Below is information about a few sections and highlights of the Big Thicket National Preserve that you shouldn't miss:

Big Thicket National Preserve and Big Thicket Information Station. 6044 FM 420 (7 miles north of Kountze); (409) 951-6700; nps.gov/bith. This is the place to go if you want to get the 411 on all things Big Thicket. The information station offers interpretive panels about the preserve and many of its plant and animal residents, advice on where to go in the preserve and what you'll see there, and information about the various boating opportunities in the Big Thicket National Preserve. Several trails are accessible here, including the Kirby Nature Trail, the 15-mile Turkey Creek Trail, and the carnivorous-plant-filled Pitcher Plant Trail. There are also several hiking trails, long and short, in this section. If you're interested in touring the Big Thicket by canoe, boat, foot, or van, contact Timber Ridge Tours. Tours depart from the information station Thursday through Monday. Call (409) 246-3107 for more information.

Beech Creek. Southeast of Woodville, off FM 2992. This plant-filled forest includes large populations of magnolias, hardwoods, and, of course, beeches. Walk along the 1-mile Beech Woods Trail to check out some of the scenery. Primitive camping is available here with a free permit. (There are no developed campgrounds in the park.)

Big Sandy Creek. On FM 1276, 3.3 miles south of US 190. An 18-mile stretch here is the only part of the Big Thicket National Preserve that allows mountain biking. That same trail can also be used for horseback riding. Take a walk along the 5.4-mile Woodland Trail, located near the northwestern edge of the unit, to see an array of plants and animals. Big Sandy Creek includes primitive campsites for those who want to rough it for the night.

Birding. Birders, rejoice: The Big Thicket National Preserve is home to one of the best birding sites along the Upper Texas Coast section of the Great Texas Coastal Birding Trail, which spans the southeast region of the state from the Big Thicket area east to the Texas-Louisiana border. (Another great site is Roy E. Larsen Sandyland Sanctuary in Silsbee, see below.) The trail has been landscaped to attract some of the area's most beautiful songbirds, including red-cockaded woodpeckers and even an occasional bald eagle flying along the Neches and Trinity Rivers. Observation platforms make it easy to view the birds with the aid of your binoculars. For more information on the trail, contact the Texas Parks and Wildlife Department at (800) 892-1112 or visit its website at tpwd.state.tx.us, where you can download a map of the Great Texas Coastal Birding Trail.

Hickory Savannah Creek Unit. A half-mile west of US 69/287; take FM 2827 to reach US 69/287. This unit is a fine example of the Big Thicket's diverse ecosystems. Here you'll see everything from wetlands to sandy soil to forests lined with longleaf pines. During the spring, you can also see a beautiful array of wildflowers. Get the lay of the land by walking the 1-mile Sundew Trail, or if you're pushing a stroller or using a wheelchair, circle the 0.25-mile trail.

Roy E. Larsen Sandyland Sanctuary. 1250 US 96 South, Silsbee; (409) 385-0445; nature.org. Created to protect and revitalize the West Gulf Coastal Plain's rapidly disappearing longleaf pine ecosystem, the Roy E. Larsen Sandyland Sanctuary sits on the old sedimentary deposits of Village Creek. Like other parts of the Big Thicket region, the biodiversity found on these 5,500-plus acres is incredible: You'll find more than 500 plant species and more than 200 animal species living in the sanctuary's swamps and forests, including one of Texas's last remaining longleaf pine forests. Bring the whole family for a picnic, to watch the birds or study nature, take a hike on the 6 miles of trails, or canoe on Village Creek. The preserve is managed by The Nature Conservancy of Texas and is designated as site No. 17 on the Upper Texas Coast phase of the Great Texas Coastal Birding Trail.

Tours. The Big Thicket National Preserve is both a little overwhelming and full of hidden gems, so the best way to navigate the area is often to take a tour. The Big Thicket park rangers offer nature talks, guided hikes, canoe trips, and other activities throughout the year; for more information call (409) 951-6700. If you're interested in a canoe tour, try Eastex Canoe Trails (1698 US 96 South, Silsbee; 409-385-4700; eastexcanoes.com). For guided hikes, try The Nature Conservancy (409-385-0445; nature.org).

where to eat

Consult the following sections on Kountze and Silsbee for restaurant recommendations.

kountze

Thanks to its location near the Big Thicket National Preserve, Kountze is known among locals as the Big Light in the Big Thicket. The town's trees are its lifeblood, with forests making up 89 percent of the area. Not surprisingly, Kountze produces more than 5.5 million board feet of lumber each year.

The trees weren't always the biggest draw here, though. When Kountze was founded in 1881, it was a railroad town through and through, and in the 1950s it piggybacked off the discovery of oil in nearby towns to experience a population boom. It has also long been the county seat of Hardin County.

"Boom" is a relative term here, mind you: Kountze had a population of only about 800 during the 1940s and just over 2,000 by 1990. Today, the town has a population approaching 2,200 and just a handful of attractions, including the nature trail–lined Indian Springs Camp and the antiques-filled Kirby-Hill House Museum, which was once home to a local lumber tycoon.

getting there

Kountze is located about 32 miles south of Woodville and 27 miles north of Beaumont on US 69/287. How you get there depends on which unit of the Big Thicket you visit. To determine the best route to take, consult a map of the Big Thicket area, available through the Big Thicket National Preserve and Big Thicket Information Station (6044 FM 420, about 7 miles north of Kountze; 409-951-6700; nps.gov/bith).

where to go

Ghost Road Scenic Drive County Park. West on TX 770 for 12 miles to Saratoga. Turn north on FM 787; the Ghost Road follows this stretch to the intersection of FM 1293. Originally named Bragg Road, this stretch of highway has long been known as Ghost Road due to unexplained lights that have been seen by residents for over a century. Some scientists have explained the lights are due to gases; lovers of all things paranormal explain the lights as due to ghosts. The ghost stories range from Spanish conquistadors in search of buried

an oil detour

Learn about one of the Big Thicket's most significant industries—oil—by making a short drive to the Oil Patch Museum in Batson, located 21 miles southwest of Kountze. On display in this tiny museum is old equipment from the oil fields, as well as photos and other memorabilia celebrating Southeast Texas's early days in the industry. Museum visits are offered by appointment only, so be sure to call (409) 262-8580 before stopping by. The museum, which looks a bit run-down from the outside, is located at TX 105 and FM 770.

gold to a honeymooner at the old Bragg Hotel who continues to search the woods for his murdered bride.

Indian Springs Camp and RV Park. 6106 Holland Cemetery Rd., just east of US 69; (409) 246-2508; indianspringscamp.net. Right across the highway from the Big Thicket Information Center (6044 FM 420), you'll find this beautiful 200-acre camp. Reaping the benefits of its Big Thicket location, the camp is lined with towering oak, bay, magnolia, cypress, hickory, beech, and pine trees. There are more than 3 miles of nature trails here, as well as obstacle courses. The biggest draw, though, is Village Creek—one of Southeast Texas's most popular canoe streams and a great place to swim and picnic. Guests can also fish in the creek and sloughs. RV and tent camping is an option, as is spending the night in a rustic log cabin.

Ken Pelt Boyhood Memories Art Gallery. 12487 Pelt Rd. (take TX 326 south for 13 miles from Kountze and then go east on FM 421 for 1.2 miles); (409) 287-3300. Artist Ken Pelt, a native son of the Big Thicket area is a self-taught painter who delights in capturing the natural wonder of the area through his folk art paintings and murals. His creations can be seen on weekdays at Pelt Farm from March through October. Call ahead to make sure the gallery is open.

Kirby-Hill House Museum. 210 W. Main St.; (409) 246-8000 or (866) 244-8442; kirbyhill house.com. John L. Kirby built this mansion for his lumber-tycoon brother John Henry Kirby in 1902, and the Kirby family lived here for the next 85 years. Today, the Hardin County Arts and Educational Foundation owns the house, which is filled with antique furniture, photos, documents, and other mementos dating back to the 1830s. Part of the house doubles as a bed-and-breakfast, with guests sleeping amid the original decor; see the Where to Stay section below for more information. Informational tours of the museum are offered weekdays; call to arrange. Special educational programs, lunches, and murder mystery theater dinners are also offered throughout the year. Call or visit the website to learn about upcoming events.

where to eat

Mama Jack's Restaurant. 215 S. Pine St., just off US 69; (409) 246-3450. Order off the menu or visit the all-you-can-eat buffet for your choice of homemade breads, chicken and dumplings, meat loaf, pork chops, potatoes, veggies, and good old-fashioned desserts like cobblers and pies. There's also a salad bar. $–$$.

where to stay

Ethridge Farm Log Cabin Bed and Breakfast. 103 S. Williford Rd. (about 3 miles south of Kountze); (409) 898-2710 or (409) 246-3978; ethridgefarm.com. Get a taste of country livin' when you stay at one of these log cabins in the woods. Ethridge Farm guests have their choice of the larger log cabin lodge, 3 cabins, and the Barn Hideaway. Your stay includes a country breakfast in the lodge, where you'll enjoy breakfast favorites like waffles, pancakes, bacon, eggs, biscuits, grits, hash browns, and juice and coffee. For an additional fee, you can enjoy a country dinner, a candlelight dinner, or time in the outdoor spa. $$.

Indian Springs Camp and RV Park. 6106 Holland Cemetery Rd., just east of US 69 and across the highway from the Big Thicket Visitor's Center; (409) 246-2508; indiansprings camp.net. Rough it by camping in your RV or a tent, or stay the night in a cabana-style cabin. Either way, you'll wake up surrounded by towering trees with lots of opportunities for hiking and exploring the Big Thicket area. See the listing in the Where to Go part of this section for more information. $–$$.

Kirby-Hill Bed and Breakfast. 210 W. Main St.; (409) 246-8000 or (866) 244-8442; kirbyhillhouse.com. Sleep surrounded by antiques in the historic Kirby-Hill mansion, which dates back to 1902 and is listed in the Where to Go section. Three rooms are available. The accommodations include a standard double bed, a sitting room, bathroom with an original claw-foot tub, use of the kitchen, and a home-style breakfast. A $30 deposit is required to hold your reservation here. $.

silsbee

When Houston businessman John Henry Kirby made his way to the area in 1893, he wanted to profit from the lumber here. But as fellow businessman Nathaniel D. Silsbee pointed out, the lack of a railroad in the area meant there was no way to transport freshly cut timber. So the duo worked together to build the Gulf, Beaumont, and Kansas City Railroad from Beaumont to San Augustine. All the railroad and lumber hustle and bustle in the area eventually resulted in the birth of a town, which locals named after Silsbee.

Today, the town remains a lumber hot spot, though its economy has diversified to include manufacturing, health care, and tourism. Much of this tourism stems from people visiting the Big Thicket, but Silsbee also attracts visitors with its historic icehouse-turned-museum and a couple of good catfish restaurants in nearby Lumberton.

getting there

From Kountze, follow TX 418 (also called 5th Street in Kountze) for just over 10 miles, then take a right at North 5th Street and follow the road for less than a mile into Silsbee. Alternatively, you can get to Silsbee by following US 287/US 69 South for about 2.7 miles, then taking a slight left at TX 327 East and follow the road for 6 miles. Take a left at 5th Street and follow the road for about a half-mile into town.

where to go

Ice House Museum. 818 Earnest Ave. at 4th Street; (409) 385-2444; icehousemuseum .org. In 1928, Gulf States Utilities built the Silsbee Ice House, which later became the property of H. C. Hopkins and C. F. Young. In its early years the Ice House produced close to 30,000 tons of ice. The rate of production declined substantially when refrigeration was invented, though the Ice House continued to produce ice for parties, recreational events, and local businesses. The Ice House finally closed in 1983.

Seven years later, Silsbee resident Helen White spearheaded an effort to turn the unused Ice House into a museum. In 1991, the Ice House became the town's first building—albeit a deteriorating one—to receive a historic designation from the Texas Historical Commission. The building was restored with the help of volunteers, who also acquired artwork and historical artifacts from the area to display in the museum.

With the help of the City of Silsbee's Economic Development Corporation, the Ice House has recently expanded to hold even more pieces and accommodate meetings, workshops, and special events. Today, visitors come to the free museum here to see historical and art exhibits, with many pieces donated by local residents. Closed Sunday through Tuesday.

where to eat

If you're looking for some home cooking, you'll find a few restaurants in Silsbee. But there are even more restaurants in nearby Lumberton, about 7 miles south of Silsbee off of US 96. To give you more options, restaurants in both towns are included here.

Catfish Cabin. 192 S. LHS Dr., Lumberton; (409) 755-6800; catfishcabin.com. The decor here might be kitschy, but the Catfish Cabin is the real deal: Ask any local, and he or she will tell you that the James family's restaurant serves up some of the freshest (and most popular) fried and grilled seafood in town. Before your meal, you'll get some fresh roasted peanuts. Feel free to throw the shells on the floor as you eat them—that's what the locals do. $–$$.

The Cottage. 5843 Old Evadale Rd. (1 block north of US 96 in Silsbee); (409) 385-9057. True to the spirit of its name, The Cottage is relaxing and cozy, with just 10 tables. Crowds flock to here to eat what the restaurant calls "most everything folks are hungry for." Around here, that means burgers, sandwiches, salads, steaks, catfish, and homemade fries. $–$$.

Katfish Kitchen. 835 N. Main St., Lumberton; (409) 751-5378. It might be a toss-up when deciding which Lumberton catfish restaurant to dine at, but this former burger shack should definitely be in the running. Full of flavor and surprisingly low on grease, the catfish here is served with slaw and hush puppies. The menu also includes other Cajun dishes, including a fairly spicy gumbo. $.

Novrozsky's. 1170 TX 327 East, Silsbee; (409) 386-6300; 441 S. Main St., Lumberton; (409) 755-1224; novrozskys.com. With locations in both Silsbee and Lumberton, this is the place to go for a good burger (including a vegetarian one of the black bean variety), chicken-fried steak, sandwich, or baked potato. This casual joint's extensive menu includes several heart-healthy options. $.

West Texas Bar-B-Que. 3078 US 96 North, Silsbee; (409) 385-0957. Well-flavored barbecue makes this family-run restaurant a local favorite. If you've got a sweet tooth, save room for dessert. The pies here are big sellers. Closed Sunday. Credit cards aren't accepted, so bring cash. $.

where to stay

Econo Lodge. 131 N. LHS Dr., Lumberton; (888) 614-1750; econolodge.com. Formerly the Lumberton Inn, the Econo Lodge offers clean, basic accommodations while you are in town. All rooms have a cable TV with free HBO, hair dryer, refrigerator, microwave, coffeemaker, and an iron and ironing board. Other amenities include free Internet, free hot breakfast, and a business center. $.

Hickory Hills Cabins. 3730 Hickory Hill Rd., Silsbee; (409) 385-0558; hickoryhillbedand breakfast.com. Seeking a place with the hominess of a bed-and-breakfast and the privacy of your own home? The Hickory Hills Cabins offer just that. Country touches decorate each newly built cabin, from the stone fireplace to the log futon to the built-in bunk beds. Each cabin can hold up to 6 people. The cabins' Big Thicket location makes this the perfect spot to clear your head and rejuvenate. $$.

east

day trip 01

east

>>> **battlegrounds & birds:**
pasadena, la porte, baytown,
anahuac

pasadena

In Spanish, Pasadena means "Land of Flowers," which may seem hard to reconcile with this Houston suburb's Ship Channel location and its ties to the shipping and petrochemical industries. But nature is one of the best reasons to come here. Pasadena, after all, is home to Armand Bayou Nature Center, where you can go hiking or kayaking and check out a dazzling collection of plants, birds, and other species in prairie, forest, marsh, and natural bayou habitats. If nature's not your thing, consider catching a show at Texas's oldest community theater, touring two of the area's historic homes, and taking a boat ride around the Port of Houston.

Visiting in May? Try to schedule your trip during the annual strawberry festival, where you can enjoy a carnival midway, live music, and a slice of an enormous strawberry shortcake. For more information, see listing in the Festivals & Celebrations appendix of this book.

getting there

Pasadena is about 15 miles southeast of downtown Houston. To reach this Houston suburb, you have two options, depending on what part of Houston you're coming from: The first option has you following I-45 South to exit 40B, where you'll merge onto I-610 East toward TX 225/Pasadena. After 1.9 miles, take exit 30 B for TX 225 East/La Porte toward

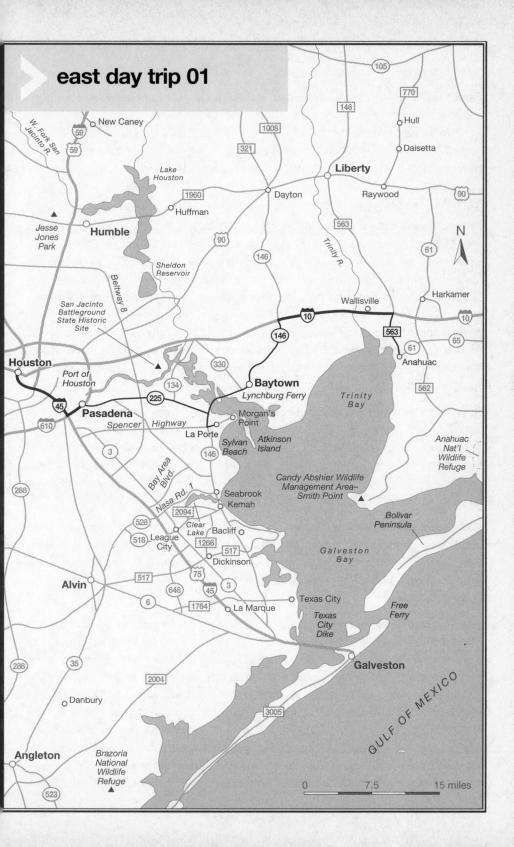

east day trip 01

Pasadena and merge onto TX 225 East. After 2.5 miles, take the Richey Street exit and merge onto La Porte Freeway and follow the signs into Pasadena.

Alternatively, you can follow I-10 East to Loop 610 South and take exit 30B (TX 225 East/La Porte) toward Pasadena; then merge onto TX 225 East and take the Richey Street exit and merge onto La Porte Freeway, following the signs to Pasadena.

where to go

Armand Bayou Nature Center. 8500 Bay Area Blvd.; (281) 474-2551; abnc.org. Named after Gulf Coast wilderness conservationist Armand Yramategui, Armand Bayou Nature Center educates visitors about different wildlife and ecosystems. While hiking along the Marsh, Prairie, Martyn, Karankawa, or Lady Bird trails, for instance, you'll learn about the forest, prairie, marsh, and natural bayou habitats that were once a dime a dozen in this area. Elsewhere in the park—along the center's boardwalk, in particular—you'll find butterfly gardens and a farm site that several European families called home during the mid-1800s. A few times a month, Armand Bayou hosts special activities: Around the full moon, visitors are invited to grab a flashlight and take a moonlit walk in search of owls, and on Saturdays you can book tours of the bayou on several pontoon boats.

Pasadena Heritage Park and Museum. 204 Main St. (1 block south of TX 225, exit at Shaver Street); (713) 472-0565; pasadenahistoricalsociety.org. The Pasadena Historical Society offers free guided tours of the homes that belonged to two of Pasadena's first families—the Pomeroys and the Parks—and which are now filled with antiques, clothing, and furniture dating back to the early 1900s. During your visit, check out the mobile drilling rig designed by the Pomeroy family around that time.

Pasadena Little Theatre. 4318 Allen Genoa Rd.; (713) 941-1PLT; pasadenalittletheatre .org. This is the oldest, continually operating community theater in the Lone Star State. Each season, it puts on about a half-dozen or so plays and musicals. Recent shows have included *Driving Miss Daisy* and *Gypsy*. Call or visit the website for information about upcoming shows.

***Sam Houston* Boat Tour.** 111 E. Loop North, Houston (Sam Houston Pavilion at the Port of Houston); (713) 670-2416; portofhouston.com. Hop onboard the M/V *Sam Houston* for a free 90-minute ride around the Port of Houston, courtesy of the Port of Houston Authority. During the air-conditioned cruise, which departs from the Sam Houston Pavilion, you can see international cargo vessels in action. Tours are offered every day except Monday and depart at 10 a.m. and 2:30 p.m. on Tuesday, Wednesday, Friday, and Saturday, and at 2:30 p.m. on Thursday and Sunday. You'll have to go through a security check prior to boarding the *Sam Houston,* so it's a good idea to arrive about a half-hour early. Occasionally, the Port Authority cancels tours due to security concerns; call ahead to make sure your tour is still scheduled to take place. The tour boat is docked for maintenance in November.

> ## a historic cabin
>
> *En route to the next stop on this trip, La Porte, stop off in Deer Park to see Patrick's Cabin (1410 Center St. between 13th and Helgra Streets; 281-479-2394; deerparktx.gov), a replica of the cabin where Sam Houston took Mexican General Santa Anna to draw up a peace treaty after the Battle of San Jacinto. The replica was built in 1985 by Deer Park employees, who made the cabin pretty authentic in both its design and furnishings. To reach Patrick's Cabin, follow TX 225 East for 3.6 miles and take the Center Street exit. Take a right at Center Street and follow the road for a little less than a mile; the cabin will be on your right.*

where to eat

Don'key's Mexican Food. 5010 Spencer Hwy.; (281) 487-1253. This always-busy hole-in-the-wall serves good, cheap Tex-Mex and some crazy strong margaritas. Don'key's offers daily lunch specials on weekdays featuring Tex-Mex classics such as taco salads, nacho plates, tacos, pechuga de pollo, and enchillada plates. Daily happy hour specials from the bar last from 11 a.m. to 4 p.m. $–$$.

Napoli. 4450 E. Sam Houston Pkwy. South; (281) 998-2223 or (281) 998-0002; napoli pasadena.com. This Italian restaurant aims to re-create the cuisine of Naples by faithfully following traditional recipes and cooking styles. Napoli's features lasagnas, pastas, and other dishes as well as vegetarian Italian creations and even Atkins-friendly dishes. On Monday nights, New York–style pizzas are buy one, get one free. $–$$.

la porte

Primarily a residential community today, this Galveston Bay town played an extremely important role in Texas history—so important that Texas as we know it might not exist otherwise. On April 21, 1836, Texas revolutionaries rode the Lynchburg Ferry here and launched a surprise attack on Mexican General Antonio López de Santa Anna and his army, who were taking a siesta at the time. Within a matter of just 18 minutes, General Sam Houston and his Texas revolutionaries decisively defeated the Mexican army and captured Santa Anna in what became known as the Battle of San Jacinto. This pivotal victory secured Texas's independence from Mexico, paving the way for Texas to become an independent country. Today, you can learn all about the Battle of San Jacinto and Texas's early history at the San Jacinto Battleground State Historic Site. Here you can also see the battleship *Texas,* which was used during World Wars I and II.

Unfortunately, one of La Porte's other big draws—Sylvan Beach—was largely destroyed by Hurricane Ike. While some parts of the beach may reopen in the future, those seeking some beach time are better off visiting Galveston (Southeast Day Trip 02) or Freeport and Surfside Beach (South Day Trip 01).

getting there

La Porte is about 14.5 miles east of Pasadena. Follow TX 225 East for 9.7 miles; then take the TX 146 South exit toward La Porte and follow the signs.

where to go

Lynchburg Ferry. From Houston, follow TX 225 East for about 10 miles from Loop 610; then head north on Independence Parkway, passing San Jacinto Battleground State Historic Site until you reach the south ferry landing; (281) 424-3521. This ferry played a key role in Texas's independence, transporting Texas revolutionaries—aka Texians—to the Battle of San Jacinto in 1836. Today, you can drive your car onto the ferry and ride across the Houston Ship Channel from Houston to Baytown and back. The ride lasts just 7 to 10 minutes, and ferries depart every 5 to 10 minutes from 4:30 a.m. to 8:15 p.m. each day. Call for more information.

San Jacinto Battleground State Historic Site. One Monument Circle; Battleship *Texas*: (281) 479-2431, San Jacinto Museum of History: (281) 479-2421; sanjacinto-museum .org. Load up on Texas history at the San Jacinto Battleground State Historic Site, which is home to the San Jacinto Museum of History, the San Jacinto Monument, and the battleship *Texas*. At this historic spot, General Sam Houston led Texas revolutionaries to defeat Mexican General Antonio López de Santa Anna and his army in just 18 minutes on April 21, 1836, in what became known as the Battle of San Jacinto. The defeat of Mexico's army here resulted in Texas's independence.

The battle is now commemorated with the world's tallest monument tower—the 570-foot San Jacinto Monument. Inside is the San Jacinto Museum of History, which is filled with artifacts from Texas's history before, after, and during the battle. The museum screens a film about the Battle of San Jacinto. Take a ride up to the observation deck at the top of the tower to get a great view of the battleground, the Houston Ship Channel, and the city of Houston.

Also located at the battleground site is the battleship *Texas,* which dates back to World War I, when she became the first US battleship to launch an aircraft and mount aircraft guns. The *Texas* also participated in World War II, including at Normandy on D-Day. Visitors can tour the deck, check out the infirmary and living quarters, and try out the unloaded antiaircraft guns on the restored battleship.

Each April, the San Jacinto Battleground State Historic Site celebrates the Battle of San Jacinto's anniversary with the largest battle reenactment in Texas. For more information consult the listing in the Festivals & Celebrations appendix.

where to eat

Gringo's Mexican Kitchen. 2631 Underwood Rd.; (281) 470-7424; gringostexmex.com. The tasty options here range from shrimp enchiladas to tortilla soup to the Southwest Shrimp & Avocado Salad to burritos, burgers, and fajitas. Gringo's serves a mean green sauce, so be sure to try it with your chips. Drink the 'ritas here slowly—they're strong. $$.

Monument Inn Restaurant. 4406 Independence Pkwy. South (previously Battleground Road); (281) 479-1521; monumentinn.com. Watch the ships navigate the Houston Ship Channel as you dine on some of the La Porte/Baytown area's best seafood. The restaurant could stand a little updating decor-wise, but the food keeps the customers coming back. Those who want oodles of seafood may opt for the All-U-Can-Eat platter filled with cold boiled shrimp, oysters on the half shell, stuffed crab, fries, bread, and fried catfish, shrimp, and oysters. The menu also includes pasta, steak, and chicken options. Whatever you order, be sure to try a cinnamon roll. $$–$$$.

baytown

Though settlers moved here as early as the 1820s, Baytown was largely undeveloped until the early 1900s. Just a few years after oil was discovered at Spindletop in nearby Beaumont (East Day Trip 02), oilmen began drilling near Baytown, along Tabbs Bay by the shoreline towns of Pelly and Goose Creek. In 1917, oilman Ross Sterling and his associates founded the Humble Oil & Refining Company (now Exxon Mobil) and built a refinery at Goose Creek. Baytown began developing around the refinery, with Humble Oil paving roads in the area.

Despite this development, Baytown remained an unincorporated community until its 1945 annexation by the neighboring town of Pelly. When Pelly and Goose Creek residents officially voted to consolidate their towns with Baytown in 1947, though, they opted to name their new city Baytown. Since the city was officially established in January 1948, its population and surface area have grown several times over. So, too, have the number of major petrochemical plants in Baytown.

But while these plants keep the local, national, and international economies pumping, there are other reasons to stop in Baytown for a leisurely visit: a winery; two spots on the Great Texas Coastal Birding Trail, both with marine creatures, to boot; a drag-racing park; an 1869 school; and artifacts from an 18th-century Spanish mission. And those are just a few of the attractions in this growing town with something for almost everyone.

bridging la porte and baytown

As you drive along TX 146 from La Porte to Baytown, you'll cross the Fred Hartman Bridge, aka TX 146 Bridge. A true engineering feat, this 1,250-foot bridge features 440-foot-tall diamond-shaped towers and runs about 2,475 feet at its main span. The US Coast Guard and local police carefully watch the bridge, which runs across the Houston Ship Channel and is traversed by about 200,000 vehicles each day.

getting there

To get to Baytown, follow TX 146 North for about 5.5 miles; then take the West Texas Avenue/Decker Drive exit and merge onto North Robert C. Lanier Drive/South Service Road and follow it for about 0.9 miles; then follow the signs.

where to go

Bayland Park Marina. 2651 S. TX 146; (281) 422-8900; baylandmarina.com. When you cross the bridge from La Porte, this marina is one of the first sights you'll see. Located just south of TX 146, Bayland Park Marina is situated around an 8-acre island near the mouth of Goose Creek. Stop by to take a stroll along the boardwalk.

Baytown Historical Museum. 220 W. Defee St.; (281) 427-8768; baytownchamber.com. This free museum makes its home in Baytown's old post office, where old artifacts and mementos tell the story of Baytown's history. Closed Sunday and Monday.

Baytown Nature Center. 6813 Bayway Dr.; (281) 424-9188; baytownnaturecenter.org. After experiencing quite a bit of damage and losing lots of oak trees to Hurricane Ike, this center has reopened, much to the delight of nature lovers. The terrain includes more than 450 acres of peninsula and 3 bays, enabling this spot on the Great Texas Coastal Birding Trail to attract more than 300 different bird species and a variety of aquatic creatures. The center also has a butterfly garden. Take the kids to the children's nature discovery center to learn about the different creatures and ecosystems. Guests of all ages can kayak, fish, canoe, crab, and picnic here. Baytown Nature Center is open daily unless the weather is exceptionally bad.

Bicentennial Park. Market Street at Lee Drive; (281) 420-6597; tourismprod.baytown.org. This spacious park was built in 1976 to celebrate America's 200th anniversary. A veterans memorial honors local residents who have served in the US military. Baytown holds its annual July 4 celebration and other special events here each year.

Eddie V. Gray Wetlands Center. 724 Market St.; (281) 420-7128; tourismprod.baytown .org. The City of Baytown owns and runs this wetlands center, which sits on the banks of Goose Creek. The center is used primarily for educational purposes, hosting schoolchildren and other visitors who want to learn about wetlands and the gators, fish, turtles, and other creatures that inhabit them. It is also a spot on the Great Texas Coastal Birding Trail. Exhibits feature butterflies, gators, and other creatures. Guided tours are offered for a fee, or guests can take self-guided tours and see the animals and facilities.

Republic of Texas Plaza. 5117 N. Main St.; tourismprod.baytown.org. Dedicated in 1986 to commemorate Texas's sesquicentennial, this park is home to a statue of early Baytown settler Ashbel Smith, the 1896 Wooster School, and the 1910 Brown-McKay House. In April, the Baytown Historical Preservation Association hosts its annual heritage festival here, complete with food and crafts.

Royal Purple Raceway. 2525 S. FM 565; (281) 383-2666; royalpurpleraceway.com. This park hosts drag-racing events on its quarter-mile drag strip and three-eighths-of-a-mile dirt oval track. Each spring, thousands of spectators come out for the National Hot Rod Association's O'Reilly Spring Nationals. Ticket prices vary depending on the event.

Wallisville Heritage Park. Exit 807 on I-10 at Wallisville (13 miles east of Baytown); (409) 389-2252; wallisville.com. On display here are old saddle-making tools and other artifacts from the 1756–1771 Spanish mission Nuestra Señora de la Luz and Presidio San Augustín de Ahumada. Also here is an 1869 school with a history library filled with genealogical records, photo negatives, archival collections from the mission, and oral histories of about a hundred of the area's oldest residents. Closed Sunday.

Yepez Vineyard. 12739 FM 2354; (281) 573-4139 or (281) 804-3410; yepezvineyard.com. This family-owned and operated winery sits on 20 acres. The 2 vineyards here grow blanc du bois and Black Spanish grape plants. Tastings are offered between the 2 vineyards, and you are welcome to bring your own snacks. Throughout the year, the vineyard hosts festivals, concerts, weddings, and other special activities. The winery's tasting room is open Friday through Sunday.

where to eat

Antonio's Italian Grill and Seafood. 2727 Baker Rd.; (281) 420-7577; antoniositaliangrill .com. Antonio's serves good Italian food in a Tuscan atmosphere. The menu includes several healthy choices for those who are watching what they eat. Service is usually quick, though Antonio's often fills up during peak times. $–$$.

El Toro Mexican Restaurant. Three locations: 7529 Bayway Dr., (281) 424-8016; 1301 Decker Dr., (281) 427-3831; 5810 Garth Rd., (281) 421-1919; eltorotexmex.com. This local chain dishes up inexpensive Tex-Mex in a casual setting. The Garth Road location is often noisier than the others. $–$$.

Pizza Bella. 4517-A Garth Rd.; (281) 402-3035; pizzabellabaytown.com. Located in the Kroger Shopping Center, this no-frills pizza place offers dough made from scratch every day and has a large lunchtime following, thanks to its reasonable prices. The flagship large pizza is only $5, and the baked lasagna is only $4.99. $.

Rooster's Steakhouse. 6 W. Texas Ave.; (281) 428-8222; roostersinc.com. This rustic meat market and restaurant is a carnivore's dream come true. The menu is packed with steaks, fried fish, chicken-fried steak, and sandwiches. There are a few baked-fish options. Closed Sunday. $–$$$.

anahuac

Standing on the mouth of the Trinity River where it meets Galveston Bay, Anahuac was first founded as a Spanish fortress in 1821. Eleven years later, Texas insurgents attacked the fort here to rescue William B. Travis, who was held captive by Mexican troops. The fort was dismantled soon after and has since been turned into a park.

The camping-friendly park is just one example of Anahuac's great outdoor opportunities. The rural town—which is the county seat of Chambers County—is also home to the 34,000-acre Anahuac National Wildlife Refuge, which enables visitors to see dozens of bird species and other wildlife in their natural habitats, ranging from coastal marshes to ancient floodplains. Each September, Anahuac celebrates some of its favorite marsh creatures— alligators—at the 3-day Texas Gatorfest. Learn more about this event in the Festivals & Celebrations appendix.

getting there

To reach the last stop on this trip, Anahuac, get back onto TX 146 North and follow it for 7.4 miles. Follow the signs for I-10 East and stay on the interstate for 11.8 miles. Take exit 810 toward FM 563/Anahuac/Liberty.

where to go

Anahuac National Wildlife Refuge. 4017 FM 563; (409) 267-3337; fws.gov/refuge/ Anahuac. A combination of bayous, coastal marshes, prairies, and ancient floodplains makes this 34,000-acre refuge a wonderful place to see hundreds of different species in their natural habitats. Located along Galveston Bay, Anahuac National Wildlife Refuge has attracted more than 250 species of birds, many of them migrants. In addition to observing the wildlife here, visitors can fish, crab, and hunt for waterfowl. Short-term overnight camping is allowed in certain parts of the refuge.

Fort Anahuac Park. 1704 S. Main St. at Trinity Bay; (409) 267-2409. Mexican troops used barracks at a fort here to hold captive William B. Travis and other Texas insurgents.

In June 1832, Col. Francis White Johnson led an attack on the fort in an attempt to get Travis released. This marked the first armed confrontation between Mexican troops and Texas revolutionaries. The fort was dismantled afterwards, and subsequent attempts to reopen it failed. In 1946, Chambers County acquired the fort site and turned it into a park, clearing the site of the fort's remains. Today, visitors use the park for picnicking, camping, and water activities.

Waterborne Education Center. 810 Miller St.; (409) 267-3547; txwaterborne.org. This local nonprofit organization seeks to educate students and the general public about Gulf Coast ecology and stewardship of natural resources. The Waterborne Education Center takes visiting groups of up to 25 persons on scientific excursions aboard 45-foot renovated Coast Guard buoy tenders. These hands-on excursions include opportunities to go trawling for fish in Galveston Bay, test the water quality and check out the wildlife in area marshes, and go seining for fish. Trips last up to 4 hours. Call for more information.

where to eat

Panther Tracks Cafe. 104 S. Main St.; (409) 267-6747. This is the kind of place where the servers know the names of their customers, who keep coming back for more. Most order the buffet, which is stocked with home-cooked favorites like chicken-fried steak, fried okra, and fried catfish. $–$$.

day trip 02

east

>>> oil & art:
beaumont

beaumont

Drive 87 miles east on I-10 from downtown Houston and you'll find yourself in Beaumont—the town that made Texas synonymous with oil. In 1901, Anthony Lucas struck oil while drilling more than 1,000 feet into a salt dome known as Spindletop. For 9 days, oil shot up in the air at a rate of 100,000 barrels per day. Needless to say, Beaumont became a boomtown, with hundreds of companies opening to drill for oil here and in the nearby towns of Orange and Port Arthur.

Two Beaumont museums—Spindletop-Gladys City Boomtown Museum and the Texas Energy Museum—explore Spindletop's history and legacy. Several other museums here explore different subjects, ranging from a famous female athlete to firefighting to old homes. Several galleries and museums give art aficionados the opportunity to see first-class works in all mediums by artists from near and far, while the many antiques shops here are sure to delight shoppers and collectors.

getting there

To reach Beaumont, drive 87 miles east on I-10 from downtown Houston. If you want to turn this into a 2- or 3-day trip, consider combining this trip with East Day Trips 03 and 04, which cover Beaumont's neighboring towns of Nederland, Port Arthur, and Orange.

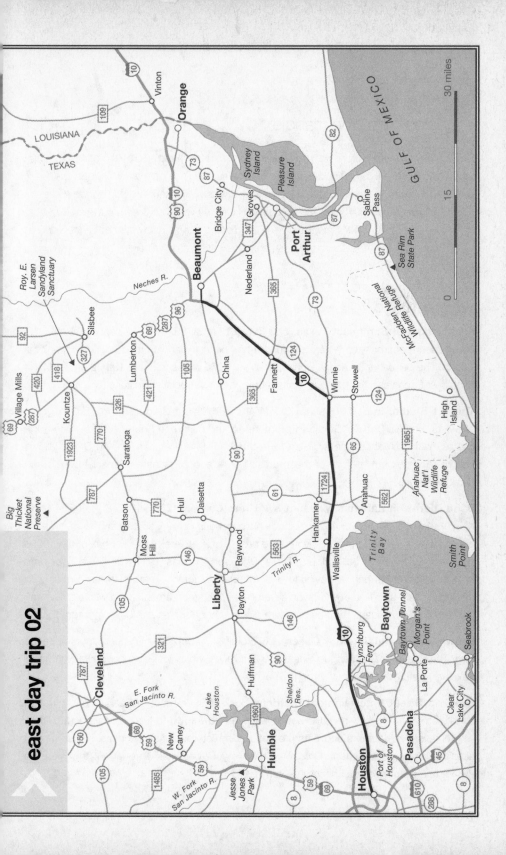

east day trip 02

> ## welcome to the triangle

*During your trip, you're likely to hear someone mention the "Golden Triangle."
Don't worry—it's nothing like the Bermuda Triangle. The nickname "Golden Tri-
angle" refers to Beaumont and the nearby towns of Port Arthur and Orange (East
Day Trips 03 and 04) and, more specifically, to the wealth brought to the area by
the discovery of oil at Spindletop in 1901. Today, people also say the "Golden" in
"Golden Triangle" refers to the gas flares seen at area oil refineries.*

where to go

Art Museum of Southeast Texas. 500 Main St.; (409) 832-3432; amset.org. While this
free museum emphasizes American work, it has been expanding its collection of regional
folk art. The permanent collection includes about 1,000 works from the 19th, 20th, and 21st
centuries. Each year, the museum hosts about 8 to 10 special exhibitions.

The Art Studio, Inc. 720 Franklin St.; (409) 838-5393; artstudio.org. In 1983 a group
of artists founded The Art Studio to promote art and culture in Southeast Texas. In addition to making studio space available to talented artists in the area, The Art Studio allows
visitors to check out exhibits of these artists' work and participate in special events and
demonstrations.

Babe Didrikson Zaharias Museum & Visitors Center. 1750 I-10 East (exit 854/M. L.
King Parkway); (409) 833-4622; babedidriksonzaharias.org. Visit this museum to learn
about the woman that the public voted the best female athlete of the first half of the 1900s
in an Associated Press poll. Mildred "Babe" Didrikson Zaharias (1911–1956), who was born
in nearby Port Arthur before moving to Beaumont at the age of 4, earned three Olympic gold
medals in track-and-field events, won several major golf tournaments, and was a three-time
basketball All-American. The free museum displays her trophies and other memorabilia.

Brown Gallery and Scurlock Gallery. 2675 Gulf St.; (409) 833-4179; beaumontartleague
.org. The Beaumont Art League runs these 2 galleries, which display the work of Southeast
Texas artists. Closed Sunday through Tuesday.

Crockett Street Entertainment District. Crockett Street east of Pearl Street; crockett
street.com. Want to go where the action is? Head downtown to this entertainment district,
where several restaurants and bars are housed in restored historic houses. If you want to
hear live music in Beaumont, Crockett Street is your best bet. Throughout the year, the
district hosts festivals and special events.

Dishman Art Museum. 1030 E. Lavaca St. on the Lamar University campus; (409) 880-8141; lamar.edu. This free gallery on the Lamar University campus houses the Eisenstadt Collection; tribal art from Africa, New Guinea, and pre-Columbian Mexico; and Robert Willis's collection of prints by European masters such as Matisse, Kandinsky, and Miró. Students' work is also displayed. Closed Saturday and Sunday.

Edison Museum. 350 Pine St.; (409) 981-3089; edisonmuseum.org. Using interactive exhibits composed of more than 1,400 artifacts, this free museum offers visitors the opportunity to better understand the life and work of Thomas Alva Edison, American inventor extraordinaire. The museum, which houses the largest collection of Edison's inventions west of the Mississippi, is located in the historic Travis Street Substation. Closed Saturday and Sunday.

Fire Museum of Texas. 400 Walnut St.; (409) 880-3927; firemuseumoftexas.org. Located inside Beaumont's old Central Fire Station, this free museum houses a large collection of old fire engines, fire bells, buckets, badges, and photographs from 1856 to the present. Also here is a 24-foot-tall fire hydrant—the world's largest—donated by Walt Disney Studios to celebrate the rerelease of the movie *101 Dalmatians.* On special occasions, the fire hydrant even sprays water. A puppet theater, safety house, and toys in the Fire Safety Activity Center teach visitors how to prevent and fight fires. Closed Saturday and Sunday, except by appointment. Call ahead if you're interested in scheduling a guided tour of the museum.

Gator Country. 21159 FM 365; (409) 794-WILD; gatorrescue.com. Take a walk on the wild side with a visit to this wildlife adventure park. Big Al, the largest alligator in captivity in the Lone Star State, lives here. Other resident creatures include 130 American alligators, 4 species of turtles, 6 species of crocodiles and caimans, snakes, a Savannah monitor lizard, and a sulcata tortoise. During your visit, you can feed the gators and even hold the babies. The park restaurant serves gator- and Cajun-inspired food. Closed Saturday and Sunday.

Griffin Berry Farm. 2394 Moore Rd.; (409) 753-2247; griffinberryfarm.com. Owners Bill and Barbara Griffin use organic methods to grow apples, grapes, pears, blueberries, peaches, satsumas, kumquats, and other produce. Crops are typically available—many for picking—in May, June, October, and November. Visit the website to find out what produce is available; then call to schedule an appointment to pick your produce of choice.

Jefferson Theatre. 345 Fannin St.; (409) 835-5483; beaumont-tx-complex.com/jefferson theatre.html. Since it was built in 1927, this theater has been known for its grand interior. In its early years, the theater screened movies such as *It's a Wonderful Life* and hosted traveling shows, orchestra performances, and theatrical performances. Though the theater faced possible destruction in the 1970s, it was rescued in 1976 by a group that called themselves the Jefferson Theatre Preservation Society and was restored in 2000. Today, the City of Beaumont runs the theater, which hosts everything from concerts to plays to movies. Jefferson Theatre is listed in the National Register of Historic Places and is a recognized Texas Historic Landmark.

John J. French Museum. 3025 French Rd.; (409) 898-0348; jjfrench.com. This place has more than a few "firsts" to its name: It is one of the first painted houses, one of the first 2-story houses, one of the first houses in the area built out of milled lumber, and the oldest restored house in Beaumont. The house in which the museum operates dates back to 1845, when it was built by pioneer and merchant John Jay French. The restored home features antique furniture, clothing, decor, and household tools that give visitors a flavor for life in the house's heyday. Also on-site are a blacksmith shop, corncrib, smokehouse, and tannery. Closed Sunday and Monday.

Julie Rogers Theatre for the Performing Arts. 765 Pearl St. (adjacent to the Beaumont Civic Center); (409) 832-0798; beaumont-tx-complex.com/julierogerstheatre.html. The Symphony of Southeast Texas, Beaumont Civic Opera, Beaumont Civic Ballet, and Beaumont Ballet Theatre all perform at this exquisite theater. Call to find out about upcoming performances. You just might have the opportunity to see a world-class show. After all, Baryshnikov has danced on the stage here before.

McFaddin-Ward House. 1906 Calder Ave. at Third Street; (409) 832-2134; mcfaddinward.org. Built in 1905–6, this beaux arts colonial-style house was home to the prominent McFaddin family for 75 years. Today, the restored manse, as well a carriage barn, retains many original furnishings. Docent-led tours last about 90 minutes, beginning at 10 and 11 a.m. and 1:30 and 2:30 p.m. Tuesday through Saturday. Each tour is limited to 8 guests, so arrive at least 10 minutes early to make sure you get a spot.

Spindletop-Gladys City Boomtown Museum. 5550 University Dr. at US 69/96/287 (on Lamar University campus); (409) 880-1750; spindletop.org. Learn how Beaumont went from being a tiny town to the lifeblood of the oil and petroleum industry in the early 1900s. Exhibits feature period clapboard buildings, including a saloon, post office, blacksmith shop, and, of course, wooden oil derricks. There's also a monument to the Lucas gusher that started it all. Closed Monday.

Texas Energy Museum. 600 Main St.; (409) 833-5100; texasenergymuseum.org. The perfect complement to the Spindletop-Gladys City Boomtown Museum, this museum educates the public about petroleum science and Spindletop's role in the birth of the modern petroleum industry. In a 21st-century twist, talking robots tell visitors about the early oil drilling in the area. Closed Monday.

Tyrrell Historical Library. 695 Pearl St.; (409) 833-2759; beaumontlibrary.org. Housed inside the beautiful Gothic-style First Baptist Church, this library's collections include thousands of Texas history books, genealogical books, archives concerning Southeast Texas, letters from the Civil War, and other rare documents. The museum is listed in the National Register of Historic Places. Closed Sunday.

where to shop

Burns Antik Haus. 2195 Calder Ave. in Olde Town; (409) 835-3080; burnsantikhaus.com. The owners travel to Europe's warehouses and farms to handpick each item sold here. The extensive collection includes art, ceramics, decorative items, glasses, rugs, furniture, lighting fixtures, and architectural ironwork. Closed Sunday and Monday, except by appointment.

11th Street Market. 2470 North 11th St.; (409) 898-2600. If you get the shopping bug but don't quite know what you want, this expansive emporium houses 29 different shops under one roof. You can find gifts, collectibles, antiques, furniture, and more, with price ranges to match. Closed Sunday and Monday.

Ella + Scott. 460 N. M. L. King Pkwy.; (409) 835-8280; shopellascott.com. This newly opened fashion boutique is housed in a historic Beaumont building and specializes in apparel and accessories from designers such as Blank Denim and Collective Concepts. Closed Sunday.

Finder's Fayre Quality Antiques and Interior Design. 1485 Calder Ave.; (409) 833-7000; findersfayre.com. This 4,000-square-foot antiques shop fills its 8 showrooms with unique items from France, England, Germany, and the US.

McManus Co. 820 N. 11th St.; (409) 833-4393; mcmanusco.com. This lighting and furniture store sells decorative antiques and items such as pillows, table runners, wall decor, and vases. McManus Co. is also a distributor of for the creations of John Medeiros of East Providence, RI, an acclaimed designer of high-quality jewelry using man-made stones set in precious metals.

where to eat

Bryan's 797. 797 N. 5th St. at Hazel; (409) 832-3900; bryans797.net. If you're looking for a nice restaurant in Beaumont, this is your place. Diners enjoy attentive service while they feast on made-to-order dishes with the freshest ingredients. The chef borrows from Asian, Chinese, Cajun, Lowcountry, and eastern European cuisine and techniques to create one-of-a-kind southern-inspired dishes. Call for reservations. $$–$$$.

Chaba Thai Cuisine. 4340 E. Lucas Dr.; (409) 899-4500. Diners here enjoy authentic, well-seasoned Thai favorites like pad thai, curries, and spring rolls. Service is quick. $–$$.

Doug Nelson's Cafe. 10025 Fannett Rd./TX 124; (409) 842-1557; facebook.com/DougNelsonCafe. For more than 30 years, locals have been stopping off here for lunch, ordering up barbecue, cornmeal-crusted shrimp and catfish, and potato salad, among other dishes. Closed Saturday and Sunday. $–$$.

Floyd's Cajun Seafood & Texas Steakhouse. 2290 I-10 South; (409) 842-0686; floyds seafood.com. With 3 locations in Southeast Texas, Floyd's offers Louisiana-inspired staples such as crawfish, fresh Gulf oysters, gumbo, and frog legs. They also serve respectable steaks and pastas. If you can't find anything you like on the extensive menu, you're probably not hungry! Closed Monday. If you are in the military, Floyd's will give you a 50 percent discount. $$–$$$.

Hamburger Depot. 1652 W. Cardinal Dr.; (409) 840-6600. Big juicy burgers and well-toasted buns here make this a hamburger lover's heaven—and a cholesterol watcher's hell. Walk up to the counter to order. $–$$.

Jack Patillo's Bar-B-Que. 2775 Washington Blvd.; (409) 833-3154. Patillo's has been around for nearly a century and is now consistently rated the best place to get barbecue in Beaumont, Port Arthur, and Orange. Some even think the food here beats out the juicy ribs in Lockhart and Austin. Patillo's smokes its barbecue and uses a special sauce recipe derived from the West Indies. $–$$.

Richard's Cafe. 1087 Magnolia St.; (409) 835-7063. Richard's serves soul food favorites like beef tips over mashed potatoes or oxtail over white rice. Owned and operated by a hard-working husband-wife team, this cafe is a local favorite and a step back into the home kitchens with regional dishes that many residents of this area have enjoyed for generations. The service is friendly. $–$$.

Suga's Deep South Cuisine & Jazz Bar. 461 Bowie St.; (409) 813-1808; sugasdeep south.com. Located in a beautifully restored historic building in downtown Beaumont, Suga's offers down-South comfort recipes with an uptown twist, such as fried Gulf shrimp in cornmeal served with a pineapple/jicama slaw, or a Berkshire pork chop roasted with pear/apple chutney and whiskey. Along with the expansive menu, Suga's is also a happening jazz venue. $$$.

Zydeco Louisiana Diner. 270 Crockett St.; (409) 835-4455; zydecolouisianadiner.com. If you're in town at lunchtime on a weekday, stop in for southern Louisiana favorites such as po'boys, gumbo, red beans and rice, jambalaya, okra, mashed potatoes, and black-eyed peas. $–$$.

where to stay

MCM Elegante Hotel & Conference Center. 2355 I-10 South; 409-842-3600; mcmel-egantebeaumont.com. The Beaumont location of this small regional chain has been named the town's best hotel for 5 years running. Guests enjoy luxury accommodations, including fine bed linens, a fitness center, a day spa, 3 restaurants, a tropical outdoor pool and hot tub, and free wireless Internet. $$.

day trip 03

east

>>> **port dreams:**
nederland, port arthur

nederland

When Port Arthur Townsite Company owner Arthur Stilwell built a railroad from Kansas City to Sabine Lake (along the Texas-Louisiana border) in the late 1880s, he had the financial backing of parties in Holland. Hoping Dutch people would settle in the region, he gave many towns along the railroad's route Dutch names. Among them was this little town just 10 miles southeast of Beaumont, which he called Nederland.

While some of the people who settled here were in fact Dutch, the area also attracted French immigrants from Louisiana and people from elsewhere in the country and state. Two museums in Nederland now celebrate the town's early French and Dutch settlers.

getting there

Nederland lies about 90 miles east of Houston. To get there, follow I-10 East to exit 849, where you'll merge onto US 287/US 69 South/US 96 South toward Port Arthur and follow the road for 6 miles. Then exit onto TX 347 East toward Nederland.

where to go

Dutch Windmill Museum. 1500 Boston Ave.; (409) 722-0279; nederlandtx.com. A 40-foot-tall replica of a Dutch windmill pays tribute to the Dutch immigrants who settled Nederland in 1898. Inside is a free museum with artifacts including wooden shoes, a trunk

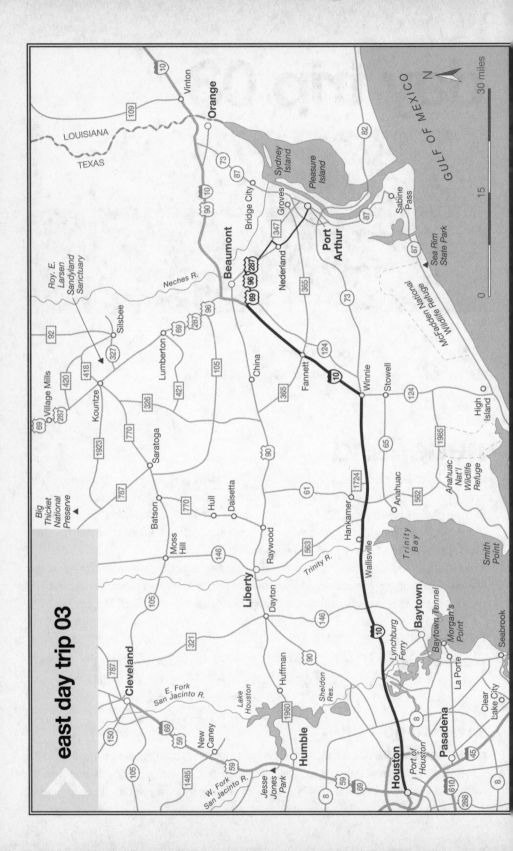

east day trip 03

brought over from Holland in the late 1800s, and memorabilia from former country-and-western musician and former Nederland resident Tex Ritter. Closed Monday in spring and summer; Monday through Wednesday in fall and winter.

La Maison Des Acadiens Museum. 1500 Boston Ave.; (409) 722-0279; nederlandtx .com. Located adjacent to the Dutch Windmill Museum, this museum opened in 1976—the US bicentennial—to honor the French who came from South Louisiana to settle Nederland. This aptly named free museum, which features old French furniture and other period pieces, is housed in a building modeled after early Acadian homes in southern Louisiana: *La Maison Des Acadiens* means "House of Acadia." Hours mirror those of the Dutch Windmill Museum (above).

where to eat

La Suprema. 3106 FM 365; (409) 722-2880; lasuprema1970.com. Four generations of the Martinez family have been serving up fresh Tex-Mex dishes in this Nederland spot. Made from time-tested family recipes, the fare here fits the bill when you are in the mood for some good Tex-Mex comfort food. Daily specials include burritos, enchiladas, tacos, and other goodies at reasonable prices. Service is quick and friendly. $–$$.

The Schooner Restaurant. 1507 S. US 69 at FM 365; (409) 722-2323; theschooner restaurant.com. Since 1947, locals have been coming to The Schooner to eat fish caught the same day, as well as steaks. While the food is a little expensive considering the area, the restaurant is extremely casual. $$–$$$.

port arthur

Although Port Arthur doesn't have a Dutch name, it is the namesake of Port Arthur Townsite Company owner Arthur Stilwell. He established the town along the edge of Sabine Lake in the late 1800s, with the hope that it would be many things—resort town, port city, and the end of the railroad line he planned to build from Kansas City to Port Arthur.

In 1900, John W. Gates began to make some of Stilwell's visions realities after he gained control of Stilwell's interest in the Port Arthur Townsite Company. Gates shelled out $1.4 million to dredge the Port Arthur canal before selling it to the US government for a mere dollar. Congress subsequently designated Port Arthur a point of entry. Today, it is part of the so-called Golden Triangle (along with Beaumont, East Day Trip 02, and Orange, East Day Trip 04). A booming port, it is home to three major refineries and remains the terminus of the Kansas City Southern Railway. It is also home to two wildlife management areas and two national wildlife refuges.

> ## where the birds are

Thanks to the marshes in the area, the Golden Triangle is home to a number of great birding sites. To learn about recent bird sightings and upcoming birding events in the area, visit the Golden Triangle Audubon's website at goldentriangle audubon.org.

getting there

You don't have to drive far to get to the next stop on this day trip—Port Arthur. Just a few miles southeast of Nederland, Port Arthur can be reached by following US 287 South/US 69 South/US 96 South roughly 6 miles until you see signs directing you around Port Arthur.

where to go

Candy Cain Abshier Wildlife Management Area (WMA). 10 Parks & Wildlife Dr.; (409) 736-2551; tpwd.state.tx.us. This 207-acre preserve sits along Galveston Bay and Trinity Bay. Thanks to the hundreds upon hundreds of birds that stop here during spring migration, it is one of the most popular spots on the Great Texas Coastal Birding Trail. A smaller number of birds pass through as they head south for the winter. A wheelchair-accessible wildlife viewing tower here allows visitors to spy on some of the creatures—birds included—that make their home among the live oaks and in the freshwater ponds here. The park was named in honor of former Texas Parks and Wildlife employee, Catherine "Candy" Cain Abshier. Take note before you visit: There are no public restrooms, and it's a good idea to bring your own water and mosquito repellent.

Golden Triangle Veterans Memorial Park. 8100 Gulfway Dr.; (409) 842-0500. This park pays tribute to 10,000 servicemen and women from the Golden Triangle who served during World Wars I and II, the Korean War, Vietnam, peacetime, and Desert Storm. A 50-foot tall Tower of Honor lists the names, ranks, and service branches of the 930 Golden Triangle residents who were killed while in service or are still missing in action. On display are tributes to different branches of service, as well as an old jet, tank, helicopter, and a 7-foot-tall US Marine statue.

Lower Neches Wildlife Management Area. Head northeast from Port Arthur on TX 87/TX 73 for about 10 miles to Bridge City, turn right on Lake Street, and drive for about 2 miles until you see the unit headquarters/sign-in station; (409) 736-2551; tpwd.state.tx.us. Here you'll find an old oil well drilling site and a wheelchair-accessible observation platform, where you can check out egrets, ducks, and herons in their natural habitat—a Sabine River marsh. Call for more information.

McFaddin and Texas Point National Wildlife Refuges (NWR). Along TX 87 at the southeastern tip of Texas, near the Louisiana border; Texas Point NWR is adjacent to Sabine Pass, about 15 miles south of Port Arthur; McFaddin NWR is 12 miles farther west; PO Box 358, Sabine Pass; (409) 971-2909; fws.gov. These 2 national wildlife refuges were established by the federal government to protect the Gulf Coast's freshwater and salt marshes and the creatures and plants that inhabit them. The 55,000-acre McFaddin NWR is the largest freshwater marsh remaining on the Texas Gulf Coast; it also includes brackish marsh. This allows McFaddin to attract one of Texas's largest populations of American alligators.

McFaddin's eastern neighbor, Texas Point NWR, includes 8,900 acres of freshwater and salt marshes, as well as wooded uplands and prairie ridges. Texas Point was previously known as Sea Rim. More than 60,000 snow geese and 23 duck species can be found here.

Thousands of migrating birds stop at the refuges to eat and rest. In addition to birding, McFaddin and Texas Point offer opportunities to fish, hunt for waterfowl, go crabbing, and view wildlife. Both wildlife refuges open each day 1 hour before sunrise and remain open 1 hour after sunset.

The headquarters for both Texas Point and McFaddin NWR is located approximately 2 miles south of Sabine Pass on TX 87. The office is closed Saturday and Sunday.

Museum of the Gulf Coast. 700 Procter St.; (409) 982-7000; museumofthegulfcoast.org. This 39,000-square-foot museum teaches visitors about the history of the Texas/Louisiana Gulf Coast region, from the Native Americans to the Europeans to the Civil War to the 20th and 21st centuries. Exhibits cover everything from natural history to decorative arts to local legends such as Janis Joplin, ZZ Top, and NFL coaches Jimmy Johnson and Bum and Wade Phillips.

Pleasure Island. South on TX 82 across Martin Luther King Bridge; (409) 982-4675; pleasure islandtx.com. This 18.5-mile man-made stretch of land is surrounded by Sabine Lake and the Sabine Neches Intracoastal Waterway, making it a recreational haven for visitors of all ages. Highlights include Lakefront Park, where you can picnic and play volleyball and basketball; Fun Island Depot, which has activities for kids; and Walter Umphrey State Park, which boasts a lighted fishing pier as well as tent and RV camping. There's also a bike trail, disc golf course, a marina, boat ramps, an RV park, and places to grab food and drinks.

Pompeiian Villa. 1953 Lakeshore Dr.; (409) 983-5977. This pink stucco home was built in 1900 for "Barbed Wire King" Isaac Elwood, who later sold it in exchange for Texas Company (Texaco) stock worth $10,000 back then (about $3 billion today). Now listed in the National Register of Historic Places, the house was modeled after homes built in Pompeii, Italy, around AD 75–80 and is furnished with pieces from the 1700s to the present. Tours are available.

Port of Port Arthur. 221 Houston Ave.; (409) 983-2011; portofportarthur.com. This recently expanded port connects with Kansas City Southern Railway to ship cargo to dozens of locations across the US and Canada. It is home to "Big Arthur," the Gulf Coast's largest gantry crane. An observation deck at the port offers a good view of the harbor. Tours of the Port of Port Arthur (try saying that three times fast!) are offered by appointment.

Queen of Peace Shrine. 801 9th Ave. in Hoa Binh Park; (409) 983-7676. To thank Port Arthur for welcoming them with open arms, Vietnamese parishioners of the Queen of Vietnamese Martyrs' Catholic Church planted beautiful gardens in Hoa Binh Park, where a statue of the Virgin Mary also stands.

Rose Hill Manor. 100 Woodworth Blvd.; (409) 985-7292. Rome H. Woodworth built this 14-room, southern Greek Revival–style home in 1906. It sits on 11 acres on the outskirts of town and includes a balcony that wraps around the house. Tours are offered daily.

Sabine Pass Battleground State Historic Site. 6100 Dick Dowling Rd. (12 miles south of Port Arthur on FM 3322/Dick Dowling Road, off TX 87); (512) 463-7948; visitsabinepass battleground.com. At this site in 1863, 46 Confederate soldiers saved Texas from penetration by Union forces. Led by Lt. Richard "Dick" Dowling, they captured 4 Union gunboats and about 350 Union soldiers. The 58-acre battleground, which is managed by the Texas Historical Commission, honors these men with a bronze statue of Lt. Dowling. Interpretive panels tell visitors about the Civil War battle.

Shrine of Our Lady of Guadalupe. 3648 Staff Sgt. Lucian Adams Dr.; patx.us/olgchurch/ shrine.htm. Our Lady of Guadalupe Catholic Church dedicated this outdoor shrine, which includes a 17-foot bronze statue of the Virgin Mary. Sculpted by Miguel Angel Macias and Douglas Clark, it stands on rocks from Mexico City's Mount Tepayac, where the Virgin Mary is believed to have appeared. A second bronze statue, measuring 7 feet high, depicts St. Juan Diego.

Texas Artists Museum. 3501 Cultural Center Dr.; (409) 983-4881; texasartistmuseum .com. Texas Artists Museum showcases work from artists who live in or hail from Port Arthur and the surrounding towns. Throughout the year, the free museum hosts special exhibits, youth programs, and events featuring musicians, singers, dancers, painters, and actors. Closed Sunday and Monday.

Vuylsteke Dutch Home. 1831 Lakeshore Dr.; (409) 984-6101. This lavish Dutch colonial– style home was built by Port Arthur's first Dutch consul in 1905. The restored home includes the original furnishings. Call ahead to schedule a free tour.

White Haven. 2545 Lakeshore Dr.; (409) 984-6101. This southern Greek Revival–style mansion is filled with furniture and porcelain dating back to the 1700s and 1800s. Call to schedule a tour.

where to eat

Boudain Hut. 5714 Gulfway Dr.; (409) 962-5079. By day, diners walk up to the window at this rustic joint to order Cajun food; by night, the place transforms into a bar with live music five nights a week. A local favorite is their Boudain Balls, Cajun sausages stuffed with rice and seasonings then deep fried. Open daily for breakfast, lunch, and dinner. $–$$.

Larry's French Market & Cajun Restaurant. 3701 Atlantic Hwy./FM 366 in Groves (about 5 miles northeast of Port Arthur); (409) 962-3381; larrysfrenchmarket.com. You'll know you're near the Louisiana border the moment you step into Larry's, which serves up Cajun favorites such as fried boudin balls, crawfish étouffée, shrimp Creole, gumbo, fried gator, and po'boys. There's live music Thursday through Saturday. Don't be shy about dancing—the locals aren't. $–$$$.

Rancho Grande. 7670 Memorial Blvd.; (409) 729-9105; ranchograndebarandgrill.com. Part of a local chain, Rancho Grande in Port Arthur offers some purely Mexican special-ties in addition to its ever-popular Tex-Mex menu. The restaurant is famous for its chicken diablo and killer margaritas. The restaurant offers a kid's menu and some "healthy" dining options as well. $$.

where to stay

Driftwood Inn & RV Park Resort. 3700 Memorial Blvd.; (409) 985-8411. The no-frills rooms at this inn and RV part include wireless Internet and digital cable; there's also a pool on-site. Pets aren't allowed in rooms, only in the RV spots. $.

Holiday Inn Park Central. 2929 Jimmy Johnson Blvd.; (409) 724-5000; holidayinn.com. This Holiday Inn offers comfortable accommodations, an outdoor pool, a fitness center, a business center, and Internet access in rooms and public spaces. The hotel's Park Cafe serves breakfast and dinner, and kids under 12 eat for free when accompanied by an adult. Room service dining is also offered. The Manhattan Lounge offer drinks and hors d'oeuvres. $$.

day trip 04

east

>>> **border treasures:**
orange

orange

Day-tripper, you're barely in Texas anymore. Orange is the easternmost city along the Texas-Louisiana border created by the Sabine River. Though the town is Texan through and through, its proximity to Louisiana is evident in the Cajun cooking and the coastal marshes that attract dozens of bird species. The Sabine Lake also offers fishing opportunities, as do the Neches and Sabine Rivers.

This hospitable town is as old as Texas, with its 1836 founding date. The town was named for wild orange groves sighted along the Sabine by Spanish and French boatmen who had visited the area many years earlier. Like nearby Beaumont (East Day Trip 02) and Port Arthur (East Day Trip 03), Orange is part of the Golden Triangle. To see just how big of a role Orange plays in the petroleum industry today, you need only take a drive along FM 1006 South. Along this stretch are several miles of plants that produce products from petroleum.

The Texas Department of Transportation's Travel Center has a location in Orange. Call (409) 883-9416, or stop in at 1708 E. I-10 (exit 879) to pick up brochures, get tips on where to fish, and more.

getting there

Travel east on I-10 from Houston for 113 miles; take Exit 877 and follow the feeder road into downtown Orange.

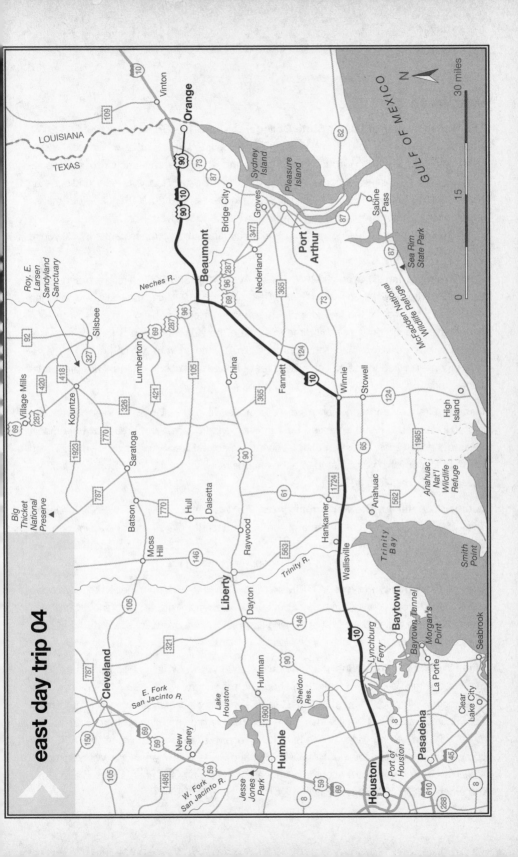

where to go

The Brown Center of Lamar State College–Orange. 4205 Park Ave.; (409) 883-2939; lsco.edu. Banker, shipbuilder, and philanthropist Edgar W. Brown Jr. and his wife, Gladys, paid more than $1 million (roughly $10 million today) for the construction of this house in 1956. The colonial-style home is made even more exquisite by its surroundings—an 88-acre garden, towering pine trees, and azaleas galore. The 20,000-square-foot manse features 20 rooms, a winding staircase, 2 porches, and 2 foyers—one decorated with a scenic mural. Lamar State College now uses the house as a conference center. Call if you're interested in visiting.

First Presbyterian Church. 902 W. Green Ave.; (409) 883-2097; firstpresorange.com. When this Greek Revival–style church was dedicated in 1912, it was the first air-conditioned public building west of the Mississippi. There was just one problem: The city of Orange didn't have enough power at that time to operate the air conditioner! So a private power plant was built next door to get the job done. Today, the church—which houses a 2,435-pipe organ—is listed in the National Register of Historic Places. Free tours are offered by appointment only.

Fishing. Orange's location along the water makes it a popular place to fish. You can find flounder, redfish, and speckled trout in Sabine Lake, bass and bream at Blue Elbow Swamp, and a variety of fish in the Neches and Sabine Rivers. For recommendations on where to fish or fishing tours, stop into the Orange Convention & Visitors Bureau at 803 W. Green Ave. or call (409) 883-1011.

Lutcher Theater for the Performing Arts. 707 Main Ave.; (409) 886-5535; lutcher.org. This 1,500-seat theater hosts some of the best concerts, plays, and operas in the area. Recent performances have included *Catch Me If You Can, A Chorus Line,* and *Biloxi Blues.* Call or visit the website to find out what's happening during your trip.

Orange Community Players. 708 Division St.; (409) 882-9137; orangecommunityplayers .com. This little community-run theater puts on several shows a year, including a Christmas production. Call to find out about upcoming shows. Recent productions include *A Salute to The Carol Burnett Show* and *The Full Monty.*

Piney Woods Country Winery & Vineyards. 3408 Willow Dr. (take I-10 East to exit 876, turn west at the bayou, and take the first right to the winery); (409) 883-5408; pineywoods wines.com. With wooded surroundings, this 25-year-old winery boasts a country ambience. The winery specializes in fruit wines made from locally grown fruits and berries. They also make a Pecan Mocha wine. Wines here have received recognition in more than 70 wine competitions, including the Houston Livestock Show & Rodeo International Wine Competition. Tours and tastings are offered; call ahead to make sure someone's available to show you around. Closed Sunday.

taking flight

If you're a serious birder, consider visiting the Sabine National Wildlife Refuge in Hackberry, Louisiana. Located about 40 miles southeast of Orange, the wetlands here are a designated "Internationally Important Bird Area" based on the sheer number of migratory waterfowl, wading birds, and other marsh birds found here each year. For more information on Sabine National Wildlife Refuge, call (337) 762-3816 or visit fws.gov/swlarefugecomplex/sabine.

Shangri La Botanical Gardens and Nature Center. 2111 W. Park Ave.; (409) 670-9113; shangrilagardens.org. Situated on 252 acres, Shangri La epitomizes tranquility. The botanical gardens include more than 300 plant species arranged in 5 different formal "rooms"; there are also 4 sculpture "rooms." Next to the gardens sits a bird blind, where you can check out the nesting birds. Stop at the Nature Center to enjoy hands-on activities. Inside the Orientation Center is a children's garden, theater, exhibition greenhouses, a garden shop, and a cafe. Closed Monday.

Stark Museum of Art. 712 Green Ave.; (409) 886-2787; starkmuseum.org. This first-class museum houses a significant collection of 19th- and 20th-century western American art, including sculptures by Frederic Remington and paintings from the Taos School of New Mexico. Stark Museum of Art is also home to sizeable collections of Native American art, rare books, manuscripts, and decorative arts. Special exhibits are held throughout the year. Admission is free.

Tony Houseman State Park and Wildlife Management Area. 1708 E. I-10 (exit 879); (409) 579-9883; tpwd.state.tx.us. This is the first stop on the Great Texas Coastal Birding Trail and a good place to see birds in the Piney Woods, particularly during the summer and during migration season (fall and spring). Unfortunately, the trails are lacking, and access is limited. You can picnic here, however. A boardwalk system enables visitors to walk out to Blue Elbow Swamp, where you can fish for bass and bream. The site is also home to the Orange location of Texas Department of Transportation's Travel Center, where you can pick up brochures, get tips on where to fish, and more.

W. H. Stark House. 610 W. Main Ave.; (409) 883-0871; whstarkhouse.org. This Queen Anne–style house dates back to 1894, when it was built by philanthropists William Henry Stark and Miriam M. Lutcher Stark, who lived here until 1936. The restored 3-story house features ornate woodwork, stained glass windows, and 15 rooms filled with the original furniture, decor, and mementos. A visit to the house and its carriage barn provides a glimpse at the lifestyles of Texas's wealthy during that era—and at the owners' dazzling collection

> ## port of orange
>
> *Orange's deepwater port lies about 42 miles inland where the Sabine-Neches and Gulf Intracoastal Waterway meet. The port isn't open to visitors, but you can catch a glimpse of the action downtown on Border Street.*

of American Brilliant Period cut glass, milk glass, Asian antiques, and porcelain. Today, the house is listed in the National Register of Historic Places and has been named a Texas Historic Landmark by the Texas Historical Commission. Tuesday through Saturday, tours begin in the carriage house. Call ahead to reserve your spot on a tour.

where to shop

Farmer's Mercantile. 702 W. Division St. at 6th Street; (409) 883-2941. Since 1928, this general store has sold an array of farming and ranching tools. Even if you don't need to buy any garden supplies or livestock feed, it's worth checking out the store, which maintains much of the same atmosphere it did 80 years ago. Closed Sunday.

where to eat

Casa Ole. 1717 16th St.; (409) 886-0642; casaole.com. With 45 restaurants in Texas and neighboring states, Casa Ole is a popular place for traditional Tex-Mex dishes. The Orange location is no exception, offering family-tested recipes and friendly service. $.

Dylan's on 9th. 8601 9th Ave.; (409) 722-1600; dylanson9th.com. Whether you are looking for lunch or dinner or a place to celebrate happy hour, Dylan's offers a full menu and friendly service as well as daily specials. A separate children's menu will keep the youngsters happy, too. $$.

Old Orange Cafe & Catering Company. 914 W. Division Ave.; (409) 883-2233; old orangecafe.com. Chef David Claybar has raised the bar for dining in Orange with his soups, sandwiches, fish, burgers, and chicken entrees. Each day's specials include a quiche (crawfish, anyone?), soup (think shrimp Creole), a "catch of the day," and another entree. Before stopping in, visit the website, which is updated with specials daily. Photos of old Orange cover the walls here, making for a comfortable, casual atmosphere with friendly service. Old Orange Cafe serves lunch Monday through Friday and brunch on Sunday; the brunch menu changes weekly. Closed Saturday. $$–$$$.

Spanky's Bar and Grill. 1703 N. 16th St.; (409) 886-2949; spankysgrill.com. Every week-day, Spanky's offers blue plate specials. For a very reasonable $8.95, diners can choose from multiple sides to accompany the southern-style entrees, which include chicken spaghetti, fried pork chops, and pot roast. $–$$.

where to stay

E House Inn. 205 College St.; (409) 886-0940; ehouseinn.com. This charming green B&B sits in the heart of downtown Orange, offering easy access to many local attractions and restaurants. The house was completely renovated in 2004, but it still features much of the original character, including its longleaf pine floors. Guests enjoy free Internet access, as well as a conference room and printing services for businesspeople. $.

Shangrila Bed & Breakfast. 907 Pine Ave.; (409) 697-0912; therogershouse.com. Though it shares a name with Orange's beloved botanical gardens, this Cape Cod–style B&B is a completely separate property—one with its own lovely floral accents and chirping birds. Guests enjoy a downtown location, a private bathroom, a garden patio, nice linens, and robes. Spa services are offered by appointment. A gourmet breakfast is served daily, and at 6:30 p.m. guests enjoy wine and cheese. Pets aren't allowed here; neither is smoking. Complimentary bicycles are available so that guests can explore the area. $.

worth more time

If you want to stretch this trip out, consider heading farther east into Louisiana to visit **Lake Charles.** Located about 2 hours and 15 minutes from downtown Houston, Lake Charles is home to many art galleries, museums, and parks. Among the best reasons to visit are the casinos (Delta Downs, Isle of Capri, and L'Auberge du Lac) and the Cajun cuisine found along the so-called Southwest Louisiana Boudin Trail. To reach Lake Charles from Orange, head east on I-10 for about 30 miles and then follow the signs.

For more information on things to do and places to stay, sleep, and shop in Lake Charles, visit visitlakecharles.org, stop by 1205 N. Lakeshore Dr., or call (800) 456-SWLA.

southeast

day trip 01

southeast

>>> **down by the bay:**
alvin, santa fe, bay area houston

alvin

First settled by the Elisha and Missouri Thomas family in 1845, Alvin has a long history in the cattle and agricultural sectors, with the Santa Fe Railroad beginning to ship cattle east from the area beginning in the 1860s. Within two decades, a growing number of men were coming to the area to get their piece of the pie—that is, prairie land where their own cattle could roam. In 1893, Alvin incorporated as a city.

In the early 1900s the local economy began to diversify, with Alvin producing strawberries, oranges, figs, pears, cape jasmine blossoms, and eventually oil. Today, Alvin's agricultural roots are still apparent at Shimek's Gardens and Froberg's Vegetable & Fruit Farm. But it's also evident that Alvin has another commodity these days: native son and baseball legend Nolan Ryan, whose career is celebrated at the Nolan Ryan Center here.

getting there

Alvin is about 30 miles south of Houston. To get there, take TX 288 South to Alvin Sugarland Road/TX 6 South. Follow the road for about 10 miles and then follow the signs into town.

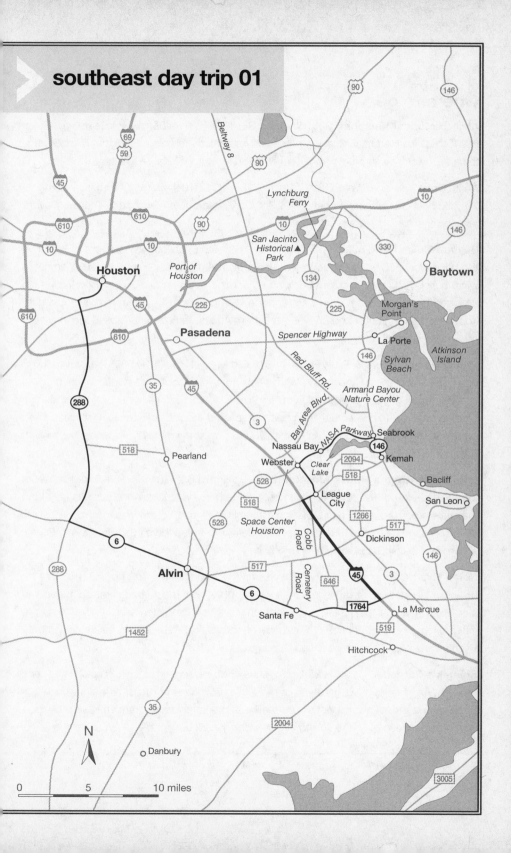

where to go

Alvin Historical Museum. 300 W. Sealy St.; (281) 331-4469; alvinmuseum.org. Since 2001, the Alvin Historical Museum has made its home in the old post office. Exhibits paint the area's history with memorabilia and other artifacts from local residents.

Alvin Opry. 8th and West Sealy Streets; (281) 331-8181; alvinopry.com. On Friday at 7 p.m., locals come here to get their fill of Opry-style country and gospel tunes. Call for reservations.

Bayou Wildlife Park. 5050 FM 517 Rd.; (281) 337-6376; bayouwildlifepark.com. Kids love this park, where 50 animal species—including giraffes, hog deer, Banteng cattle, lemurs, a white buffalo, and rhinos—roam freely on 80 acres of prairie and woods. Visitors can take a guided tour of the park on a tram and feed the animals. Pony rides are available daily from March through July and on weekends from August to February. Closed Monday from August through February 1.

Froberg's Vegetable & Fruit Farm. 11875 Old Manvel Rd.; (281) 585-3531. Even if you don't need groceries—and really, who wants to think about *that* while day-tripping?— Froberg's is worth a stop. In addition to selling great fresh produce (most of it grown locally), Froberg's serves up homemade fried pies, hot roasted peanuts, canned jams, pickles, fresh pecans, and other treats. You can even pick your own strawberries here during the harvest. Call for more information.

Marguerite Rogers House Museum. 113 E. Dumble St.; (281) 585-2803; alvinmuseum .org. This restored historic house was built in 1900 in the Queen Anne style, largely from materials culled from the nearby Oscar Cummings House, which was destroyed by the 1900 hurricane. The Alvin Museum Society offers docent-led tours on Thursday and Friday, as well as the first Saturday of each month.

Nolan Ryan Center. 2925 TX 35 Bypass at Alvin Community College; (281) 388-1134; nolanryanfoundation.org/museum.htm. Learn about Alvin's most famous resident, baseball star Nolan Ryan, at this museum. During your visit, you can catch a ball in the interactive catch-pitch exhibit and check out a variety of photos and multimedia presentations about Ryan's career. Closed Saturday and Sunday.

Shimek's Gardens. 3122 CR 237; (281) 331-4395; cityscope.net/~neshimek. Harvey and Nell Shimek have filled this garden with more than 850 kinds of roses, as well as hundreds of roses and other flower varieties. Butterflies and hummingbirds frequently stop by for a sniff. Visit between May and July to see everything in bloom.

be street-smart

Don't be surprised if you recognize some of the Alvin street names from your old history books. Many north-south streets here are named after Confederate generals, while many east-west streets were named after area railroad investors and land developers.

where to shop

Alvin Antique Center and Marketplace. 2500 S. TX 35 Loop; (281) 388-0537; alvin antiquecenter.com. This 55,000-square-foot antiques mall could keep you busy for hours. It's filled with every kind of antique imaginable. Closed Monday.

Laid Back Books. 2320 Mustang Rd. (between the TX 35 Loop and Gordon Street); (281) 756-8778; laidbackbooks.com. Used books in every imaginable genre are stacked from floor to ceiling in a remodeled house dating back to the 1930s. Everything is surprisingly well organized. Closed Sunday and Monday.

Native American Expressions. 2500 S. Loop 35; (281) 331-9788; nativeamerican expressions.net. This shop sells a variety of handmade Native American and western arts and crafts, including dream catchers, jewelry, breastplates, tomahawks, and prints.

where to eat

Joe's Barbeque Company. 1400 E. TX 6; (281) 331-9626; joesbarbequecompany.com. For more than 30 years, this roadhouse restaurant has been serving barbecue, brisket, sausage, ribs, ham, turkey, burgers, chicken, baked potatoes, and cobbler. The food may not be as good as some of Houston's best barbecue joints, but locals say it's by far the best place to get barbecue in the Alvin area. $–$$.

Julia's Family Restaurant. 406 E. TX 6; (281) 585-6073. This local favorite serves country cooking with a smile. Be sure to save room for one of Julia's homemade desserts. $–$$.

santa fe

Named for the Atchison, Topeka and Santa Fe Railway that passed through the area in 1877, this growing Galveston County community wasn't incorporated until 1978. In its early days, the area's primary industry was agriculture. These days, the area has diversified and benefits from its location near NASA and Texas City refineries. But the best reason to visit

Santa Fe is still related to agriculture: The town is home to the award-winning Haak Vineyards & Winery, which produces reds, whites, and rosés.

getting there

Santa Fe is only about 9 miles southeast of Alvin. To get there, follow TX 6 South for about 9 miles.

where to go

Haak Vineyards & Winery. 6310 Ave. T; (409) 925-1401; haakwine.com. When Raymond Haak read about a hybrid grape that grew well in dry, hot environments, he paved the way for his winery to become one of the first to produce blanc du bois. Since opening in 1973, Haak Vineyards & Winery has expanded to more than 11,000 square feet, and the winery has branched out to produce a number of reds, whites, and rosés. In the last few years, Haak's wines have won more than two dozen awards at national and international wine competitions, including the Finger Lakes International Wine Competition, the Lone Star International Wine Competition, and Texas Open Wine Judging.

Tours are offered throughout the day on weekdays and every hour on the hour (until 1 hour before closing) on weekends. Tours are $10; under 21 years free. During your visit you can also taste some of Haak's wines and pick up a few bottles in the gift shop.

where to eat

Gilhooley's Restaurant. 222 9th St., Dickinson; (281) 339-3813. This laid-back joint serves a variety of Gulf Coast seafood, but if you order only one thing off the menu, be sure it's the oysters. $$.

Sherry's Busy Bee Cafe. 12350 TX 6; (409) 925-6330. *Texas Monthly* named Sherry's one of the Lone Star State's 40 best small-town cafes, and it's easy to see why: Guests enjoy a friendly atmosphere, greasy burgers on homemade buns, fried chicken, fried squash, and tasty homemade desserts like peanut butter pie. $.

bay area houston

Don't go looking for the "Bay Area Houston" or "Bay Area" on Texas maps. You probably won't find it. That's because it's a fairly new designation used to refer to the area surrounding Galveston Bay and Clear Lake. It includes the towns of Kemah, Seabrook, La Porte, League City, and Nassau Bay, as well as the section of Houston sometimes referred to as Clear Lake.

This area is filled with gems—enough that you could stretch this trip an extra day, or forgo the first two stops on this day trip to spend more time in the Bay Area. One of these gems is NASA's Johnson Space Center and its visitor center, Space Center Houston, where you could spend a whole day enjoying interactive exhibits about the history of space flight.

A second gem can be found in the fishing town of Kemah: the Kemah Boardwalk, where the carnival rides, shops, restaurants, an aquarium, and other attractions could keep you busy for an entire day.

The other gems are of the water variety: The 2,000-acre Clear Lake, which empties into Galveston Bay, is the country's third-largest recreational boating basin, with more than 9,000 marina slips. Visitors come to Clear Lake and Galveston Bay to row, Jet Ski, water-ski, and fish, too. Throw in a line here, and you're likely to reel in a fingerling channel catfish or a largemouth bass.

getting there

There are a few different routes from Santa Fe to the Bay Area, but most of them require a lot of turns on many different streets. The easiest way to get there—especially considering you're already navigating some unfamiliar tiny-town terrain—is to take FM 1764 to the Gulf Freeway/I-45 North and follow the freeway for 8.1 miles. Then take exit 23 toward League City/FM 518 and take a right at FM 518 East/West Main Street and follow it for about 1.2 miles until you're in League City. From League City, you can go elsewhere in the Bay Area by heading northwest on TX 3 North toward FM 518 West/Magnolia Street for 2.6 miles and then taking a right at East NASA Parkway (NASA Road 1 East) and following the signs.

To get to Seabrook, head east on NASA Parkway and follow the signs. Continue on to Kemah by driving 1.5 miles south on TX 146 South.

where to go

Big League Dreams Sports Complex. 1150 Big League Dreams Pkwy. (off Calder Road/exit 22 off I-45), League City; (281) 316-3400; bigleaguedreams.com. Baseball fans, this one's for you: This sports complex is home to replicas of 13 famous major league ballparks, so you can imagine you're in the big leagues as you run from base to base. With fields for volleyball, soccer, hockey, basketball, and other sports, there's something for almost every athlete or wannabe athlete in your family.

Butler Longhorn Museum. 1220 Coryell St., League City; (281) 332-1393; butlerlonghorn museum.com. This is the first museum dedicated to the Texas longhorn. Exhibits here cover the history of the area and the Texas longhorn and include sculptures, art, and longhorn artifacts. Ten acres of trails surround the museum, offering opportunities to hike and picnic.

***Captain Kidd* Topsail Schooner.** On the corner of TX 146 and 6th Street in Kemah (in slip A29); (281) 334-5433; captkiddcharters.com. This 55-foot topsail schooner offers 2-hour public sails around Galveston Bay throughout the year. For a particularly special trip, opt for one of the sunset sails. Day sails cost $25 per person, and sunset sails cost $30 per person. Call ahead to make reservations. Private charters are available on a first-come, first-served basis.

Challenger 7 Memorial Park. 2301 W. NASA Pkwy., Webster; (713) 440-1587; hcp1.net/
Parks/ChallengerSevenMemorial.aspx. This park honors the seven astronauts who died
when the space shuttle *Challenger* exploded midair in 1986. The memorial here uses the
exact colors from the mission logo designed by the astronauts themselves. The park is also
home to an Audubon Society–sanctioned bird sanctuary, hiking trails, a picnic area, and a
man-made pond that has been stocked with largemouth bass and catfish just waiting to
be fished out on your rod.

Clear Creek Winery, Vineyard & Resort. 709 Harris Ave., Kemah; 281-334-8300; clear
creekvineyard.com. Clear Creek offers visitors a chance to tour one of the largest wineries
in the state and sample their current wines in four different tasting areas. While sipping their
products you can watch the winemakers at work in Clear Creek's glassed-in fermentation
and bottling room. Or, you can stroll the winery grounds and demonstration vineyards. A
restaurant and a bed-and-breakfast are also on the grounds. The winery is open Tuesday
through Sunday.

Helen's Gardens. 701 E. Main St. at Kansas Avenue, League City; (281) 554-1188. Find
your Zen place as you walk through well-manicured gardens, which boast an array of flowers, a waterfall, and birdhouses. The League City Garden Club and the Parks Department
keep the garden looking good.

Kemah Boardwalk. 215 Kipp Ave., Kemah; (877) 285-3624; kemahboardwalk.com.
There's a reason Houstonians love to visit this entertainment district: From restaurants
to carnival rides and boardwalk games to shops and an aquarium, there are plenty of
fun activities sure to please everyone in your crew. At the Stingray Reef you can watch,
touch, and even feed the stingrays as they swim past. Add to the thrills with a trip to the
amusement park here, where you can climb on a rock wall and ride the 2-story carousel,
the C.P. Huntington train, a Ferris wheel, roller coasters, and the quick-falling Drop Zone.
Several souvenir shops around the amusement park sell T-shirts, toys, western getup, and
tchotchkes.

For some wet and wild fun, take a ride on the Boardwalk Beast. Designed to look like
a shark, this open-deck boat speeds out into Galveston Bay at 40 miles an hour, ensuring
plenty of water from the bay showers those on board. For a slower, drier ride, board the
Boardwalk Beast in the evening. Tickets for the Boardwalk Beast can be purchased on-site.

If you want to kick back and grab a bite to eat during your visit, you've got plenty of
options along the boardwalk. Currently, there are about 10 restaurants (plus a couple of
coffee shops), all of which are owned by Landry's. Options range from Tex-Mex at the
Cadillac Bar to seafood at The Aquarium or Landry's Seafood House. Other restaurants
include Pizza Oven, Joe's Crab Shack, Saltgrass Steak House, Red Sushi, and the afford-
able Lighthouse Buffet.

caution: name change ahead

Drivers, beware: Up until a few years ago, NASA Parkway, the street on which Space Center Houston is located, was called NASA Road 1, and some maps and GPS systems still don't account for the name change.

Each year, the Kemah Boardwalk hosts special events and festivals, including an Easter egg hunt, car shows, and a special July 4 fireworks display. The Kemah Boardwalk is closed Christmas and Thanksgiving Day.

Railean Distillery. 341 5th St., San Leon; (713) 545-2742; railean.com. This local rum distillery offers tours, where you can learn how rum is made and sample Railean White Rum, Railean Reserve XO, and Railean Small Cask Reserve. The distillery recently began making another product line: American Agave Spirits, made from 100 percent blue agave. Tours and tastings are available by appointment only. Be aware that there's no air-conditioning here.

The distillery is about 10 miles south of Kemah. To get there, follow TX 146 South for about 3.5 miles; then take a left at FM 646 West/Grand Avenue and follow it for 1.3 miles. Take a right at West Bayshore Drive/FM 646 and follow the road for about 3.7 miles. Take another right at 9th Street/FM 517 and, after about 0.9 miles, turn left at Avenue I/FM 517.

Space Center Houston. 1601 NASA Pkwy., Houston; (281) 244-2100; spacecenter.org. Space Center Houston is the official visitor's center of the Lyndon B. Johnson Space Center, the hundred-building complex where every NASA astronaut trains and where NASA's Mission Control makes its home. You could easily spend the better part of a day here learning about human spaceflight through the dozens of exhibits and interactive activities. Among the exhibits here are The Feel of Space, which gives visitors the chance to see how astronauts shower, eat, and live in space; and the Blast Off Theater, where simulated shuttle exhaust blows into the room as you watch live updates about current missions on shuttle monitors. On display are old spacesuits and hardware from old shuttles. A new feature is the Design Zone, an interactive exhibit that explores the relationship between math and creativity. You can also get a close-up look at NASA's day-to-day operations by participating in the 4- to 5-hour Level Nine Tour (available weekdays only), which takes you inside Mission Control and to the Neutral Buoyancy Lab where the astronauts train.

Space City Rock Climbing. 201 Hobbs Rd., Ste. A1, League City; (281) 316-0377; spacecityrockclimbing.com. Visit one of the only rock gyms in town and climb more than 6,000 square feet of faux rocks and boulders. The gym offers climbing opportunities for guests of all skill levels, and special programs and lessons are available.

> ## pelicans ahead
>
> *Large fiberglass pelicans seem to line the streets of Seabrook. In total, there are more than two dozen of these colorful creatures around town. One looks like a scuba diver, another like Uncle Sam, and still another like a pirate. Each of these colorful creatures was decorated by a different artist. You can learn more about the pelicans—and download a map of their locations—online at seabrookpelican path.com.*

Water sports. Water recreation enthusiasts from across Texas consider **Clear Lake** one of the state's best spots for water sports, and it's easy to see why. With this inlet spanning 2,000 acres and including more than 9,000 marina slips, Clear Lake is the third-largest basin in the US for recreational boating. The Bay Area is also a popular spot for rowing, Jet Skiing, waterskiing, and fishing for fingerling channel catfish and largemouth bass.

Several companies in the area serve visitors interested in these sorts of recreational activities. If you're interested in fishing, try **South Coast Sailing Adventures** (507 Bradford Ave., Kemah; 281-334-4606) or visit **Sylvan Beach Park,** where you'll find a bait shop and a lighted fishing pier that juts out a quarter mile into Galveston Bay (636 N. Bayshore Dr., La Porte; 281-326-6539). Interested in sailing? Try the **Bay Area Rowing Center** (2517 NASA Pkwy., Seabrook; 281-532-1518; houstonrowing.com) or contact **All Points of Sail Sailing School** at Lakeside, which offers sailing classes, certification, charters, and kayaking (2517 NASA Pkwy., Seabrook; 281-532-1518; lakesidesailing.com). If you're looking for a park where you can camp and partake in all of your favorite water sports, check out **Clear Lake Park Boat Ramp** (5001 NASA Pkwy., Clear Lake), where you can camp, fish, boat, bike, and picnic. For additional recommendations, contact the **Bay Area Houston Convention & Visitors Bureau** at (281) 474-9700 or visitbayareahouston.com.

West Bay Common School Children's Museum. 210 N. Kansas Ave., League City; (281) 554-2994; oneroomschoolhouse.org. Go back to school at this 1898 schoolhouse museum, where teachers dressed in period costume conduct classes. Visitors of all ages can participate in a pen-and-ink lesson, practice reading at the recitation bench, and compete in a spelling bee. Stop at the Barn Museum to see artifacts from the area's early years. The gift shop here sells turn-of-the-century school memorabilia. The League City Historical Society runs the award-winning museum, which is open weekdays, and by special appointment.

where to shop

Aroma Garden Creations. 609 Bradford Ave., Kemah; (281) 756-7627; kemahsoaplady .com. In this boutique, you'll find handmade soaps, bath salts, sarongs, and other accessories and food delicacies.

Kemah Boardwalk. 215 Kipp Ave., Kemah; (877) 285-3624; kemahboardwalk.com. If you're looking for kitschy souvenirs, western wear, T-shirts, and hats, you're sure to find them in the shops and kiosks at the Kemah Boardwalk.

Kemah Farmer's Market. 204 FM 2094 (corner of TX 146 and FM 2094), Kemah; (281) 538-5605; kemahfarmersmarket.com. Every Saturday this open-air market fills with vendors of all kinds. In addition to produce, you'll find antiques and arts and crafts as well as lots of happy shoppers. Be sure to bring cash as many vendors don't accept plastic. If you run out, there is an ATM on hand.

Rose's Seafood Market. 415 Waterfront Dr., Seabrook; (281) 474-3536; rosesseafood .com. If you want to pick up some seafood to cook at home, this is the place to go. This family-run market sells the freshest seafood around. You'll find everything from live blue crab and shark to fresh salmon, red snapper, and sushi-grade tuna here.

where to eat

Coffee Oasis. 4650 NASA Pkwy., Seabrook; (281) 532-1439; coffee-oasis.com. Enjoy free wireless Internet and occasional live music while you eat a sandwich, soup, salad, or wrap and sip some coffee. $.

El Centinela Mexican Restaurant. 104 TX 3 North, League City; (281) 554-9286. This may not be the best Mexican food in the area, but if you're looking for breakfast options, the huevos rancheros, chorizo and eggs, and breakfast tacos are worth a try. $–$$.

Frenchies. 1041 NASA Pkwy., Houston (on the northeast corner of NASA Parkway and El Camino Real); (281) 486-7144; frenchiesvillacapri.com. This neighborhood Italian restaurant has been around since 1979 and has been serving many of the same customers for 30 years. Located just a mile west of NASA, Frenchies counts many NASA staffers and astronauts among its regulars and pays tribute to them with photos on the wall. The menu is filled with simple, home-cooked dishes that you don't have to get dressed up to eat. Save room for the tiramisu. Closed Sunday. $–$$.

The Italian Cafe. 4622 NASA Pkwy., Seabrook; (281) 326-1618; theitaliancafe.com. Dine here for Italian favorites that are consistently well-cooked and full of flavor. The menu includes pasta, chicken dishes, salads, seafood, and meatball and blackened chicken po'boys. Closed Sunday and Monday. $–$$$.

Kemah Boardwalk. 215 Kipp Ave., Kemah; (877) 285-3624; kemahboardwalk.com. Whether you're in the mood for fine or casual dining, seafood or Tex-Mex, you'll almost certainly find what you're looking for at the Kemah Boardwalk. Landry's owns all of the restaurants here, which include the Tex-Mex favorite Cadillac Bar (281-334-9094); the family-friendly Joe's Crab Shack (281-334-2881); local seafood and oyster bar favorite The Flying Dutchman (281-334-7575, closed Monday); Red Sushi (281-334-6708, closed Monday); the casual Pizza Oven (281-334-2228); breakfast spot Bayside Grille (281-334-5351); Landry's Seafood House (281-334-2513); The Aquarium seafood restaurant (281-334-9010); and Saltgrass Steak House (281-538-5441). $–$$$.

Mamacita's Restaurant. 515 E. NASA Pkwy., Webster; (281) 332-5362; mamacitas mexicanrestaurant.com. Name your favorite Tex-Mex dish, and you're sure to find it at Mamacita's, where vegetarian, meat, and chicken options abound. The service is quick, the space is clean, and the margaritas are strong at this family-friendly hot spot. $–$$.

Red River Bar-B-Que Company. 1911 E. Main St., League City; (281) 332-8086; redriver bbq.com. Listeners of Houston's Mix 96.5 radio station named the barbecue here the best in Houston. In addition to barbecue, the menu boasts sausage, pork, turkey, ham, chicken, burgers, baked potatoes, po'boys, steaks, fried seafood, and all of your favorite barbecue sides. Be sure to save room for a slice of pie. $–$$.

Seabrook Classic Cafe. 2511 NASA Pkwy., Seabrook; (281) 326-1512; seabrookclassic cafe.com. Satisfy everyone in your group with this menu full of sandwiches, soups, salads, fish tacos, burgers, and seafood. Breakfast options include *migas,* huevos rancheros, biscuits and homemade gravy, and eggs served every which way. $–$$.

Sudie's Seafood House. 352 Gulf Freeway North, League City; (281) 338-5100; sudies .com. For more than 25 years, locals have been coming to this family-owned restaurant for seafood and steak made however you like it—fried, grilled, and blackened. The menu also includes 3 types of gumbo, fried pickles and mushrooms, and burgers. $$–$$$.

T-Bone Tom's Steakhouse. 707 TX 146, Kemah; (281) 334-2133; tbonetoms.com. Widely considered one of the best barbecue places in the area, T-Bone Tom's has been featured on the Food Network's *Diners, Drive-ins, and Dives.* While the place is a steak house in name, it's the barbecue, sausage, brisket, and chopped beef sandwiches that make this place a local favorite, along with live music on Friday and Saturday nights. $–$$.

Villa Capri on Clear Lake. 3713 NASA Pkwy., Seabrook; (281) 326-2373; frenchiesvilla capri.com. Brought to you by the same family that owns Frenchies, this Italian restaurant sits right on Clear Lake, making for some lovely scenery. Portions are generous, and the service is friendly. You can get away with wearing shorts and flip-flops or something much fancier here. Closed Monday. $$–$$$.

where to stay

Clipper House Inn. 710 Bradford Ave., Kemah; (281) 334-2517; clipperhouseinn.com. Looking for a romantic getaway? Guests here stay in one of 6 1930s cottages, each named for famous clipper ships and decorated with antiques and decorative pieces from around the world. An on-site boutique winery adds to the romance of the place and well-tended gardens fill the area, creating a soothing environment not far from the Kemah Boardwalk. $$.

Kemah Boardwalk Inn. No. 8 Kemah Waterfront, Kemah; (281) 334-9880; kemahboard walkinn.com. Stay here and you'll wake up right by the boardwalk and enjoy great views of Galveston Bay. The rooms and suites are decorated to make you feel like you're at the beach and come with all the usual amenities—satellite TV, private balconies, quality linens, and wireless Internet. $$.

The Old Parsonage Guest Houses. 1113 Hall St., Seabrook; (713) 206-1105; seabrook accommodation.com. Escape here for all of the amenities of home—and none of the stress. Guests stay in 2-bedroom guesthouses, each with its own private bathroom, kitchen, and living room. Upon arrival, you'll receive a basket filled with snacks and a bottle of wine. A continental breakfast is also included in your stay. $$.

day trip 02

southeast

life's a beach:
galveston

galveston

Galveston needs no introduction for most Houstonians. Located 50 miles southeast of Houston off I-45, this island sits right on the Gulf of Mexico. Historically, this location has been both a blessing and a curse for the beach town's tourism industry. First, the blessings: Galveston boasts beaches for partiers, families, luxury-seekers, and day-trippers, and visitors and locals can partake in just about every water and beach activity imaginable here. Restaurants here serve seafood caught in the Gulf—often the same day it's served—and hotels and condos offer views that will make you feel like you're a thousand miles away from Houston.

Galveston's curses, of course, have made headlines all too recently: In 1900, a powerful hurricane destroyed much of the island, which up until then, had been a more significant town—economically, socially, and politically speaking—than Houston. When the city rebuilt, a seawall was added to protect it from future Gulf storms. In 2008, a little over a century later, another hurricane—Ike—battered the island town. While Hurricane Ike destroyed or severely damaged many beaches, attractions, and homes, Galveston and its people have proven resilient, working hard to rebuild and clean up their town and welcome visitors back to this popular spot for day and weekend escapes from the city.

In welcoming visitors back, Galveston isn't just luring tourists to its beaches. The town is also home to several museums and many architecturally exquisite Victorian homes and

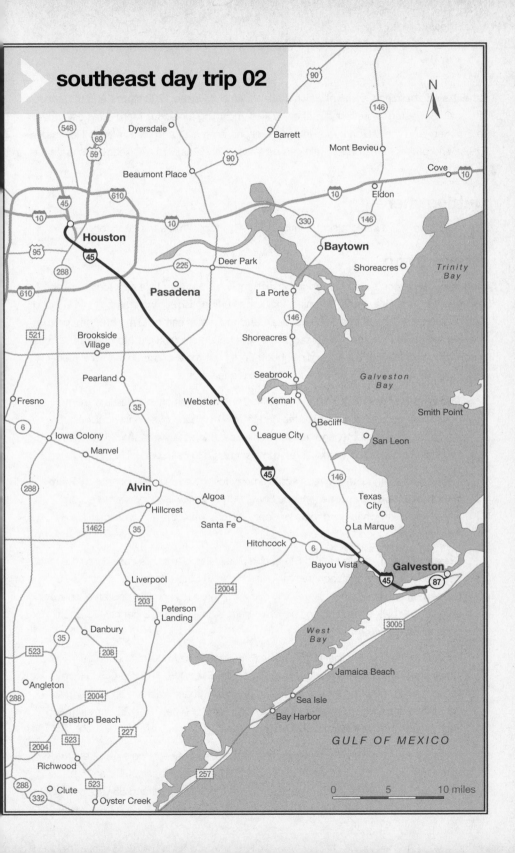

southeast day trip 02

other historic buildings, some of which managed to survive the 1900 storm. And throughout the year, Galveston hosts festivals of every kind, including a raucous Mardi Gras celebration in February and the Victorian era–infused Dickens on the Strand festival each December. These and other Galveston festivals can be found in the Festivals & Celebrations appendix of this book.

getting there

From Houston, it's a straight shot southeast on I-45 for 50 miles to Galveston.

where to go

Beaches. Galveston's Gulf of Mexico location makes it a great place to lie on the beach or partake in your favorite water activities, including surfing, fishing, waterskiing, and boating. Sure, the beaches here aren't always clean and the water can be dirty, but they promise fun and are close to home. Some sections of the beach are restricted to guests at private resorts and residents of beachfront neighborhoods, but most of the beach here is open to the public. If you're looking for a beach, here are a few to try:

The East Beach (1923 Boddeker Rd.; 409-797-5111) is often called the "party beach" because, well, it's where the party's at. The beach often hosts outdoor concerts, special events, and festivals. This beach tends to attract a wilder crowd since drinking is actually legal here. Admission is $8 in cash per car.

If you prefer to imagine you're at some snazzy resort beyond US borders, try **Palm Beach at Moody Gardens** (1 Hope Blvd.; 800-582-4673; moodygardens.com), where you'll find white sand, blue lagoons, spas, a waterfall, and a children's area. Admission is included with a day pass.

Stewart Beach, located at 6th Street and Seawall Boulevard, is considered the best beach for families. Each summer, it hosts sand castle contests, volleyball tournaments, and other family-friendly events. There's also a children's area, souvenir shop, snack bar, restrooms, and showers here. Admission is $8 per car. For more information call (409) 797-5182.

On the west end of the island, the Texas Parks and Wildlife Department runs **Galveston Island State Park,** located at 14901 FM 3005. This is a great place to see wildlife, including birds and ducks, raccoons, marsh rabbits, and even the occasional armadillo. Admission is $5 per person. Call (409) 737-1222 or visit tpwd .state.tx.us for more information.

Surfers, take note: The city allows surfing at beaches between the 17th Street and 21st Street rock groins, between the western edge of the Flagship Pier at 25th Street and the 29th Street rock groin, between the 29th Street and 53rd Street rock

the old fort

During your visit to the Bolivar Peninsula, visit Fort Travis Seashore Park, which is located on the peninsula's western end near the ferry landing. The fort, named for Battle of the Alamo commander William B. Travis, was built in 1899 and served as a station for troops during World Wars I and II. Today, you can still see some of the old bunkers here while you picnic, camp, play ball, or fish along the rocky shore. The park, located at 900 TX 87, is open daily. Call (409) 684-1333 for more information.

groins, and at beaches west of 91st Street. If you need to rent a surfboard, stop into one of the many surf shops along Seawall Boulevard, or try **Strictly Hardcore Surf Specialties** at 3702 Ave. R (409-763-1559), just a few blocks from Seawall Boulevard.

Want to catch some fish? Your best bet is to head out to one of the beachfront jetties or visit one of the commercial fishing piers here. Try **Seawolf Park Fishing Pier,** the **Galveston Fishing Pier,** or the **61st Street Fishing Pier.**

For additional recommendations on renting gear or help finding the ideal spot for your water activity of choice, contact the **Galveston Island Visitors Center** at (888) 425-4753 or visit galveston.com.

Bishop's Palace. 1402 Broadway; (409) 762-2475; galveston.com/bishopspalace. Named one of the country's 100 most important buildings by the American Institute of Architects, this ornate castle was built between 1886 and 1892. Today, the Galveston Historical Foundation manages the property as a museum. Take a tour to learn about the building's unique design and see the magnificent furnishings and decor inside the house, including a fireplace lined with pure silver. Guided tours are offered daily at 12:30 and 3:30 p.m.

Bolivar Ferry. (409) 795-2230; txdot.gov. Ride one of the free diesel ferries from the east end of Galveston to the Bolivar Peninsula and back. This isn't always the best-smelling ride, but it's fun to watch the seagulls, as well as the occasional porpoise in the water, and get an unusual look at the area. The ferries, which connect two parts of TX 87, leave about every 20 minutes. You can drive your car onto one or step onboard the 185-foot-long ferry as a passenger. The ride lasts about 18 minutes each way. To reach the ferry landing, follow I-45 South out of Houston until it turns into Broadway (after you cross the causeway to Galveston Island at the "0" mile marker). Follow Broadway, and you'll see signs directing you toward the landing.

goin' to the dogs

Galveston's beautiful beaches call out to all traveling bowsers, so feel free to bring Fido! Dogs need to be leashed at all times (on leashes no longer than 6 feet). Be aware that on Bay Harbor, Miramar, Stavenger, and Point San Luis beaches, cars are permitted on the sand. Have fun splashing in the surf but watch for the occasional jellyfish and tar bells (which can be removed from dog fur with vegetable oil).

Galveston Railroad Museum. 2602 Santa Fe Place; (409) 765-5700; galvestonrrmuseum .com. This museum covers all things railroad related. Exhibits include the restored Santa Fe Depot and multimedia presentations on Galveston's role in the railroad and shipping industries. Nearly three dozen vintage railroad cars and steam engines sit on old tracks, and you can get a feel for 1930s railroad culture by walking through the People's Gallery, where models re-create the hustle and bustle of the old depots.

The Grand 1894 Opera House. 2020 Postoffice St.; (409) 765-1894 or (800) 821-1894; thegrand.com. Galveston's 1894 opera house is a true survivor. It has withstood the hurricanes of 1900 and 1915, Hurricanes Carla, Alicia, and Ike, and occasional periods of neglect. Today, the fully restored opera house is one of Texas's last remaining theaters built in the late 1800s, a feat that has earned it a place in the National Register of Historic Places. Throughout the year, the theater hosts symphony performances, ballets, plays and musicals like *Cats* and *A Chorus Line,* and concerts by the likes of Ronnie Milsap and Johnny Mathis. Call or visit the website to find out about shows during your visit.

Lone Star Flight Museum and Texas Hall of Fame. 2002 Terminal Dr. (at Galveston's Scholes International Airport); (409) 740-7722 or (888) FLY-LSFM; lsfm.org. Learn about aviation's glory days with a visit to this museum. On display are more than two dozen restored vintage aircraft such as bombers, wartime "executive" aircraft, and a Grumman F82F Bearcat. Visit the Dee and Betty Howard Aviation Art Collection to view over 90 aircraft paintings by well-known military artists.

Michel B. Menard Home. 1604 33rd St.; (409) 762-3933; galvestonhistory.org. Built in 1838 for one of Galveston's founders—Michel B. Menard—this is now the oldest house in Galveston; it is listed in the National Register of Historic Places. Built in the Greek Revival style, it is filled with decor and furniture from the first half of the 1800s. Though the house faced almost certain demolition due to disrepair in the early 1990s, the Galveston Historical Foundation and the house's current owners collaborated to restore it. Today it is open to the public as a museum and is often rented for special events.

Moody Gardens. 1 Hope Blvd.; (800) 582-4673; moodygardens.com. If you want to be able to eat, drink, sleep, and do a million other activities in one place, this is the place to go. Moody Gardens is part hotel, part spa, and part convention center—and part a little of everything else. Here you'll find restaurants; an aquarium housed in a pyramid; IMAX 3-D, 4-D, and Ridefilm theaters; a golf course; the fun-filled science Discovery Museum; and, on Palm Beach, blue water, waterfalls, and some of the island's whitest sand. One of the biggest draws here is Moody Gardens' Rain Forest Pyramid where you will see 1,000 species of exotic plants and animals from the rain forests of the world. The *Colonel* Paddlewheel Boat, listed in the "tours" section below, also departs from Moody Gardens. Throughout the year, Moody Gardens hosts special events, including the Festival of Lights, which takes place each November and December (see listing in the Festivals & Celebrations appendix). Moody Gardens is open every day of the year—holidays included. One- and two-day passes are available, as well as tickets for individual attractions. Avoid long lines by purchasing your tickets online beforehand.

Moody Mansion. 2618 Broadway; (409) 762-7668; moodymansion.org. This exquisite 28,000-square-foot, 4-story manse dates back to 1895. The Moodys—financial giants and philanthropists who had their hands in cotton, insurance, banking, ranching, and hotels— purchased the house following the infamous 1900 hurricane, and the house remained in the family until 1986. Today the family's touches can be seen throughout the exquisite property, which is operated by the Mary Moody Northen Endowment and the Moody Foundation. The mansion, which is often rented for special events, is open daily for 1-hour tours that take you through 20 impressively decorated rooms. Throughout the year, Moody Mansion hosts special exhibits on the Moody family, the industries in which they were involved, and Galveston.

***Ocean Star* Offshore Drilling Rig & Museum.** Next to Pier 19 on Harborside Drive; (409) 766-STAR; oceanstaroec.com. If you've ever wanted to understand how oil and gas are produced offshore, this museum run by the Offshore Energy Center will answer your questions. You'll start your visit by boarding an old drilling rig and watching a video about oil production before heading inside the museum. Then you'll check out exhibits covering drilling practices, marine transport, and environmental protection.

Pier 21 Theater. Harborside Drive and 21st Street on the second floor; (409) 763-8808; galvestonhistory.org. It's hard to visit Galveston without seeing the 1900 hurricane's effect on the city. (Ditto for Hurricane Ike these days.) To learn more about the storm that has shaped and defined Galveston for more than a century, head down to Pier 21 Theater. Every hour on the hour, the theater screens a documentary called *The Great Storm,* which uses visual and sound effects, eyewitness accounts, and old photographs to highlight the storm's deadly legacy.

If you've got time to spare, stick around to watch *The Pirate Island of Jean Laffite* and learn about one of the area's most infamous and not entirely understood pirates. Screenings of *The Pirate Island* take place every hour on the half-hour.

Both films are the work of the Galveston Historical Foundation and are screened every day (ask about combination tickets). A third film offering has recently been added: *Galveston: Gateway on the Gulf.* This movie documents Galveston's role as the entry point for more than 200,000 immigrants who entered the US between 1835 and 1935 through Galveston.

Rosenberg Library. 2310 Sealy Ave.; (409) 763-8854; rosenberg-library.org. This was the first free public library in the Lone Star State. It houses rare books, art, and original letters and other written documents from the likes of General Sam Houston and Stephen F. Austin. Since Hurricane Ike, the library has been collecting Galvestonians' memories and stories about the deadly 2008 storm.

Schlitterbahn Galveston Water Park. 2109 Lockheed Rd.; (409) 770-9283; schlitterbahn .com/gal. If you love the water but want to steer clear of the beach for whatever reason, this water park offers an excellent alternative for guests of all ages. Schlitterbahn is divided into three zones—Blastenhoff, Surfenburg, and the heated indoor section of the park, Wasserfest. Each section features an array of slides and water activities that range from lackadaisical to wild in their intensity. There are a number of activities designed specifically for your children. You can purchase food at concessions here, but you can save money by bringing your own cooler filled with drinks and snacks. The entire park is open from late April to late September, and Wasserfest is open from March to April and late September to early January.

Texas Seaport Museum. Pier 21, No. 8; (409) 763-1877; galvestonhistory.org. The museum is home to the *Elissa,* a restored barque dating back to 1877. When she was sailing, the *Elissa* visited Galveston, and now she's returned, this time serving as a museum featuring 19th-century maritime technology. During your visit, walk the *Elissa*'s decks and view exhibits and a video about her history. You can also search the immigration database here to find any of your relatives who immigrated to the US through Galveston.

Tours. Sometimes the best way to get the lay of the land (and sea) is to take a tour. A number of companies provide tours of Galveston, some on land, others by water. The **Treasure Isle Tour Train** (409-221-0282) will take you around the city for an hour and a half and show you the sights, new and old. The always-humorous **Galveston Island Duck Tours** (409-621-4771; galvestonducks.com) will take you around town by both land and water, while **Galveston Harbour Tours** (409-765-8687) provides harbor tours for birders and those interested in local marine life. Departing from Moody Gardens each weekday at 1 p.m. (1 and 3 p.m. on weekends) is the **Colonel Paddlewheel Boat** (1 Hope Blvd.; 800-582-4673; moodygardens.com), a triple-decker boat that travels around the bay for narrated 45-minute sightseeing cruises. No matter which tour you take, call ahead to make reservations.

where to shop

Galveston is home to dozens of shops and galleries—far too many to list here. Below you'll find descriptions of Galveston's 3 major shopping districts. If you'd like a complete list of shops and galleries, contact the Galveston Island Visitors Center at (888) 425-4753 or visit galveston.com.

Postoffice Street. This historic downtown district runs along Postoffice Street, starting around 23rd Street. Lining Postoffice Street are antiques shops and art galleries featuring sculptures, paintings, and almost every other medium imaginable. Chic coffee shops, restaurants, and bars are also sprinkled throughout the area, making it easy to take a snack break.

Seawall Boulevard. The Seawall may be best known as the island's man-made storm protection, but the street it runs along—Seawall Boulevard—also attracts the attention of shoppers looking for beach gear and rentals, as well as every Galveston Island souvenir imaginable.

The Strand. This historic shopping and entertainment district spans 5 blocks along Avenue B/Strand Street from 20th to 25th Street. Many of the Victorian buildings lining the area are occupied by shops—some selling souvenirs, others selling art, gifts, or clothes.

where to eat

Benno's on the Beach. 1200 Seawall Blvd.; (409) 762-4621; bennosofgalveston.com. This hole-in-the-wall family restaurant serves Cajun-style seafood. Portions are huge, and the food is pretty cheap for seafood. Beware, though: There's often a line to get in. $$.

Gino's Italian Restaurant and Pizzeria. 6124 Ave. S; (409) 762-6481; ginositalianfood .com. This is the place to go for casual Italian in Galveston. The extensive menu is filled with classic Italian dishes, including homemade pastas and pizzas. Free delivery is available. $$–$$$.

MOD Coffeehouse. 2126 Postoffice St.; (409) 765-5659; modcoffeehouse.com. Visit this hip coffeehouse during lunch for specials such as spanakopita, tamale pie, and baked mac and cheese that puts Easy Mac to shame. There's free wireless Internet for customers here. $.

The Mosquito Cafe. 628 14th St.; (409) 763-1010; mosquitocafe.com. After suffering some serious damage during Hurricane Ike, this local favorite is back and looking more charming than ever. The eclectic menu includes gourmet sandwiches, salads, fish, and other American favorites such as mac and cheese. $$.

Rudy & Paco. 2028 Postoffice St.; (409) 762-3696; rudyandpaco.com. This is one of Galveston's finest restaurants. The menu includes steak and seafood with a Central and

South American twist. Think red snapper ceviche, roasted poblano and squash bisque, or grilled Gulf shrimp with Creole sauce. If you show up for dinner in shorts, you'll be asked to sit at the bar, as the dining room requires dressier attire. $$$.

Shrimp n Stuff. 39th Boulevard and Avenue O; (409) 763-2805; shrimpnstuff.com. For more than 30 years, this is where the locals have been going for seafood. The unpretentious menu includes a lot of greasy, fried dishes, including popcorn shrimp po'boys, the fried oyster dinner, and hush puppies, but there are a fair number of non-fried po'boy, dinner plate, and gumbo options, too. $–$$.

Yaga's Cafe and Bar. 2314 Strand St.; (409)762-6676; yagaspresents.com/yagascafe. For a fun, inexpensive meal, try this Jamaican-inspired restaurant. The menu consists of delicious pizzas, sandwiches (burritos and fish tacos included), shrimp, salad, and burgers—including those of the vegetarian and breakfast varieties—as well as the ever-popular mixed drinks. Service is quick. $.

where to stay

Coppersmith Inn. 1914 Ave. M; (409) 763-7004 or (800) 515-7444; coppersmithinn.com. This bed-and-breakfast is situated in a historic Queen Anne–style home built in 1887 with 14-foot ceilings, stained glass windows, and impressive Victorian woodwork. The main house has 3 suites on the second floor, and the adjacent Carriage House and Clara's Cottage offer enhanced privacy. All rooms and suites have cable TV, free wireless Internet, and antique feather beds. $$.

The Galvestonian Condominiums. 1401 E. Beach Dr.; (409) 765-6161; galvestonian .com. This luxurious resort sits just minutes from The Strand shopping and entertainment district. Whether you're visiting for a couple days or looking to buy a condo, you can choose from a variety of views and floor plans, all of which include a full kitchen and private balconies. $$$.

Hotel Galvez & Spa: A Wyndham Historic Hotel. 2024 Seawall Blvd.; (409) 765-7721; wyndham.com. Since 1911, this has been considered one of the Galveston's elite hotels. Each of the 224 rooms and suites is beautifully decorated, and guests have access to the resort-worthy pool and Jacuzzis. The spa here caters to those in need of extra pampering. $$.

Moody Gardens Hotel, Spa, & Convention Center. 7 Hope Blvd.; (409) 741-8484; moodygardenshotel.com. Stay here for luxurious rooms and easy access to everything Moody Gardens has to offer—white beaches, the Aquarium and Rainforest Pyramids, a golf course, restaurants, shops, a spa, and seasonal special events. $$.

The San Luis Resort, Spa & Conference Center. 5222 Seawall Blvd.; (800) 445-0090; sanluisresort.com. If you want to hit the beach along the Seawall, it doesn't get much better than the San Luis. This luxurious hotel offers great ocean views, a spa and salon, a lighted tennis court and a fitness center, and a resort-worthy swimming pool. $$$.

The Tremont House: A Wyndham Grand Hotel. 2300 Ship's Mechanic Row; (409) 763-0300; wyndham.com. Wake up just steps from Galveston's Strand district. Though the hotel is no longer in its original building, it occupies a building that's a landmark itself—the Leon and H. Blum Building, which dates back to 1879. Guests enjoy all of the luxury and pampering that's to be expected of a Wyndham hotel, with several extra doses of history and beautiful architecture. They also can return home to share some celebrity lore: Past lodgers have included Ulysses S. Grant, Sam Houston, Anna Pavlova, and Buffalo Bill. $$.

Vacation rentals. If you want to rent a house on the beach and stretch your trip out a few days, there are several companies in the area that can help you find the perfect place. Try **Castaways Resort Properties** (17614 San Luis Pass Rd.; 409-737-5300 or 800-380-5100; castawaysgroup.com), or **Sand 'N Sea Properties** (4127 Pirates Beach and 13706 FM 3005; 409-797-5500 or 800-880-2554; sandnsea.com). The **Galveston Convention and Visitors Bureau** (409-797-5145; galveston.com/vacationrentals) is also a contact point for rentals.

south

day trip 01

south

wet & wild:
angleton, lake jackson, freeport &
surfside beach

angleton

When Stephen F. Austin and his first colonists landed at the mouth of the Brazos River in 1821, they are believed to have found themselves in what is now Surfside Beach, just down the road from Angleton. Today, Angleton pays tribute to their arrival with a 60-foot statue in Henry William Munson Park.

Though Brazoria was initially the seat of Brazoria County, that honor moved to Angleton in 1896. The vote to move the county seat was so controversial that court records reportedly had to be moved to Angleton in the middle of the night, out of fear that the move's opponents might destroy them. The Brazoria County Historical Museum tells the history of the county in what is believed to be the oldest remaining building in town.

getting there

Angleton is 45 miles south of Houston, just off TX 288. To get there, follow TX 288 South and then take the FM 523 exit toward Alvin/Angleton and follow the signs.

where to go

Brazoria County Historical Museum. 100 E. Cedar St.; (979) 864-1208; bchm.org. Learn about Brazoria County's rich cultural history here, including the role that the area

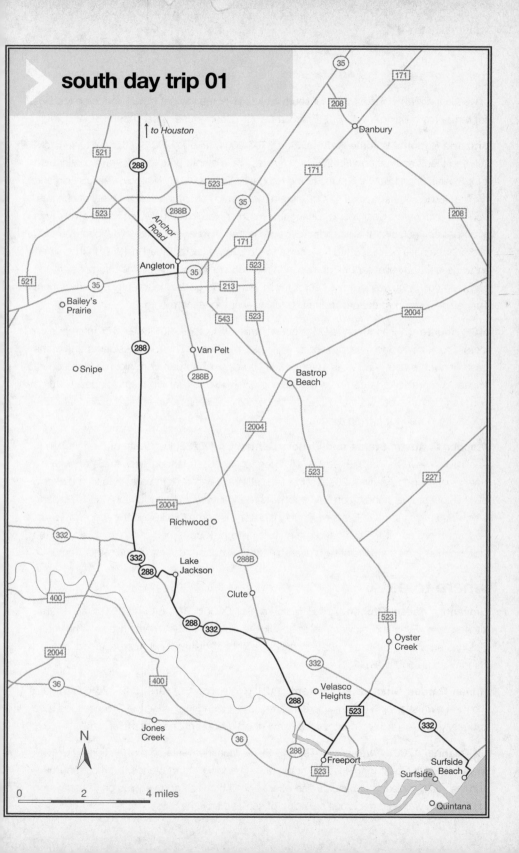

south day trip 01

↑ to Houston

521
288

523

288B
35

523

Anchor Road

Angleton

35

521

35

Bailey's Prairie

288

Van Pelt

Snipe

288B

171
35

171

523

213

543   523

Danbury

35

171

208

208

2004

Bastrop Beach

2004

523

227

2004

Richwood

332

332
288

Lake Jackson

288B

Clute

400

288   332

2004

36

400

288B

523

Oyster Creek

332

Velasco Heights

523

Jones Creek

36

288

523

Freeport

288

Surfside

Surfside Beach

332

Quintana

N

0   2   4 miles

played in the birth of Texas. The museum makes its home in what is believed to be the old-est remaining building—the 1897 Brazoria County Courthouse. Closed Sunday.

Brazoria National Wildlife Refuge. 24907 FM 2004, take TX 288 South from Lake Jackson and then head east on FM 2004 for 5 miles. Take a right onto FM 523 and continue on it for 8 miles; then follow the signs to the refuge; (979) 964-4011; fws.gov. The US Fish and Wildlife Service manages this 42,000-acre refuge, which encompasses a variety of habitats. You can spot gators year-round. During the summer, you'll also be able to spot a variety of bird species, including the seaside sparrow, horned lark, egrets, and white ibis; over 300 bird species have been spotted here since the refuge was established in 1966. In the winter, snow geese, gadwalls, sandhill cranes, and mottled ducks flock here. The refuge has hiking trails and can be accessed by boat for those wanting to go fishing, crabbing, or oystering. The refuge is open to the public the first full weekend of each month.

MSR Houston. 1 Performance Dr. (a quarter-mile off TX 288); 281-369-0677; msrhouston .com. Stock car racing fans, take note: This 2.38-mile road course is considered one of the best—if not *the* best—in Texas. It features 17 turns, which span from slow to high speed. Those who prefer karts can race around the 0.7-mile track, which also includes 17 turns and can be run clockwise and counterclockwise. Call before you visit; occasionally, the tracks are closed for private events.

***Stephen F. Austin Statue* and Visitors Center.** Off TX 288, just south of the Stephen F. Austin Highway/TX 35; (979) 239-8718. Stephen F. Austin landed near Angleton with his first colonists in the early 1820s. Today, he's still watching over the area, albeit in the form of a 60-foot statue standing on a 12-foot-tall base in Henry William Munson Park. The park, which also pays tribute to Brazoria County's history, is home to a lake in the shape of Texas. To learn more about the park and the statue, or to pick up a map of the area, stop at the visitor center. The statue is always available for viewing, but call for visitor center hours.

where to eat

Giovanni's Italian Kitchen. 729 E. Mulberry St. (TX 35); (979) 849-3332; giovannisitalian kitchen.com. Even the pickiest eater should be able to find something here. The menu includes an array of pastas, pizzas, chicken and beef dishes, and fresh seafood. Closed Sunday and Monday. $$–$$$.

Hunan Garden Chinese Restaurant. 1121 N. Velasco St.; (979) 849-1738. Disregard the run-down shopping center where this restaurant stands because the Chinese food here is pretty good, especially in a town with few good dining options. Try the egg rolls. $–$$.

La Casona. 1708 N. Velasco; (979) 848-9979; lacasonafiesta.com. Traditional Tex-Mex meets the Gulf Coast in this festive restaurant. In addition to the tacos, burritos, and que-sadillas you'd expect, La Casona also offers boiled crawfish and veggies on Tuesday and Thursday as well as a generous selection of seafood anytime. $$.

lake jackson

Established in 1941, Lake Jackson is by far one of the newest towns included in this book. The Brazoria County town was built so that the Dow Chemical Company could expand its operations—and so that its thousands of employees would have a place to live. Instead of trying to develop the other towns in Brazoria County, Alden B. Dow and others decided to start a new town on the site of the old Lake Jackson Plantation. They chose the location—just 13 miles from the Gulf of Mexico—partly because its elevation allowed good drainage, partly because it was inland enough to protect the plants from Gulf storms, and also because the wooded area was attractive.

In developing the town, Dow sought to cut down as few trees as possible. Thanks to the company's commitment, Lake Jackson remains a great place to bird-watch and hike. It's also home to the Texas Parks and Wildlife Department–run Texas Sea Park, where those interested in marine life can tour the aquarium, fish hatchery, and nature center.

getting there

Lake Jackson is less than 12 miles from Angleton. To get there, take TX 288 South for 9.4 miles. Then take a left at South Yaupon Street and, after about 0.4 miles, a right at Center Way.

where to go

Gulf Coast Bird Observatory. 103 W. TX 332; (979) 480-0999; gcbo.org. Spanning more than 30 acres in Columbia Bottomland Forest, this little slice of birder heaven was built to protect birds and their natural habitats along the Gulf Coast. Visit the Interpretive Center to learn about the birds that frequent the area. Grab a map and take a hike on the trails, where you'll see some of the preserve's permanent residents as well as birds that have migrated— or are migrating—south for the winter. Admission is free. The observatory is open weekdays, as well as the third Saturday of every month from 8 a.m. to noon for bird banding.

Lake Jackson Historical Museum. 249 Circle Way; (979) 297-1570; lakejacksonmuseum .org. Learn about Lake Jackson's storied past through interactive exhibits, including a flight simulator that lets you see the area from the air and a theater where you can watch home movies made here in the 1940s. Closed Monday. Admission is free.

Lake Jackson Plantation Archaeological Site. From TX 332, drive northeast on FM 2400 for 1 mile; (979) 297-1570 (Lake Jackson Historical Museum); texasbeyondhistory .net/jackson. In 1844, Abner and Margaret Jackson built the Lake Jackson Plantation, which became a booming sugar refinery. To better understand the plantation and the sugar industry, the University of Houston–Clear Lake and the Brazosport, Houston, and Texas Archeological Societies have teamed up to conduct archaeological digs here. Today, the 4-acre area—which includes 12 structures—is a State Archeological Landmark. The site is

> ## welcome to brazosport
>
> *The name Brazosport is often used to refer to nine southern Brazoria communities—Lake Jackson, Freeport, Brazoria, Surfside, Oyster Creek, Quintana, Richwood, Clute, and Jones Creek. Keep this in mind if you see "Brazosport" on a map (which doesn't happen very often) or hear someone mention it.*

open to the public only on the first Saturday of each month from 10 a.m. until dusk. Free walking tours are offered during that time. The tours are handicap accessible.

Sea Center Texas. 300 Medical Dr. (intersection of Plantation and Medical Drives); (979) 292-0100; tpwd.state.tx.us. The Texas Parks and Wildlife Department runs this marine aquarium, fish hatchery, and nature center to educate the public about the state's marine resources and to protect them. The spotted speckled trout and juvenile red drum spawned from the hatchery here are used to stock bays around the state.

The visitor center houses a number of interpretive displays, aquariums, and a so-called touch tank where visitors can "pet" some of the marine life. Visit the Gulf aquarium to see nurse sharks, gray snappers, moray eels, and Atlantic spadefish, among others. To add some extra fun to your visit, take an aquarium scavenger hunt; pick up a booklet here for instructions.

Be sure to visit the wetland area of the Sea Center if you're a birder. More than 150 bird species have been spotted in this vibrant part of the Great Texas Coastal Birding Trail. The marshes also have a tendency to attract frogs, butterflies, and damselflies. Bring a picnic and lunch in the outdoor pavilion here.

Throughout the year, Sea Center Texas offers special activities for children and adults, including fly-fishing workshops and catch-and-release youth fishing events. Closed Monday; reservations are required to visit the hatchery. Admission is free, but donations are appreciated.

Wilderness Park. Off TX 332, 1 mile west of Lake Jackson. This municipal park is a lovely place to have a picnic, fish, or do a little exploring. Wander along the trails at this 482-acre city park and you may run into wild pigs, deer, and—along the Brazos River—gators.

where to eat

Andy's Kitchen. 415 This Way; (979) 299-2355. If you're counting calories, this isn't the place to eat. The word "fried" appears on the menu here often, with dishes such as fried chicken, chicken-fried steak, and chicken-fried chicken. Non-fried options include meat loaf, pot roast, and mashed potatoes. Closed Monday. $$.

Apples Way. 145 Oyster Creek Dr., Ste. 6; (979) 297-0072. This tearoom has become a Lake Jackson staple. Offering a menu filled with soups, sandwiches, salads, and quiches, Apples Way attracts a large lunchtime crowd who come for the daily specials. Even so, service is quick and efficient. $.

River Point. 111 Abner Jackson Pkwy. (behind Lowe's); (979) 299-7444. Come here for good seafood, including some of the well-seasoned fried variety. Make sure you sample their fried pickles (served as an appetizer) or the boudin balls. In addition to their seafood, River Point also specializes in steaks. $$–$$$.

Wurst Haus. 102 This Way; (979) 297-3003; wursthaus.net. Located at the intersection of This Way and That Way—seriously!—Wurst Haus serves an array of German favorites such as schnitzel, Hungarian goulash, and a variety of wursts. Those who aren't big on German cuisine also have plenty of options, including several pasta dishes, seafood, and steak. $$–$$$.

where to stay

Cherotel Grand Mariner Hotel. 925 TX 332; (979) 297-1161 or (800) 544-2119; cherotel .com. This is a fairly standard hotel, though more upscale than most of the chains in the area. The Cherotel features a full-service restaurant and bar, a heated outdoor pool, and an exercise room. $.

Valcour Verandas Bed & Breakfast. 2307 Whitetail Ln.; (979) 798-2248; valcourplantation .com. Take a trip back to 1846 during your stay at this B&B, which is located on land settled by Stephen F. Austin's original colonists. A 2-story veranda wraps around the oak tree–lined mansion. Each guest room includes a private bathroom. $.

worth more time

If you love science, make a detour on this day trip and head over to **Clute.** The city is per-haps best known as home of the **Great Texas Mosquito Festival,** held each summer. (See listing in the Festivals & Celebrations appendix for more information.) The town is also home to the **Brazosport Planetarium** (400 College Blvd.; 979-265-3376; bcfas.org) and

diy accommodations

There are a number of RV parks around Brazoria County. For a list of these do-it-yourself accommodations, contact the Brazosport Convention & Visitors Council (300 Abner Jackson Pkwy.; 979-285-2501 or 888-477-2505; visitbrazosport.com).

grab your tank

Looking for a place to scuba dive? Head about 3 miles southwest of Lake Jackson to Clute, where you'll find the aptly named Mammoth Lake Scuba Park. Divers here get to explore an F-5 jet, sunken fire trucks, caves, and even a replica of a Columbian mammoth. Mammoth Lake Scuba uses the park as its training facility. The park is located at 330 N. Dixie Dr. For more information call (979) 266-9771 or visit mammothlakescuba.com.

the **Brazosport Museum of Natural Science** (400 College Blvd.; 979-265-7831; bcfas .org), which boasts the largest shell collection on display in the South, as well as dinosaur skeletons, wildlife, and rock and mineral exhibits. For more information on Clute, contact the Clute Visitors Bureau at (979) 265-2508 or (888) 462-5883 or visit goclute.com.

To get to Clute from Lake Jackson, follow Oyster Creek Drive to Angleton Drive/Old Angleton Road, and take a right. Drive about 1.4 miles and turn left on East Main Street. In total, it's just over a 3-mile drive.

To resume this day trip from Clute, take the Nolan Ryan Expressway/TX 288 South to FM 523 North/North Gulf Boulevard. Stay on the farm-to-market road for about 1 mile and then take a right at North Velasco Boulevard.

freeport & surfside beach

If you love to spend time on the water, you're in luck. The neighboring communities of Freeport and Surfside Beach sit right on the Gulf of Mexico, and both boast fairly clean beaches.

With its many boat ramps, marina, and deep-sea fishing boats, Freeport is considered one of the best places to fish in the Lone Star State. For information on charter fishing trips and dives, contact **Easy Going Charters** (307 Pompano Ln. in Surfside Beach; 979-233-2947 or 800-293-2947; easygulffishing.com).

Freeport is also a popular town among birders. Every year, birders visit Freeport in hopes of seeing unusual species, especially during the Freeport Audubon Christmas Bird Count (see the Festivals & Celebrations appendix). In the past, Freeport has hosted one of the highest numbers of bird species in the nation.

Just a few miles southeast of Freeport is the village of Surfside Beach, a laid-back beach community that is steeped in Texas history. Stephen F. Austin's original 300 settlers are believed to have first landed on Texas soil here. This is also where the first skirmish leading up to the Texas Revolution was fought and where Santa Anna signed the Treaty of Velasco, which formally recognized Texas's independence.

getting there

If you don't take the detour through Clute, follow the Nolan Ryan Expressway/TX 288 South about 6 miles to FM 523 North/North Gulf Boulevard. Stay on there for about a mile and then take a right at North Velasco Boulevard to come into Freeport.

To reach Surfside Beach from Freeport, take FM 523 North to TX 332 East; then take a right and stay on TX 332 East for 3.7 miles. Take a right at Fort Velasco Drive and, to reach the beach, take the second left at Whelk Street, which turns into Beach Drive.

where to go

Dow Black Skimmer Colony. 2301 N. Brazosport Blvd., Freeport; (979) 238-4159; dow .com. Birders, take note: Since 1968, black skimmers have been flocking here every spring to make a temporary home at the Dow Chemical Company's plant. Dow was kind enough to convert a parking lot into a permanent nesting ground and now welcomes the public to see what is believed to be the largest skimmer nesting ground inside an industrial complex. Each summer, hundreds of skimmers are born here.

Freeport Historical Museum. 311 East Park St., Freeport; (979) 233-0066; freeport.tx .us. This free museum was opened in 2009 and contains exhibits on the early history of the Freeport area. Highlights include models of a "swing bridge" and an early lighthouse as well as lots of historical photos and other memorabilia. Closed Monday and Tuesday.

Justin Hurst Wildlife Management Area. From Freeport, take TX 36 west for 5 miles to Jones Creek; (979) 233-8729; tpwd.state.tx.us. The nearly 12,000 acres here are located on land that the Mexican government gave Stephen F. Austin in 1830 and which was later operated as a slave plantation. Today, the Texas Parks and Wildlife Department operates this wildlife management area as part of the Central Coast Wetlands Ecosystem Project, which seeks to preserve coastal wildlife for public benefit. As you wander through the park, check out the large number of indigenous and migratory species, many of which are waterfowl. It is possible to hunt and fish here with a valid license. **Beware:** There are no restrooms, and you should bring your own drinking water.

Quintana Beach County Park. 330 5th St., Quintana (from TX 288, take FM 1495 south 1.7 miles; then take CR 723 east 3 miles to the park entrance); (979) 233-1461 or (800) 872-7578; brazoria-county.com/parks/quintana. This 45-acre park was the site of Fort Bates in 1862 and remains the home of the 1942 Freeport Harbor Defense, the historic Coveney House and its natural history museum, and the Seaburn House, which is now the park office. But the main reason people come here is for easy beach access and the camping facilities. The county-run park sits along the beach, offering a wooden lighted fishing pier, off-beach parking, grills and picnic tables, restrooms and showers, full-service RV campsites, a playground, and elevated wheelchair-accessible boardwalks. Call ahead to make reservations if you want to camp here.

> ## detour for history

> *If you're fascinated by early Texas history, head about 17 miles northwest of Freeport (via TX 36) to visit the Brazoria Museum. Located inside the Brazoria Civic Center, this museum features exhibits on early plantation life, Texas's first female railroad doctor, early city history, Mexican land deeds, the Civil War, and more. The museum is located at 202 W. Smith St. For more information call (979) 236-1154 or visit brazoriahf.org/civiccenter/museum.html. Closed Sunday.*

San Bernard National Wildlife Refuge. From Freeport, take TX 36 South and head southwest on FM 2611. Take a left on FM 2918 and a right on CR 306; (979) 964-3639; fws.gov. Located on the Great Texas Coastal Birding Trail, this 34,679-acre refuge was established in 1969 to protect indigenous birds, as well as those that migrate here during the winter months. The refuge is composed of habitats ranging from freshwater lakes and salt marshes to coastal prairie and bottomland forest. More than 250 species of birds have been spotted here, including snow and blue geese, herons, egrets, and terns. Drive around the Moccasin Pond Loop to see some of the wildlife at work and at play, or come here to hunt, fish, or hike.

Scuba Diving at Flower Garden Banks National Marine Sanctuary. Scuba divers can see manta rays, whale sharks, and enormous coral heads in this national marine sanctuary. But because the sanctuary is located in the middle of the Gulf of Mexico, about 100 miles from land, it's only accessible via boat. Luckily, you can take a diving trip on the Freeport-based M/V *Fling* (contact Fling Charters at 979-233-4445 or flingcharters.com). To learn more about the Flower Garden Banks National Marine Sanctuary, call (409) 621-5151 or visit flowergarden.noaa.gov.

Shrimp Boat Monument. At the head of the Brazosport harbor channel on TX 288 in Freeport. Known as *Mystery,* this 60-foot shrimp trawler is on display to celebrate the area's role in the shrimp industry. When it was built in Louisiana in 1940, it was considered the top of the line. The 40-ton boat is built from cypress and brought in millions of pounds of Gulf Coast shrimp before being retired in 1964.

Surfside Beach. Between TX 332 and 15th Street, Surfside Beach; (979) 233-1531; surfsidetx.org. Surf, frolic in the water, sail, fish, look for shells, and watch the birds on this beach. The Intracoastal Shoreline creates the southern border of the Brazoria National Wildlife Refuge, which, with 226 species, boasts one of the country's highest Audubon Christmas bird counts in a 12-hour period.

where to eat

Kitty's Purple Cow Cafe. 323 Ocean Ave., Freeport; (979) 233-9161. Attracting an even mix of visitors and locals since 1983, Kitty's purple house along the beach is a cheerful, upbeat place to enjoy a burger. You can also choose from several seafood specialties an a generous wine and beer list. Kitty's is open daily until 10 p.m. $–$$.

On The River Restaurant. 919 W. 2nd St., Freeport; (979) 233-1352; ontheriverrestaurant .com. Feast on sandwiches, burgers, and seafood galore at this restaurant, which *Texas Monthly* named one of the 40 best small town cafes. Try the fried pickles. $$.

Pirates Alley Cafe. 100 Francis Cove, Surfside Beach; (979) 239-2233; piratesalleytx.com. This 2-story cafe sits right on the beach, making it the perfect place to grab a bite before you head back out to the water or while you watch the sunset. Sit on one of the decks while you enjoy a sandwich, burger, salad, or Blue Bell ice cream. $–$$.

Red Snapper Inn. 402 Bluewater Hwy., Surfside Beach; (979) 239-3226; redsnapperinn .com. Around here, the saying is "Our fish spent last night in the Gulf," which is good news for you. Diners enjoy fresh Gulf seafood made almost any way they like it—charbroiled, grilled, deep fried, or sautéed. Red Snapper Inn also serves a variety of po'boys. $–$$$.

Texas Burrito Factory. 218 W. Broad St., Freeport; (979) 233-3300; texasburritofactory .com. This family owned and operated establishment is a friendly place to have lunch; build your own burrito in a rustic building that dates back to the 1930s. Not only are there lots of ingredients to choose from, Texas Burrito Factory also offers an amazing array of tortillas to choose from including traditional flour, cheddar jalapeño, tomato basil, garlic and more. $.

where to stay

There are a few chain hotels, but most are not very clean. If you want an overnight trip, consider staying in Lake Jackson. If you want to stay a few days, consider renting a beach house in Surfside Beach. For leads, contact **Beach Resort Services** (409 E. TX 332, No. 2, Surfside Beach; 800-382-9283; beachresortservices.com) or **Corona Del Mar Beach Properties** (877-517-8737 or 979-871-3058; coronadelmarsurfside.com).

worth more time

This day trip covers a lot of territory as it is, but if you want to pack in a little more nature time, head about 50 miles west to **Matagorda County** and **Bay City.** The beaches here offer great fishing, as well as surfing, boating, and birding. Definitely worthy of a visit is the **Matagorda County Birding Nature Center** (1.7 miles west of Bay City on TX 35 next to LeTulle Park; 979-245-3336; mcbnc.org), which attracts an array of birds and other wildlife with its gardens and wetland areas. For more information on Matagorda County and Bay

City, contact the Bay City Chamber of Commerce (201 7th St.; 979-245-8333 or 800-806-8333; baycitychamber.org) or check out visitmatagordacounty.com.

To reach Bay City and the surrounding area from Freeport, follow TX 36 for 23 miles; get onto TX 35 West and stay on it for about 23 miles, and then follow the signs.

southwest

day trip 01

southwest

pioneer country:
west columbia, rosenberg &
richmond

west columbia

The birthplace of the Republic of Texas is 56 miles southwest of Houston in West Columbia. Known simply as Columbia during the Texas Revolution, this town was the site of the Republic's first capitol in 1836. It was here that General Sam Houston was inaugurated as the Republic's first president, Stephen F. Austin was sworn in as secretary of state, and the first congress was sworn in. Within 3 months, the state capital moved to Harrisburg (now Houston), but the capital legacy continues to define West Columbia at the Capitol of Texas Park and a replica of the first Texas capitol.

getting there

West Columbia is about 56 miles southwest of Houston. To get there, take TX 288 South for 41 miles; then take the TX 35 exit toward Angleton/West Columbia/Bay City. You'll see signs for TX 35 South—take a right at TX 35 West and follow it for 12 miles.

where to go

Ammon Underwood House. On the river side of Main Street, East Columbia; (979) 345-3921. Dating back to 1835, this is one of the oldest frame houses in Texas. It was occupied for some 50 years by pioneer and successful cotton plantation owner Ammon Underwood.

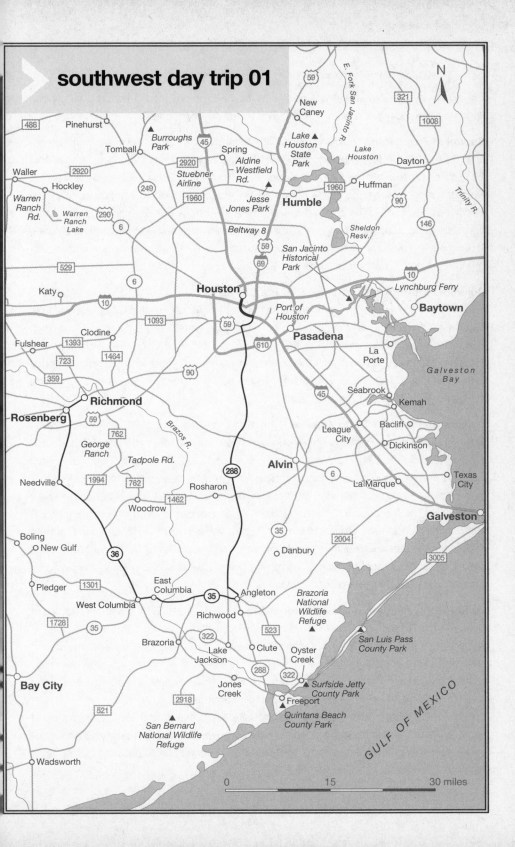

The house, which stayed in the Underwood family for more than a hundred years, has endured three moves. It is open to the public by appointment only.

Capitol of Texas Park. Northeast corner of 17th and Brazos Streets in front of Walgreens; (979) 345-3123; westcolumbiatx.org. This addition to West Columbia was dedicated in April 2009 to commemorate the first 9 years of the Republic of Texas—especially the period when the republic's first congress convened here before moving to Harrisburg, the town that became Houston. The park is located on the site of Texas's first capitol. Take a walk down the path here, and you'll see 20 different granite markers, each illustrating different facts about the early republic. Also incorporated into the park is a 19th-century cistern discovered during the building process.

Columbia Historical Museum. 247 E. Brazos Ave.; (979) 345-6125 or (979) 345-3123; columbiahistoricalmuseum.com. Want to learn more about the role that Columbia played in Texas's early years? This is the place to go. The museum features a diorama of the town in the 1820s, old artifacts from life in the Victorian era, and exhibits on the ranching and oil industries as well as the doctors, military personnel, and firefighters who have been integral to the area's development. Exhibits change regularly. The museum is housed in a stone and marble bank building that dates back to 1950.

Replica of the First State Capitol. 14th Street at Hamilton; (979) 345-3921. When Columbia became the capital of the Republic of Texas in 1836, the congress met in a building that Leman Kelsey had built from clapboard around 1833. The capitol was where Sam Houston was sworn in as president and Stephen F. Austin as secretary of state. Within 3 months of the Republic's birth, the government moved to Harrisburg, the city we now know as Houston. The first capitol of the Republic of Texas was destroyed by the infamous 1900 storm, but a replica was built nearby in 1977. Today, you can visit the replica, which features a room like the one Austin used as his office, with furniture similar to what might have been used in the original capitol building. The replica of the state capitol is open to the public by appointment only, Monday through Friday.

Varner-Hogg Plantation State Historic Site. 1702 N. 13th St. (2 miles north of West Columbia on FM 2852); (979) 345-4656; visitvarnerhoggplantation.com. Situated on 66 acres along Varner Creek, this plantation dates back to 1824, when the Varner family moved here to raise livestock and distill rum from sugarcane. After the Varners sold the plantation in 1834, its history became particularly storied, with William H. Patton holding Santa Anna here for more than a month after the Battle of San Jacinto.

In 1902, Governor James Hogg purchased the plantation and used it as a second home for his family, including daughter Ima Hogg, who refurbished the house and donated it to the state. Today, the Varner-Hogg Plantation State Historic Site is managed by the Texas Historical Commission. Closed Monday.

no place like historic homes

Given that West Columbia was the Republic of Texas's first capital, it should come as no surprise that the area is lined with historic sites and homes. Pick up a map of these historic sites—complete with descriptions—at the West Columbia Chamber of Commerce (202 E. Brazos Ave.; 979-345-3921; westcolumbiachamber.com), and take a drive around town to check them out.

where to eat

Elmo's Grill. 454 S. 17th St.; (979) 345-5127; westbrazosfoods.com/elmos.html. Elmo's serves inexpensive burgers and Mexican food based on traditional recipes. The food probably isn't the best you've ever eaten, but the service is friendly and quick and the locals seem to like it. Whatever you order, you'll probably want to finish it off with an old-fashioned milk shake made from Blue Bell ice cream. Elmo's features daily specials Monday through Thursday. Bring cash because Elmo's doesn't accept credit cards. $.

Scott's BBQ & Catering. 226 E. Brazos Ave.; (979) 345-6162; scottsbbq.com. Owner Scott Leopold caters a lot of events in the area, and locals know his shop is also a good place to get a good barbecue plate or sandwiches. Alternatively, you can order your favorite meat by the pound. $–$$.

where to stay

Columbia Lakes Resort Hotel. 180 Freeman Blvd.; (979) 345-5151; columbialakesgolf .com. Situated on 2,000 tree-lined acres, this resort is a beautiful place to rest your head and indulge in your favorite recreational activities. There's a golf course, a tennis complex with 8 courts, and a 300-acre lake stocked with trophy bass just waiting to be caught. $$.

rosenberg & richmond

Continue your trip back to Texas's early days with a visit to the neighboring Fort Bend County towns of Richmond and Rosenberg. In 1822, the area became home to the first settlement by members of Stephen F. Austin's colony, the Old 300. Fifteen years later Richmond became a city, its name borrowed from that of Richmond, England. Within the next few years, Richmond, Texas, began to establish itself as a ranching and cattle center. Rosenberg emerged in 1880, after the Gulf, Colorado & Santa Fe Railway came to the area.

Today, a trip to Rosenberg and Richmond is really a celebration of the area's early years. In addition to the many historic buildings in both towns, you'll find artifacts of the early days at the Rosenberg Railroad Museum, Decker Park, and the Fort Bend Museum. You also won't want to miss a chance to tour the 23,000-acre George Historical Ranch, which has been around since 1824—more than a decade before Texas became an independent nation.

getting there

The next stop on this day trip, Rosenberg, is about 32 miles north of West Columbia. It's a straight shot on TX 36 North, so just hop on the highway and follow the signs.

Rosenberg and Richmond are next-door neighbors. To reach Richmond from Rosenberg, follow US 90 Alternate East for about 3.6 miles.

where to go

Brazos Bend State Park. 21901 FM 762 in Needville (just south of Rosenberg); (979) 553-5102; tpwd.state.tx.us. Outdoor enthusiasts consider this one of Texas's best state-run parks. The 5,000-acre park's Brazos River location makes it a popular place to fish and spot alligators and freshwater snakes. While hiking or biking along the 20 miles of trails here, you're likely to spot coyotes, bobcats, deer, foxes, and more than 275 bird species. Visit the Nature Center to sign up for a free guided hike on the weekend or to learn about the local wildlife in the Habitats and Niches display. It is also possible to camp here. Camping fees range from $12 to $25 per night for individuals and families, depending on which campsite you use.

Brazos Bend State Park is also home to the George Observatory, a joint project of the Texas Parks and Wildlife Department, the George Foundation, and the Houston Museum of Natural Sciences. It houses the Gueymard Telescope, one of the world's largest telescopes, as well as the Challenger Learning Center for Space Science Education, where young visitors can go on simulated space missions. The telescope is open to the public on Saturday from 3 to 10:30 p.m. For more information on the George Observatory, contact the museum at (713) 639-4629 or hmns.org.

Decker Park. 500 block of Preston in Richmond. Catch a glimpse of a number of historic buildings as you walk through Decker Park, where you'll spot the 1850s McNabb Home, an old railroad depot dating back to 1901, and the 1896 county jail, which now houses the Richmond Police Department.

Fort Bend Museum. 500 Houston St., Richmond; (281) 342-6478; fortbendmuseum.org. Learn about Fort Bend County from 1822 through 1945 here. Exhibits focus on Stephen F. Austin and his colonists in the area's early years, the Texas Revolution, the Civil War, the sugar industry, and more. On-site are 3 historic houses—the 1840s Long-Smith Cottage, the 1883 Moore House, and the 1882–83 McFarlane House. Closed Sunday and Monday.

George Ranch Historical Park. 10215 FM 762, approximately 9 miles south of Richmond; (281) 343-0218; georgeranch.org. This 23,000-acre working ranch dates back to 1824, when Henry and Nancy Jones made it their home. Today, you can see the original home, as well as those of three generations of the Jones's descendants. While you tour the ranch, watch the cowboys rope, sort, and tend cattle; then visit an authentic general store or grab a burger at the Dinner Belle Cafe. To get from one place to the next here, you can ride in a tractor-drawn tram or, if you prefer, walk. The park hosts special meals and events throughout the year. Call or visit the website to see if anything special is happening during your visit. Closed Sunday and Monday.

Rosenberg Railroad Museum. 1921 Ave. F, Rosenberg; (281) 633-2846; rosenbergrr museum.org. This museum covers the history of railroads in the area, with exhibits featuring old photographs, buttons, badges, tools, train parts, timetables, and other objects from the depots that were once located here, as well as information about the people who worked at and traveled through them. The museum building was modeled after the old Union Depot, which was used by the Santa Fe and Southern Pacific railroads from 1883 until 1917. Closed Monday.

where to shop

Enchanted Forest. 10611 FM 2759, Richmond; (281) 937-9449; myenchanted.com. This sister nursery to Enchanted Gardens specializes in shrubs, trees, and other plants that grow well along the Gulf Coast. Stop in at the gift shop to find a variety of candles, soaps, floral-scented and inspired home items, and yard art.

Enchanted Gardens. 6420 FM 359; Richmond; (281) 341-1206; myenchanted.com. Gardeners, take note: Enchanted Gardens is one of the most beautiful and best nurseries in the Houston area. Here you'll find a variety of fresh herbs and vegetables, shrubbery, succulents, roses, perennials, and annuals. Be sure to visit the gift shop for unique gifts and yard art.

Rosenberg's Historic Downtown District. Avenue G between 2nd and 3rd Street in downtown Rosenberg; shoprosenberg.net. Take a walk around downtown Rosenberg, where you'll find cute shops selling antiques and collectibles, jewelry, clothes, furniture, books, and gifts. Most of the shops are along Avenue G and 2nd and 3rd Streets.

where to eat

Another Time Soda Fountain. 800 3rd St., Rosenberg; (281) 232-2999; anothertimesoda fountain.com. Take a trip back to the good ol' days while you feast on burgers, fountain drinks, and '50s-style shakes and malts. Closed Monday and Tuesday. $–$$.

> ## sip and sniff

*If you're a wine aficionado, consider stopping at **Circle S Vineyards** in Sugar Land on your way back to Houston. Dave and Helen Stacy use methods passed down from Dave's father to produce a collection of reds, whites, and seasonal treats such as blackberry port and jalapeño wine. The family vineyards that produce the grapes used here are located in Tuscany and Centerville, Texas. During your visit, you'll enjoy a winery tour and tastings. You can also hang out in one of the living rooms and play a board game or listen to jazz while you sip vino. Circle S Vineyards is located at 9920 US 90 Alternate, No. B-268, in Sugar Land. To get there, follow US 90 Alternate East about 12 miles. For more information call (281) 265-9463 or visit circlesvineyards.com.*

Bob's Taco Station. 1901 Ave. H, Rosenberg; (281) 232-8555; bobstacos.com. Since 1991, locals have counted on this family-run joint for good breakfast tacos, tamales, tacos, and other Tex-Mex favorites. Bob's serves breakfast and lunch and is open for dinner on Friday and Saturday. Closed Monday. $–$$.

Karl's at the Riverbend. 5011 FM 723, Richmond; (281) 238-9300; karlsrb.com. This Zagat-rated restaurant serves American and European dishes, which means you can find everything from beef Wellington, fettuccine Alfredo, and venison to wiener schnitzel to veal Marsala here. Whatever you get, be sure to save room for the apple strudel. Reservations recommended. $$$.

The Swinging Door. 3818 FM 359 Rd., Richmond; (281) 342-4758; swingingdoor.com. Since 1973, people have been coming here from across Houston and farther to dine on pecan-smoked barbecue. This rustic restaurant serves sandwiches—including peanut butter and jelly for kids and those who don't eat meat—as well as plates with meat and veggies. There are also a la carte and family-style options. On occasion, the Swinging Door also offers comedy shows and country-and-western dancing. Call for more information. Closed Monday and Tuesday. $–$$.

where to stay

La Quinta Inn & Suites. 28332 Southwest Fwy. 59, Rosenberg; (832) 595-6111; lq.com. This chain property offers a lot of value for a modest price including free wireless Internet, a fitness center, a pool, a business center, and complimentary breakfast. The 3-story property has 56 rooms and 16 suites with refrigerators, microwave ovens, and premium cable TV channels. Pets are welcome here, and the hotel also offers free parking. $$.

west

day trip 01

west

farmlands:
katy, brookshire, san felipe, sealy

katy

Katy is an increasingly popular master-planned suburb. Though the City of Katy was not incorporated until 1945, the area was first settled in 1872. At the turn of the century, rice farming was introduced to the area, and Katy has been a rice farming center ever since. It is also home to one of Texas's biggest oil fields, many parks, and the Katy Prairie—a popular spot for birding and hunting.

getting there

Drive 28 miles west of downtown Houston on I-10.

where to go

City of Katy Railroad Park and Railroad Museum. 5615 1st St.; (281) 391-8400; cityof katy.com. This nicely landscaped little park is home to an old red caboose. Also here is the restored Missouri-Kansas-Texas Depot, which doubles as Katy's Information and Tourist Center. Closed Sunday.

Katy Heritage Museum. 6002 George Bush Dr.; (281) 391-4884; cityofkaty.com/visit-us/ museums. Take a trip back to Katy's early days as an agricultural town when you check out exhibits featuring old farming equipment, buggies, pictures, and other antiques. The

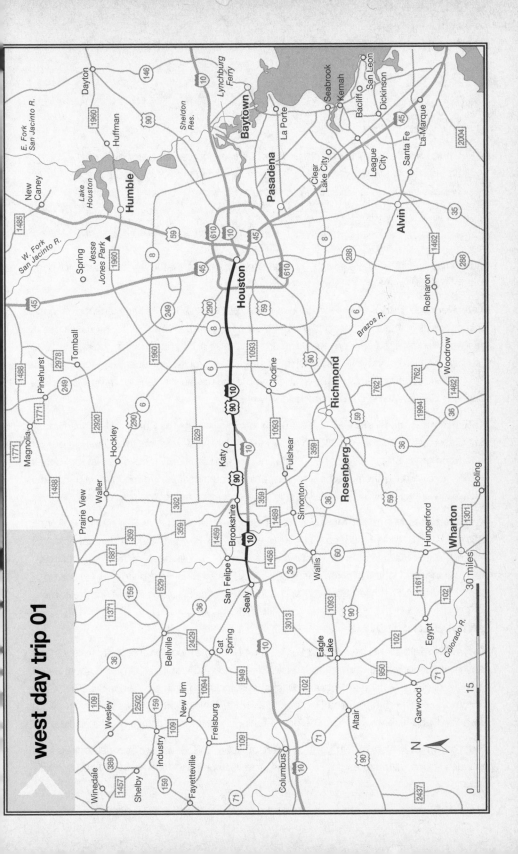

> ## first saturday

On the first Saturday of each month, local artists and vendors set up booths among the historic homes in Katy Heritage Park, and the Katy Heritage Society unlocks the homes to offer free public tours. For more information visit katyheritage society.com.

museum is open Tuesday through Thursday and on the first Saturday and Sunday of each month. Call for hours.

Katy Heritage Park. 5990 George Bush Dr.; (281) 391-2550; katyheritagesociety.com. This park was just established in 2003, but it's loaded with heritage. On the premises of this beautifully landscaped park are a pavilion and several restored buildings, including the 1898 Featherston House, the 1898 Wright House, the 1916 Stockdick House, and the Old Katy Post Office. Each December, this is where you can find the city Christmas tree standing. Concerts and special events are occasionally held here.

Katy Prairie Conservancy. (713) 523-6135; katyprairie.org. The Katy Prairie Conservancy has preserved 14 tracts—13,000 acres worth—of land just west of Houston and north of I-10. Each area attracts a variety of wildlife, including dozens of bird species that make their homes here. Among them are bald eagles, painted buntings, and, during the winter, snow geese and ducks. Visit the website or call for directions to one of the prairie preserves.

Katy Veterans Memorial Museum. 6202 George Bush Dr. (VFW Community Building); (281) 391-VETS. Nicknamed the "G.I. Joe Museum," this is where you'll find military exhibits covering all the major international conflicts in which the US has been involved. The museum also tells the story of the 130 members of the local Veterans of Foreign Wars who served in combat for the US. Closed Saturday and Sunday. Admission is free (donations welcome).

where to shop

Katy Mills Mall. 5000 Katy Mills Circle; (281) 644-5000; simon.com/mall/katy-mills. One of the largest shopping centers in the Houston area, Katy Mills spans 1.3 million square feet. Many—but not all—of the tenants are outlet stores, including Neiman Marcus Last Call, Saks Fifth Avenue's OFF 5th, Banana Republic, Calvin Klein, Nike, and Old Navy. There's also a Bass Pro Shop here, much to the delight of fishing, hunting, and camping enthusiasts.

Old Town Katy. Also known as the "Heart of Katy," this downtown district is filled with antiques shops, gifts stores, artists' shops, and restaurants. It lies north of I-10, primarily from Avenues A through D going east-west and from about Pin Oak Road to 4th Street going north.

where to eat

China Cottage. 637 S. Mason Rd.; (281) 492-7832; china-cottage.com. Authentic, inexpensive Chinese food makes this restaurant a serious crowd-pleaser. The menu includes Mongolian, Cantonese, Szechuan, and Shanghai-inspired dishes. $–$$.

Kenzo Sushi Bistro. 23501 Cinco Ranch Blvd., #R140; (281) 371-8200; kenzosushi.com. If you like a dash of cool with your sushi, Kenzo is your place. Within its ultra-minimalist interior you'll find a forward-thinking Asian fusion menu and a huge array of sushi choices. $$.

The Original Marini's Empanada House. 3522 S. Mason Rd., No. 100; (281) 391-4273; theoriginalmarinisempanadahouse.com. If you like empanadas, this is the place to go. Marini's serves empanadas stuffed with just about everything imaginable—brisket, ham and cheese, and avocados, to name just a few fillings. There are many vegetarian options. Those with a sweet tooth may prefer the various dessert empanadas. Closed Monday. $.

The Wine Next Door. 23501 Cinco Ranch Blvd.; (281) 395-4100; thewinenextdoor.com. This unpretentious wine bar serves boutique wines by the glass, bottle, or flight. Those who are hungry can try some of the cheeses and dry-cured Italian meats served here, or order in from nearby restaurants such as Perry's Steakhouse and Fish City Grill. $–$$$.

brookshire

With a population of just 3,450 in 2000 and an area of only about 3.5 square miles, Brookshire is a true small town—and a rural one, too. The Waller County town was built here on fertile soil back in the early 1880s, and it continues to reap the benefits of this land. In addition to growing peanuts, soybeans, and rice, Brookshire is home to cattle farms and oil and gas fields.

Fittingly, one of the most popular attractions here is Dewberry Farm, where families go to get a fun taste of country life. Other attractions include the Waller County Historical Museum and a model airplane field.

getting there

Brookshire is about 8 miles directly west of Katy. For a scenic (and actually quicker) route, head west on US 90 for about 7.5 miles until you find yourself in Brookshire.

Alternatively, you can hop back on I-10 West and take exit 732 for FM 359 toward Brookshire. Take a right at FM 359 North/Waller Avenue and follow the road for about a half-mile.

where to go

Bomber Field. About 13 miles northwest of Brookshire in Monaville (follow FM 359 to Monaville, and then take a left at FM1877); (713) 826-4256; bomberfieldusa.com. Model airplane lovers, take note: Bomber Field hosts radio-controlled aircraft "fly-ins." Call for dates.

Dewberry Farm. 7705 FM 362; (281) 934-3276; dewberryfarm.com. Day-trippers with kids will find tons to do at this fun-packed farm: Climb a 12-foot hay mountain, ride the longest barrel train in Texas, pan for semiprecious gems, shoot corn from cannons, rope a runaway calf, take a hayride, get lost in a maze, or feed some farm animals. On Saturday, Dewberry Farm holds pig races on its pig race track. The farm also offers a variety of seasonal activities, including a lighted pumpkin stroll and an opportunity to pick a pumpkin from the pumpkin patch in the fall, and the chance to pick and cut your own Christmas tree (dewberrychristmastrees.com).

Waller County Historical Museum. 906 Cooper St.; (281) 934-2826; wallercountyhistory .org. This museum is located in a 1910 home that once belonged to Dr. Paul Donigan, a physician, and his wife, Rebecca. Some rooms use period furnishings to re-create period scenes (including Dr. Donigan's office); others showcase exhibits featuring old photographs and memorabilia. There's also a research library here. The museum is a registered Texas Historic Landmark.

where to eat

The Cafe at Brookwood. 1752 FM 1489; (281) 375-2400; brookwoodcommunity.org/ shop-eat/the-cafe-at-brookwood. Located on the Brookwood Community campus, this cafe boasts gourmet food served by the community's smiling students, all of whom are here to learn to make a living in spite of their physical or mental challenges. Entrees include everything from Chicken Crepes Contessa to burgers to the Texas Gold Sandwich (grilled chicken, brie, and candied jalapeños grilled on ciabatta bread). The cafe serves lunch to the public from 11 a.m. to 2 p.m. 7 days a week. Call ahead to make reservations. $$–$$$.

Repka's: An Original Country Store. 8184 Buller Rd.; (281) 934-4499; repkas.com. Locals love the hot 'n' spicy crawfish at this southern seafood joint. Other popular (and by no means healthy) options include pork cracklings, fried alligator, fried oysters, frog legs, chicken-fried steak, fried catfish, étouffée, red beans and rice, shrimp, seafood platters, crawfish pie, and bread pudding. Closed Monday and Tuesday. $–$$$.

where to stay

Eve's Garden B&B. 603 Kenney Ave.; (281) 934-3569; evesgardentexas.com. Guests may stay in one of 3 rooms here or, for extra privacy, the private loft dubbed The Nest. The B&B is decorated in a country floral motif in keeping with the guest room names: Robin's Nest, Fern Hollow, and Ruby Begonia's Room. Outside is a lovely garden that is often used for weddings; in the winter an outdoor fireplace keeps guests warm while they take in the evening scenery. Continental breakfast is included. $.

La Quinta Inn & Suites. 721 FM 1489; (281) 375-8888; lq.com. One of only a couple of chain hotels in Brookshire, this 3-story La Quinta covers all the basics as well as offering some nice perks such as complimentary breakfast and newspaper, a fitness center, free wireless Internet, and pet-friendly policies. Each room and suite is equipped with a microwave oven, mini-refrigerator, and flat-screen TV. $$.

san felipe

If you're a fiend for early Texas history, you'll appreciate San Felipe. This little town—née San Felipe de Austin—was named for Stephen F. Austin, who picked it as the first site (and capital) of his colony in 1823. Meetings that laid the groundwork for the Texas Declaration of Independence were held here in the early 1830s, and many notable Texans—including William B. Travis—lived and worked here between 1823 and 1836. As a result, this former social, political, and economic hub is known as the "Cradle of Texas Liberty" and the "Birthplace of Anglo-American Settlement in Texas" by locals and historians.

Austin chose San Felipe as the capital of his settlement based on its central location, freshwater sources, and elevation, which was believed to give locals the ability to easily defend against possible intruders from the bottomlands. In the end, San Felipe's elevation didn't prove to be much help. In 1836, Mexican general Santa Anna's army began invading San Felipe, so locals burned down the town to prevent the Mexican army's occupation. The town was rebuilt shortly thereafter, but by then it was too late: Other Texas towns—including West Columbia, Houston, Huntsville, and Austin—had become more prominent, so San Felipe never did regain its old glory. To learn more about San Felipe's storied early history, visit colonialcapitaloftexas.com.

getting there

San Felipe lies just 11 to 13 miles west of Brookshire, depending on the route you take. The quickest route is to head west on I-10 for about 9 miles; then take exit 723 toward FM 1458/San Felipe/Frydek and turn right on FM 1458.

For a slightly more scenic, pastoral drive, follow Bains Street/FM 359 North about 3.7 miles and then continue onto 2nd Street/FM 1458 for about 8.5 miles.

where to go

San Felipe de Austin State Historic Site. 15945 FM 1458; (979) 885-2181; visitsanfelipe deaustin.com. This small park, operated by the Texas Historical Commission, is home to the original San Felipe town site. Here you can see a statue of Stephen F. Austin, a log cabin replica of his headquarters, and the 1847 J. J. Josey Store, which is now a museum. At the end of October, the site celebrates Stephen F. Austin's birthday with a heritage celebration; see listing in the Festivals & Celebrations appendix for more information. This site is usually open Tuesday through Saturday during daylight hours, but the museum isn't always open during that time, so call ahead. Admission is free.

Stephen F. Austin State Park. Park Road 38 (From I-10 West, head north on FM 1458; then take a left on Park Road 38); (979) 885-3613; tpwd.state.tx.us. Located on the Brazos River not far from the San Felipe de Austin State Historic Site, Stephen F. Austin State Park is a nice place to have a picnic, bike, camp for the day or overnight, hike, convene with nature, and fish. The park offers family-friendly programs on Friday evenings; on Saturday mornings kids aged 13 and under (and their parents) are invited to participate in a nature hike for kids.

where to eat

There isn't much in the way of dining options in San Felipe. Your best bet is to grab something in Brookshire, or at the last stop on this day trip, Sealy.

sealy

In 1879, Gulf, Colorado, & Santa Fe Railway president George Sealy needed some land for additional railroad lines and a depot. So he purchased some from San Felipe de Austin, and with that, a new town was born (and named for the railroad magnate, of course). With Sealy becoming an important stop between Galveston and Temple, the railroad brought lots of jobs to the area. It also brought Czech and German settlers, who began farming and ranching here.

Sealy is still very much a rural town today, but it also boasts a few intriguing attractions, including the Haynes Mattress Factory, where cotton gin builder Daniel Haynes invented the cotton mattress.

getting there

To get to Sealy, return to I-10 West and follow it for 2.6 miles until you reach exit 720 for TX 36 toward Sealy/Bellville. Follow TX 36 for a little less than a half-mile, then take a left at Meyer Street and follow the road into town.

where to go

Attwater Prairie Chicken National Wildlife Refuge. In Eagle Lake (head south from Sealy on TX 36 to FM 3013 and go west for 10 miles); (979) 234-3021; fws.gov. This 10,541-acre refuge is one of the biggest—and last—coastal prairie habitats in Southeast Texas. As the refuge's name suggests, it was created to protect the nearly extinct Attwater's prairie chicken, once one of the most populous birds in the Texas/Louisiana tallgrass prairie ecosystem. The refuge offers prairie and wetlands trails for hiking and wildlife viewing. There is also a 5-mile car tour route. Stop into the visitor center to pick up a wildflower identification guide and see more than a hundred taxidermy bird mounts. Closed Saturday and Sunday.

Frydek Catholic Cemetery & Grotto. On the St. Mary's Catholic Church grounds, FM 1458, 1 mile south of I-10, Frydek; (979) 885-3131. A few miles south of Sealy in the community of Frydek, this limestone grotto was built to honor 67 soldiers from the Frydek Parish who served in World War II. A reminder of the area's Czech heritage, the grotto celebrates the fact that all the soldiers returned home safely from the war.

Haynes Mattress Factory. 305 N. Hardeman St. Welcome to the birthplace of the modern mattress. This is where, in 1885, cotton gin builder Daniel Haynes created a machine that compressed cotton for use in mattresses. He later sold his patents to a group that formed their own mattress-making company and called it Sealy. Haynes opened another mattress factory shortly thereafter and used his own name. Today, you can still see the original factory and most of the old equipment in tours arranged through the Sealy and Historic Austin County Convention & Visitors Bureau; for more information, call (979) 885-3222.

Heritage Park/Santa Fe Park Museum. East of downtown at 211 Main St.; (979) 885-3222. This property is home to an old red caboose, an early maintainer railcar, the old jail, and other artifacts from Sealy's early days. The museum is open by appointment only, so call ahead.

Lonestar Motorsports Park. 120 Old Columbus Rd. South; (979) 877-0922; lonestar motorsportspark.com. Those who like to see fast and furious racing will enjoy visiting this motor sports park, which hosts car, motorcycle, and drag racing on a drag strip sanctioned by the International Hot Rod Association. Call to find out about upcoming events at the track.

where to eat

Maribelli's Y Italia Restaurant. 2353 TX 36 South; (979) 627-7665. Don't be deterred by Maribelli's strip mall location. Many consider this Italian spot the best restaurant in Sealy. It features a full Italian menu for lunch and dinner and also offers a moderately-priced lunch buffet. $$.

Tony's Family Restaurant. 1629 Meyer St. (TX 36); (979) 885-4140; tonysfamilyrestaurant
.com. Home-cooked burgers, chicken-fried steak, and other country favorites make this a
popular place to eat breakfast, lunch, and dinner. At lunchtime, diners can opt for the all-
you-can-eat buffet. The parking lot can accommodate RVs. $–$$.

day trip 02

west

>>> **calm waters & shady oaks:**
columbus

columbus

In Columbus, the self-declared City of Live Oaks, you'll find yourself surrounded by beautiful live oak trees, restored Victorian buildings, and—in the spring and early summer—fields upon fields of bluebonnets, Indian paintbrushes, Indian blankets, and sunflowers.

The historic town dates back to 1823, when it was settled by members of Stephen F. Austin's first colony. Today, it is the seat of Colorado County and home to a number of art galleries and museums, enabling it to make *Texas Monthly*'s list of the best small towns for art.

The Colorado River runs through Columbus, creating opportunities for kayaking, canoeing, and tubing, as well as hunting, fishing, and nature study.

getting there

Drive about 70 miles west of downtown Houston along I-10 and exit onto US 90 West.

where to go

Abram Alley Log Cabin. 1224 Bowie St. Abram Alley, one of Stephen F. Austin's original settlers, built this log cabin in 1836, after his first home was burned down during the Texas Revolution. The restored cabin is considered a great example of early Texas craftsmanship

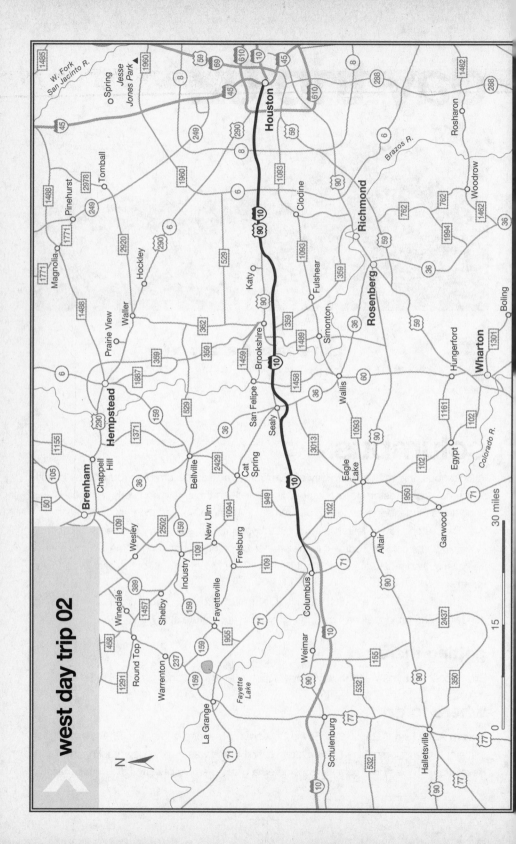

west day trip 02

what's in a name

Originally called Beason's Crossing, Columbus's name has long been the subject of dispute. Some claim the town was named in honor of Christopher Columbus, while others maintain that it derived from the influx of settlers from Columbus, Ohio.

and is a Texas Historic Landmark. The cabin is run by the Columbus Historical Preservation Trust; call (979) 732-8385 for more information. Closed Sunday.

Beason's Park. Access point just off US 90, left of the Colorado River; (979) 732-2604; lcra .org. This park is the exit point for kayakers on the Columbus Paddling Trail (see below). The Colorado River runs right through the park, making this a pretty place to picnic, throw in a line from the pier, or launch kayaks, canoes, and floats. The park does not allow overnight camping.

Colorado County Courthouse. On the courthouse square downtown; (979) 732-5135. This majestic courthouse stands in the center of town among magnolia trees. Built in 1891 in Second Empire style, the courthouse boasts a Tiffany-style stained glass dome above the original judge's bench in the second-floor district courtroom. The courthouse is a registered Texas Historic Landmark and is open during business hours Monday through Friday. When this book went to press, the courthouse was closed for renovations; call before you visit.

Columbus City Cemetery. On Walnut Street, near the center of town. Columbus City Cemetery—aka Old City Cemetery—is eerily enchanting, with old headstones and large oak trees dotting the property. Among those buried here are many Confederate soldiers and people who died during the 1873 yellow fever outbreak. A 1913 flood washed away many of the grave markers, so there are believed to be at least 500 unmarked graves. Around Halloween each year, the Nesbitt Memorial Library hosts a nighttime historical tour, the Live Oaks and Dead Folks Tour, which visits either the Old City Cemetery or the Odd Fellows Rest Cemetery (1516 Montezuma St.). During your visit, be sure to watch your step, as the uneven ground is a hazard for klutzes and a magnet for snakes.

Columbus Paddling Trail. tpwd.state.tx.us. Nature lovers and outdoorsy types won't want to miss the chance to paddle or go tubing down this inland trail on the Colorado River. The 6.5-mile paddle trail, maintained by the Texas Parks and Wildlife Department, offers a unique opportunity to check out a variety of trees and flowers, as well as birds ranging from vultures to flycatchers to ibis to roseate spoonbills. You can also fish for alligator gar, shad, sunfish, channel catfish, bluegill, Guadeloupe bass, carp, longnose gar, and yellow catfish.

The water tends to be fairly calm, though there are some smaller rapids here and there. Bring a picnic lunch and stop to eat on one of the islands along the trail.

Canoes, kayaks, and tubes can be rented from **Howell Canoe Livery** (804 Robson St.; 979-732-3816; howellcanoe.com). Call to reserve your watercraft; a deposit is required. The trail's starting point is at the TX 71 Business crossing under the North River Bridge; look for the boat ramp signs. The takeout point is Beason's Park on Walnut Street near the East River Bridge; see the Beason's Park write-up above.

Dilue Rose Harris House Museum. 602 Washington St. The Columbus Historical Preservation Trust maintains this 1860 Greek Revival–style cottage. It was the home of Dilue Rose Harris, nicknamed "Woman of the Texas Revolution" after she wrote about her family's experiences leading up to the war. The cottage features "tabby" concrete construction, unusual for that time. Call the Columbus Historical Preservation Trust at (979) 732-5135 with questions or to schedule a visit.

1886 Stafford Opera House. 425 Spring St.; (979) 732-5135. Galveston architect Nicholas J. Clayton designed this elegant building for cattleman and banker Robert Stafford in 1886. The state's largest flat-floored opera house, it has since been restored, maintaining its copper French mansard roof. Each month, the 1886 Stafford Opera House hosts dinner theater shows put on by troupes from Austin, Fredericksburg, and Deer Park. The opera house doubles as a museum and the town's visitor center and chamber of commerce.

Live Oak Art Center. 1014 Milam St.; (979) 732-8398; liveoakartcenter.org. Opened by Columbus residents in 1954, this gallery is the heart of the local arts scene. Live Oak Art Center showcases the work of emerging and more established artists who hail from the area and well beyond Texas and even US borders. Exhibits change regularly. To get the community involved, the gallery often holds "meet the artist" events and exhibit openings. Live Oak Art Center also offers workshops for people of all ages, regardless of art skill.

Nesbitt Memorial Library. 529 Washington St.; (979) 732-3392; library.columbustexas .net. This local library is home to Colorado County's sizeable collection of historical and genealogical archives. Also here is a collection of fine art and more than 200 dolls donated by Lee Quinn Nesbitt. The library frequently hosts special events, including author talks, musical performances, and the annual Live Oaks and Dead Folks cemetery tour, which you can read more about in the Columbus City Cemetery listing above.

Santa Claus Museum. 604 Washington St.; (979) 732-4458; facebook.com/santaclaus museumgiftshop. Mary Elizabeth Hopkins has collected more than 1,500 representations of Santa Claus, beginning with a Santa she received in 1913 when she was just 6 months old. Her collection—including figurines, Norman Rockwell prints, and Pez dispensers—is on display here, along with videos and interactive kiosks. The museum is open Thursday through Saturday year-round.

catch the (radio) waves!

Want to learn more abut the historic sites you're visiting when you're out and about in Columbus? Many historic sites here now have radio transmitters that broadcast prerecorded messages, chock-full of information about the site. Just look for the blue signs at each site, and tune in to the specific AM frequency. Call the Chamber of Commerce (979-732-8385) for more information.

where to shop

Donna's Attic. 735 Walnut St.; (979) 733-8864. Find something to spruce up your home for the next holiday here. Or shop for gifts, purses, and jewelry. The collection here is eclectic and changes often but you can count on finding quirky, unique gifts for special occasions. Donna's is also a distributor of Yellow Box shoes, Kameleon silver jewelry and Miss Me jeans.

Grand Oaks Antiques and Gifts. 1034 Milam St.; (979) 732-9181. More than 40 dealers sell everything under the sun here including antique estate items. Look for art works, handcrafted gift items, craft consignment items, dishes, pottery and glassware, musical instruments, religious icons, holiday gift items, home decor selections and scrapbooking treasures. Closed Saturday.

Home Design Studio. 920 Milam St.; (979) 732-5001; countrytimehomes.com. Prepare to be overwhelmed: This shop sells just about everything you could want for your home, yourself, or a gift. Among the items for sale are pajamas, wine glasses, children's toys and gift items, food, frames, candles, cookbooks, bath products, and home decor.

Turner-Chapman Gallery. 1038 Milam St.; (979) 733-0400; turnerchapmangallery.com. This gallery sells an array of photographs, paintings, pottery, lithographs, and giclées by artists such as co-owner Kenneth Turner, Charles Ford, Lynda Counts, and Paulina Kearney. It is located in the 1852 building that the Fehrenkamp grocery store once occupied.

where to eat

Jerry Mikeska's Bar-B-Q. Off I-10 West at exit 698; (979) 732-3108; jerrymikeskas.com. Mikeska's isn't much to look at from the outside, but the tender, smoky barbecue has fans all over Southeast and Central Texas. If you're not big on taxidermy, beware: Mikeska's has gone a little overboard with the dead animal heads, which line the walls from the moment you enter. $–$$.

Nancy's Steak House. 2536 TX 71 South; (979) 732-9700; nancyssteakhouse.com. Specializing in certified Angus beef, Nancy's has attracted a loyal dining crowd thanks to an extensive menu which, in addition to steaks, includes seafood, chicken dishes such as Spinach Chicken (grilled chicken breast with sautéed spinach), and a full bar. $$–$$$.

Roasters Chicken & Grill. 1206 Fannin St.; (979) 733-9464; roasterschicken.com. This family-friendly sports bar serves salads, burgers, wraps, and most things chicken, wings and gizzards included. Want to try a little of everything? Opt for the lunch buffet or, on Friday nights, the dinner buffet. There's karaoke on Saturday night. $–$$.

Schobels Restaurant. 2020 Milam St.; (979) 732-2385; schobelsrestaurant.com. Football fan? You probably know the Schobels—Aaron Schobel (Buffalo Bills), Matt Schobel (Philadelphia Eagles), and Bo Schobel (Indianapolis Colts). This German-American restaurant is owned by their family, so diners occasionally see these NFL stars eating here during the off-season. Since opening in 1979, the restaurant has attracted diners with country favorites like meat loaf, chicken-fried steak, and mashed potatoes, as well as some of the best veggies in town. The restaurant serves breakfast, lunch, and dinner, and you can order off the menu or opt for the buffet and pile an endless supply of food on your plate. $–$$.

where to stay

Lodge on Lake Siesta. 634 Spring St.; (979) 732-2726 or (888) 677-0593; lodgeonlake siesta.com. This eclectic lodge draws inspiration from the Adirondacks and Maine in its design, but the place also features a number of Texas decorative touches, including animal heads and antlers, shutters from the Texas capitol that are used as a closet door, and a bathroom clad in burnt orange as homage to the University of Texas. Sit on the screened-in porch and you're likely to see some wildlife scamper or fly past. The suites here sleep 4 to 6 people. Two night minimum stay required, and pricing varies seasonally and depending on the number of people traveling with you. $$–$$$.

Magnolia Oaks Bed & Breakfast and the Little Red House. 634 Spring St.; (979) 732-2726 or (888) 677-0593; magnoliaoaks.com. This charming Victorian house dates back to 1890, but it offers modern amenities such as a Jacuzzi. For a little R&R, sit on the swing in the garden or play croquet. Next door to Magnolia Oaks stands its sister lodging space, the Little Red House. This enchanting 1860s cottage features a ceiling painted with Texas wildflowers. $$.

day trip 03

west

>>> **czech territory:**
la grange, schulenburg

la grange

Like many other Texas towns in this area, La Grange is a culturally rich town. It sits on an old Indian camp where the east-west Indian trail called La Bahia Road crossed the Colorado River. This location makes for lovely birding, hiking, biking, and kayaking opportunities.

La Grange was first settled in the 1820s by Colonel John H. Moore as part of Stephen F. Austin's colony. The town began to develop in the early 1830s and became the seat of Fayette County in 1837. Like many towns in those days, La Grange was built around a square. Today, life in La Grange still revolves in many ways around the square, where you'll find numerous shops, restaurants, and other attractions.

Some say the town was named after Moore's hometown in Tennessee; others suggest it was named after the French estate of American Revolution hero General Lafayette, for whom the county is named. Over the years, La Grange attracted a number of Czech and German settlers, a fact that's evident at the Texas Czech Heritage & Cultural Center and in the *kolaches* and pigs in a blanket sold at Weikel's Store and Bakery.

getting there

La Grange is about 100 miles northwest of downtown Houston. While you can take I-10 to Schulenburg and then travel up US 77 to La Grange, you'll end up missing out on some of

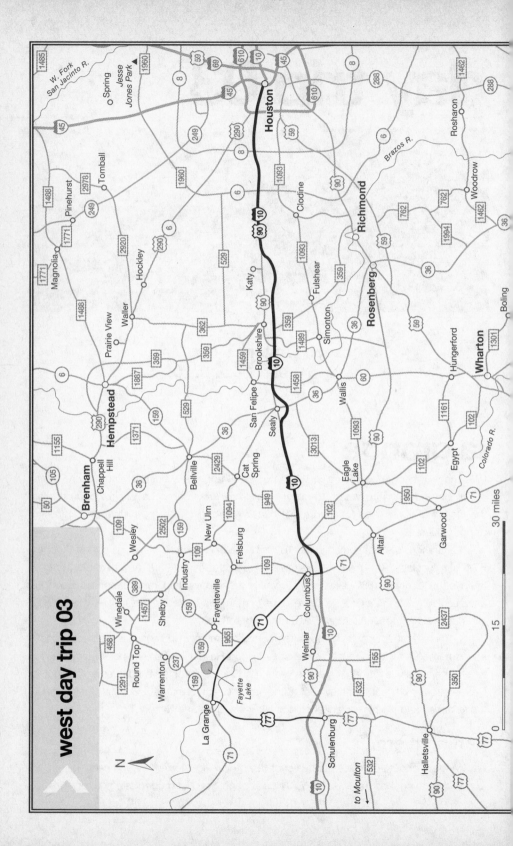

west day trip 03

the stops along TX 71. Instead, follow I-10 West toward San Antonio until you see the sign for TX 71 West toward La Grange/Austin. Take that exit and follow TX 71 West for about 23 miles; then take the ramp to TX 71 Business/La Grange and take a slight left. Continue to follow TX 71 Business West until it turns into East Travis Street.

where to go

Biking. With 12 different bike paths running through the area, La Grange is an excellent place to go biking. The trails vary in distance and terrain. To download maps of area biking routes, visit lagrangetx.org/visitors.

Fayette Heritage Museum and Archives. 855 S. Jefferson St.; (979) 968-6418; cityoflg .com/Departments-Library.htm. The museum and archives here are intended to help users better understand the history of Fayette County. There is a collection of local art, along with genealogical archives, microfilm, historic photos, and special exhibits on Fayette County. Closed Monday.

Itsy Bitsy Burro Company. 1751 Lidiak Rd., between La Grange and Schulenburg; (979) 247-4965; lildonk.com. Since 1991, owners Tonnie and Jerry Willrich have been breeding miniature donkeys that are 33 inches tall or smaller. The Willriches breed the donkeys (which they also sell) to be affectionate, making this a good place to bring kids. However, you must call to make an appointment before stopping by. The ranch is tricky to find, so ask the Willriches for directions.

The Jersey Barnyard. 3117 TX 159; (979) 249-3017 or (800) 382-2880; texasjersey.com. Bring the kids to visit the barnyard, take a hayride, milk a cow, and pet and feed the animals. Among the animals you'll meet at this working dairy farm is Belle, the cow seen on commercials for Blue Bell ice cream. During your visit, enjoy some ice cream and stop at the gift shop and garden center. Guided tours are offered 4 times daily; if you show up at an unscheduled time, you can take a self-guided tour.

KatySweet Confectioners. 4321 TX 71 West; (979) 242-5172 or (800) 419-2056, katy sweet.com. Got a sweet tooth? If you call ahead, you can tour this candy factory—and sample some fudge and pralines.

Lifechek Drug. 148 N. Washington St. (across from the courthouse in town square); (979) 968-5835. Originally named Hermes Drug Store when William Hermes founded it in 1856, this is the oldest operating pharmacy in the Lone Star State. While some of the fixtures remain, remodeling has given the drugstore a 21st-century look and feel.

Monument Hill and Kreische Brewery State Historic Sites. 414 TX 92 Loop; (979) 968-5658; tpwd.state.tx.us. These 2 sites, located just 1 mile south of La Grange, span a total of 40.4 acres. A tomb at **Monument Hill** pays tribute to the Texans who lost their lives in the 1842 Dawson Massacre outside of San Antonio and the Meir Expedition, considered

historic muster oak tree

La Grange is home to many beautiful old oaks, but the one that's found on the northeast corner of the town square is particularly special. Beneath this tree in 1842, Captain Nicholas Dawson literally rallied the troops, rounding up 53 men to help Texas fight Mexican troops.

the most disastrous border confrontation between Texas and Mexico during Texas's years as an independent country. During your visit, take advantage of the opportunity to picnic, study nature, check out some ruins, and look for the more than 50 species of birds.

Adjacent to Monument Hill is **Kreische Brewery State Historic Site,** which became Texas's first brewery when it was built on Monument Hill sometime between 1860 and 1870. The restored brewery is open Saturday for guided tours. Tours of the Kreische House are held on first and second Sundays. Admission to both sites is free.

N. W. Faison House. 822 S. Jefferson St./TX 77; faisonhouse.org. Nathaniel Faison, who participated in the Dawson expedition against Mexico in the late 1860s, is believed to have built this house in the 1840s. He later deeded the property to his black housekeeper, Louisiana Brown, who sold it to Faison's brother Peter in 1872. Members of Peter's family lived here until 1961. Parts of the restored house are typical of Texas pioneers' homes during the 1840s; other parts are more ornate, suggesting different parts of the house were built at different times. The house is open to the public on the second Saturday of each month and by appointment; call the La Grange Area Chamber of Commerce (979-968-5756) to schedule a visit.

Rosemary's Vineyard and Winery. 5501 TX 71 East; (979) 249-2109; wines-made-in-texas.com. Rosemary's bills itself as "Fayette County's first little winery." It produces Merlots, Chardonnays, Blanc du Bois, Ruby Port, a Lenoir, and a sweet Muscadine wine. All the grapes are picked and processed on-site by hand. Visit Thursday through Sunday for a tasting, or call to schedule an appointment.

Texas Czech Heritage & Cultural Center. 250 W. Fairgrounds Rd. (at the entrance to the Fayette County Fairgrounds); (979) 968-9399 or (888) 785-4500; czechtexas.org. If you've got some Czech blood, you'll want to check—no, *Czech*—this out. Here you can see the names of Czech settlers who helped found La Grange, visit a replica of a Czech village, trace your Czech ancestry in the library, visit the amphitheater, and take a self-guided walking tour in Czech and English. The center is open Monday through Saturday and by appointment.

Water sports. The Colorado River runs through La Grange, which makes for some good kayaking and canoeing. If you're interested in renting a kayak, call (979) 968-5600. Prefer to rent a canoe? Try (979) 247-4128. And for those who like to fish, opportunities to catch bass abound at Fayette Lake. For more information on fishing here, call Prairie Park at (979) 249-3344.

where to shop

Le Petite Gourmet Shoppe. 134 N. Washington St.; (979) 968-4000; lepetitegourmet shoppe.com. Located in a historic building on the square, this little shop is a slice of foodie heaven. It carries an array of kitchen gadgets, cookware, cutlery, coffee, tea, and gifts.

Second Chance Emporium. 529 W. Travis St.; (979) 968-6070. This thrift store sells pre-owned clothes and other secondhand items. It is run by a group of local churches, which donate the proceeds to local charities. Second Chance Emporium is open on Friday and Saturday only from 9 a.m. to 3 p.m.

where to eat

Bistro 108. 108 S. Main St.; (979) 968-9108; bistro108.com. This charming restaurant is a good place to go for a nice meal while you're in the area. Entrees like pecan-crusted catfish and bacon-wrapped pork tenderloin and daily soup specials like chicken tortilla and poblano corn chowder make this one of the most popular restaurants in town. Closed Monday. $$$.

La Grange Smokehouse. 4315 E. TX 71; (979) 249-5777; lagrangesmokehouse.com. Stop in for hot links, brisket, and ribs on Saturday and Sunday; the rest of the week, you can grab smoked and fresh meats to go. $–$$.

Latte on the Square. 219 W. Travis St.; (979) 968-9545; latteonthesquare.com. This cute little coffee shop serves coffee, espresso, hot chocolate, and tea, as well as smoothies, breakfast favorite likes eggs and ham, paninis, wraps, salads, and ice cream. $–$$.

Weikel's Store and Bakery. 2247 W. TX 71; (979) 968-9413; weikels.com. Thanks in part to the renowned *kolaches* and pigs in a blanket made and sold here, this family-run operation is a popular stop between Houston and Austin. Be prepared to wait in line to order. The store sells home decor items, T-shirts, and University of Texas paraphernalia. $.

where to stay

Brendan Manor Bed & Breakfast. 345 E. Travis St.; (979) 968-2028 or (866) 658-1100; brendanmanor.com. Stay in one of 5 bedrooms at the historic Bradshaw/Killough home, where you'll sleep among antiques galore and enjoy a full breakfast every day. $$.

Texana Trails & Lodging. 2647 Kallus Rd.; (979) 247-4457; texanatrailslodge.com. This Colorado River Valley homestead dates back to 1835—before Texas won its independence from Mexico. Guests stay in a stone Georgian Revival–style house, the newly built lodge, or the 1850 stone stable. All are exquisitely decorated to create a sophisticated country ambience. $$.

schulenburg

As its nickname—"Gateway to the Rolling Hills"—suggests, Schulenburg is a rural area—and a rather charming one at that. The landscape is dotted with cattle farms, painted churches, dance halls, and open fields that sprout wildflowers each spring.

The Kesiah Crier and James Lyons families were the first settlers here, making their homes on a land grant from the Mexican government in 1831. The town of Schulenburg wasn't incorporated until 1875, after the Galveston, Harrisburg and San Antonio Railroad purchased land here and built a depot on a section that had been owned by Louis Schulenburg, who became the town's namesake. Schulenburg, Texas, attracted many German and Czech settlers in its early years, and their culture continues to manifest itself here, from the polka music to the painted churches to the *kolaches* sold in local bakeries to the town's name.

getting there

Schulenburg is directly south of La Grange. To get there, follow US 77 South for about 16.5 miles.

where to go

Chaloupka Farm. 784 CR 251 in Moulton (14 miles southeast of Schulenburg); (361) 798-6131 or (361) 772-4718; rockycreekmaze.com. A 15-foot hay slide, a barrel train, hayrides, wildflowers, and seasonal events like the haunted maze make for plenty of family fun. Call ahead to inquire about hours, as the farm maintains a variable seasonal schedule.

Historic homes. Schulenburg is home to more than a dozen historic landmarks, and you can get a complete list of them from the **Schulenburg Chamber of Commerce** (618 N. Main St.; 979-743-4514 or 866-504-5294; schulenburgchamber.org). Among the landmarks are 2 notable houses: **Old Anderson Place** (510 S. Main St.) was originally owned by William B. and Rosetta Anderson, who built it before 1857. Subsequent owners included Schulenburg's namesake, Louis Schulenburg, and T. W. Pierce, one of the main investors for the Galveston, Houston & San Antonio Railroad. Austrian immigrants built the **Gus Cranz Mansion** (710 West Ave.) in 1874, with a facade reminiscent of an Austrian villa. Cranz's son-in-law, Hugh Roy Cullen, may be familiar to Houstonians: He endowed the University of Houston. Neither Old Anderson Place nor the Gus Cranz Mansion is open to the public, but you can drive past and steal a look or two.

heartbreak hotel?

Schulenburg's strangest structure is the venerable Von Minden Hotel (607 Lyons Ave.; 979-743-3714). Local lore insists that the hotel is haunted by the ghosts of its original owners, Ruby and Ben Speckles. Another story recalls a returning World War II soldier who waited in vain for his sweetheart to join him there. After waiting all night, the soldier committed suicide by jumping from an upper-floor window. This was purported to be the inspiration for the Elvis Presley song "Heartbreak Hotel."

Painted Churches Tour. schulenburgchamber.org/tours/churches. There's no need to travel all the way to Europe to see some exquisitely decorated churches. Fayette County is home to 4 boldly hued "painted" churches—that is, churches with faux-finished interiors that were painted by roving artists. Each church has its own unique design. The Schulenburg Chamber of Commerce offers a map to guide you to these churches—**Sts. Cyril and Methodius Church** in Dubina, **St. John the Baptist Catholic Church** in Ammannsville, **St. Mary's Catholic Church** in High Hill, and **St. Mary's Parish** in Praha. All are still active. They are open for self-guided tours Monday through Saturday; please be respectful of any religious activities taking place during your visit. To learn more about the churches or to schedule a guided tour, stop by the Chamber of Commerce at 618 N. Main St. or call (866) 504-5294 or (979) 743-4514. For more information check out klru.org/paintedchurches/index.html.

Stanzel Model Aircraft Museum. 311 Baumgarten St.; (979) 743-6559; stanzelmuseum .org. If you're fascinated with airplanes (especially of the toy variety), this museum is a must-see. Your visit will begin with a multimedia presentation about flight history and its impact on Victor and Joe Stanzel, the museum's namesakes, who owned a toy factory here for more than half a century. The duo were especially known for the model aircraft they designed. You'll then move to the museum's factory section to learn how model aircraft were originally developed and manufactured in the Stanzels' farmhouse. In total, there are more than 30 exhibits—some interactive—here. Also on-site is the restored late 19th-century home that belonged to the Stanzels' grandparents. The museum is open Monday, Wednesday, Friday, and Saturday.

Texas Polka Music Museum. 625 N. Main St.; (979) 743-4752; texaspolkamuseum.com. This new museum features memorabilia related to all things polka—instruments, old band uniforms, recordings, band photos and schedules, and polka DJ playlists and program notes. The museum is open Thursday through Saturday.

> ## fiddles and dominos
>
> *If you're a fiddling or dominos fanatic (or better yet, both!), head down to Hallettsville, located 17 miles south of Schulenburg on US 77 South. This German/Czech community is home to the Texas Championship Dominoes Hall of Fame and the Texas Fiddlers Hall of Fame—both conveniently located at Knights of Columbus Hall on US 77 South. For more information call (361) 798-2311 or visit kchall.com.*

where to shop

The Flower Box. 615 N. Main St.; (979) 743-3219 or (800) 432-8440; schulenburgflowers .com. This popular shop sells candles, cards, Texana, and gifts; they also offer craft sessions on occasion.

Harold's Coins. 710 Lyons Ave.: (979) 743-4800; haroldscoins.com. Harold's buys and sells just about every coin imaginable. If you want something they don't have, they'll try to get it for you.

Potter Country Store. 716 N. US 77 and 16 N. Kessler Ave.; (877) 743-2660; potter countrystore.com. Stop at these 2 locations to buy freshly shelled pecans, as well as pecan fudge, roasted cinnamon sugar pecans, chocolate-covered pecans, and other homemade treats made with Potter's pecans.

Texas Rustic. 102 N. Kessler Ave.; (979) 743-4846; texas-rustic.com. As the name of this shop suggests, this is the place to find your Texas-themed items whether it is furniture, home decor accessories, glassware, metal signs, or that deer-antler chandelier you've been craving. Closed Sunday and Monday.

where to eat

City Market. 109 Kessler Ave.; (979) 743-3440 or (800) 793-3440; citymarketsch.com. This meat market makes its own sausage, producing 10,000 pounds each week and selling it in dry, summer, and jalapeño varieties. On weekdays, City Market serves brisket and barbecued sausage for lunch, but the best day to lunch here is on Saturday, when the barbecue dishes include brisket, pork shoulder, turkey breast, sirloin, sausage, turkey, and ribs. Closed Sunday. $–$$.

Frank's Restaurant. Intersection of I-10 and US 77; (979) 743-3555. The burgers, chicken-fried steak, and other home-cooked favorites, along with the smiling servers, make this a reliable favorite for those traveling along I-10. $–$$.

Iron Horse Filling Station. 405 W. Summit St.; (979) 743-4392; ironhorsefillingstation
.com. This casual restaurant serves grilled sandwiches, pizza, soup, and salad, and during
breakfast, coffee and muffins. Iron Horse doesn't serve any fried food, but those who crave
something of that variety may opt for the non-fried, guilt-free burger and fries. Closed for
dinner Monday through Wednesday and all day Sunday. $–$$.

Sengelmann Hall. 531 N. Main St.; (979) 743-2300; sengelmannhall.com. Food, beer,
live music, and dancing: Sengelmann Hall's got it all. This charming joint is located inside
a restored 1890s dance hall that's filled with charm. The saloon and *biergarten* here serve
pre-Prohibition cocktails, the famous Sengelmann Hall Punch, and a variety of Texas micro-
brews and Czech and German beers. In the restaurant, executive chef Kenny Kopecky creates a new menu for each season. The cuisine tends to reflect Texas, German, and Czech
influences, with dishes ranging from the chicken-fried rib eye to duck quesadillas to Czech-
style potato pancakes and goulash. The menu includes vegetarian options, and the kitchen
can usually accommodate special dietary requests. Whatever you order, save room for one
of the homemade Czech desserts. After dinner Thursday through Sunday, head upstairs to
listen to some live music and tap your feet in the dance hall. $–$$$.

where to stay

Mimi's Bed & Breakfast. 2925 Piano Bridge Rd.; (979) 743-9539; mimisbedandbreakfast
.com. Mimi's offers guests accommodations in 1 of 3 turn-of-the-20th-century farm-
houses—Ludvik's Place (3140 Piano Bridge Rd.), Dog Run (5601 Mensik Rd.), and Adie's
Place (1601 High Hill Rd.). Your stay includes a continental breakfast of *kolaches* or pigs in
a blanket and coffee, tea, and juice. $$.

Wildlife Guesthouse. 7707 W. US 90; (979) 224-6234; wguesthouse.com. Get your
fill of country living at this 60-acre exotic wildlife ranch. There are 2 bedrooms in the
2,000-square-foot Wildlife Guesthouse. Bring your horse to ride or borrow one of the golf
carts to check out the scenery and the deer, antelope, wild turkeys, ducks, and geese that
live here. Pets are allowed here, but kids aren't. $$$.

worth more time

If you love beer and want to stretch this trip out beyond the 2-hour limit of this book, head
down to **Shiner.** Located about 127 miles southwest of downtown Houston, Shiner is
home of the aptly named **Shiner Beer,** brewed by the **Spoetzl Brewery** (603 E. Brewery
St.; 361-594-3383) since 1909. The independent brewery—the oldest in the Lone Star
State—offers tours on weekdays at designated times, which change seasonally. To learn
more call (800) 5-SHINER or visit shiner.com.

Dubbed the "cleanest little city in Texas," Shiner is home to a few other attractions,
including a historic opera house and two museums that celebrate the town's history. To

learn more about Shiner, visit shinertx.com or contact the Shiner Chamber of Commerce at 817 N. Ave. E or (361) 594-4180.

Shiner is located about 32 miles southwest of Schulenburg. To get there, you have a few options: You can follow I-10 West for about 11.5 miles, take exit 661 for FM 609 toward TX 95/Flatonia/Smithville, and follow TX 95 South for about a mile. Or you can follow US 77 South for 17.2 miles; then get onto US 90 Alternate West and follow it for just over 14 miles.

Alternatively, you can follow FM 957 for about 10 miles until you reach FM 532; then follow FM 532 for about 10 miles until you reach South Lavaca Drive/TX 95 South, which you'll follow for about 10 more miles until you see the signs for Shiner.

northwest

day trip 01

northwest

bluebonnets & blue bell:
chappell hill, brenham, burton

chappell hill

Chappell Hill is a small town with a picture-perfect backdrop, no matter the season. During March and April, the town lights up with seemingly endless fields of Indian paintbrushes and bluebonnets. It even celebrates its botanical glories by hosting Texas's official Bluebonnet Festival, complete with more than 300 juried artists, in mid-April. In the fall Chappell Hill fills up with fall decorations for the Scarecrow Festival, and in the winter, lights and teddy bears abound for the Holiday Home Tour and Teddy Bear Parade. And though the Chappell Hill Lavender Farm delivers a soothing aroma and purple fields year-round, it's during the annual Lavender and Wine Fest each August that Texans trek here from miles away to discover what locals consider one of their great treasures. (Find details about all these events in the Festivals & Celebrations appendix of this guide.)

These are just a few of the reasons why visitors love to visit this hospitable little agricultural town. Even if there are no festivals taking place during your visit, this Washington County town is sure to charm. Located in the heart of Stephen F. Austin's original colony, Chappell Hill looks relatively unchanged from its early days. A designated National Register Historic District, Main Street is dotted with old buildings that now serve as restaurants, art galleries, and shops, where the salespeople will take the time to ask about your day and point you to the town's best spots. The scenery, friendly people, and change of pace are so enchanting that you just might want to extend your visit by spending a night or two at one of the area's many bed-and-breakfasts.

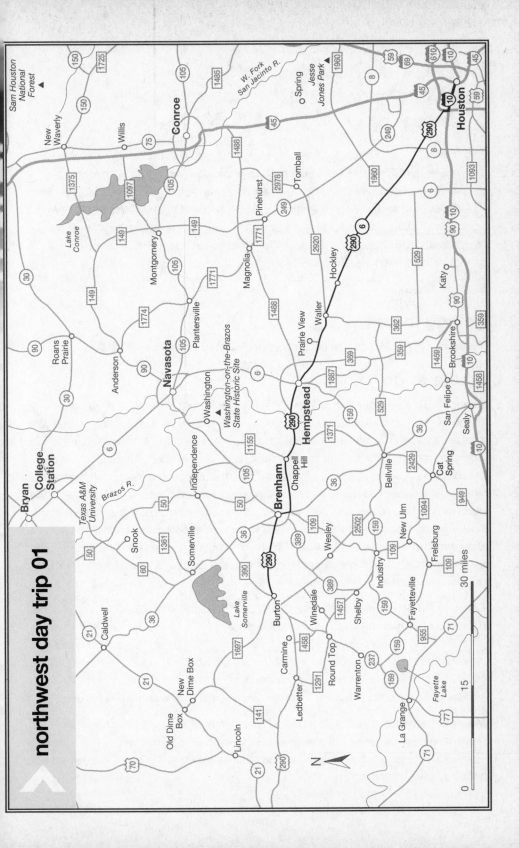

northwest day trip 01

> ## sausage country
>
> *If you love some good Polish sausage—and can stomach seeing how it's made—visit* **Chappell Hill Sausage Company.** *The owner, Mike Kopycinski, a third-generation American, makes Polish sausages like his grandfather enjoyed in the old country before coming to Texas in the 1800s. Although Chappell Hill Sausage Company doesn't offer tours, you can stop in and watch as the staff makes the sausage. Chappell Hill Sausage Company is located at 4255 Sausage Ln. For more information call (979) 836-5830 or visit chsausage.com.*

getting there

To reach Chappell Hill, drive about an hour northwest of Houston on US 290.

where to go

Chappell Hill Lavender Farm. 2250 Dillard Rd., Brenham; (979) 251-8114; chappellhill lavender.com. You can practically smell your way to this farm, where the fields are lined with lavender. Cut your own for $5 a bundle, and then consider using it in some of the farm's renowned recipes for treats like lavender lemonade, lavender pecan crisps, and lavender chocolate-chip cookies. During your visit, picnic in the gazebo and stop into the gift shop, where lavender-scented soaps and gifts abound. In August, Chappell Hill Lavender Farm hosts its annual Lavender and Wine Fest, which you can learn more about in the Festivals & Celebrations appendix of this book. Though the farm is located in Chappell Hill, it has a Brenham address, so be sure to input "Brenham" rather than "Chappell Hill" into your GPS. Be aware, though, that some mapping programs, such as Google Maps, identify the lavender farm's location as Washington, Texas.

Chappell Hill Museum & Historical Society. 9220 Poplar St.; (979) 836-6033; chappell hillhistoricalsociety.com/museum.html. Get schooled in early Texas history at Chappell Hill's first public school building, which now serves as a museum. The school building itself dates back to 1927, but the items on display here go back a bit further. Permanent exhibits illuminate Chappell Hill's history, especially the Civil War period, Reconstruction, Polish immigration in the area, and 2 old schools from the area. Closed Monday and Tuesday.

Masonic Cemetery. On Old Chappell Hill Road, north of FM 2447. This cemetery is the final resting place of relatives of Alamo heroes Davy Crockett and William B. Travis, as well as many Confederate soldiers. In 2000, the grounds also became home to a monument honoring Travis and his son.

where the wildflowers are

Every spring Washington County lights up with Indian paintbrushes, bluebonnets, and other flowers. To find out where the best wildflower patches are, download a visitor guide from visitbrenhamtexas.com, visit the Washington County Visitor Center at 115 W. Main St. in Brenham, or pick up a brochure at one of the shops or restaurants in the area.

Old Rock Store. 5070 Main St. at Cedar; (979) 836-6033; chappellhillhistoricalsociety .com/store.html. This historic sandstone and cedar property has been used for many different things. When it was built in 1869, it was a general store. It later served as a feed store, a butcher shop, and the Chappell Hill Post Office. Today, it's essentially a museum, though the small space is also available for rental for meetings and special events. Inside hang two beautifully stitched wall panels that represent the town's history. Two local artists designed the 30-foot-by-6-foot hangings in the early 1970s. Call to schedule a visit.

where to shop

Bluebonnet House & Garden Center. 5095 Main St. (FM 1155); (979) 836-2554; blue bonnethouse.net. Since 1992, this gift shop has been selling fine linens, handmade ceramics, seasonal decor, candles, jewelry, quilts, plants, and unique garden art, hanging baskets, and planters. Many gifts here incorporate images of bluebonnets. Some items are kitschy, but if you're willing to look, you're likely to find something good.

The Brazos Star. On Main Street next to Bluebonnet House & Garden Center; (713) 301- 5073; brazosstar.com. You'll find a little of everything here—crafts, antiques, old baseball and basketball cards, bracelets made of old silverware, picture frames, candles, collectibles, and then some. While some of the antiques seem cluttered, don't let that keep you away. There are some great finds here, and owner Mary Louise Young and her staff are very friendly. Ask for tips on what to do in the area, and they're sure to give you some good advice. The Brazos Star building is listed on the National Registry of Historic Places. It is open Saturday and Sunday only, except for the occasional Friday during bluebonnet and wildflower season in March and April.

The Stagecoach Inn. 4950 Main St. (FM 1155); (979) 830-8861; thestagecoachinn.com. This historic inn doubles as a private residence and an antiques shop. Stop in to see some of the beautiful 18th- and 19th-century antiques, reproductions of furniture from this period, lighting fixtures, and decor that owner Eileen Evans has hand-selected to sell in the shop here.

Texana Cigar & Coffee Co. 5080 Main St. (FM 1155); (888) 845-0853. Stop at this shop for some Texana coffee or some cigars that remind us of how Chappell Hill got put on the map: Legend has it that Chappell Hill's namesake, Robert Wooding Chappell, looked down from a hill 130 years ago, saw the fertile land, and decided to use it for a tobacco plantation—the only one ever attempted in the Lone Star State. Legend or not, he built a booming tobacco plantation—and in turn, the town of Chappell Hill. The Texana Cigars sold here are made from Cuban-seed tobacco that is farmed in Nicaragua.

where to eat

Bevers Kitchen & Gifts. 5162 Main St.; (979) 836-4178; bevers-kitchen.com. Burgers, chicken-fried steak, chili, and sandwiches are some of the biggest draws here, but Bevers Kitchen also caters to customers who are watching what they eat. The chalkboard here lists daily Weight Watchers' specials and a "Mediterranean Health Style" special; the menu also includes salads, veggie burgers, and a veggie plate. Whatever you order, save room for a slice of homemade pie. Closed Sunday. $.

Chappell Hill Meat Market & Cafe. Highway 290 at FM 1155; (979) 836-0850. Stop in here for good burgers, barbecue, and the famous country sausage, which has been made here by the Kopycinski family since 1939. Since then, the cafe and market were moved to its current location on Highway 290, but links master Mike Kopycinski and his wife, Cissy, still serve their customers some of the best grub in town. $–$$.

The Lazy Mule Saloon. 9002 FM 1371; (979) 421-9200 or (713) 240-6926; lazymulesaloon .bzzp.net/contact.html. Formerly known as the Second Fiddle Bar & Grill, this hole-in-the-wall serves cold beer and bar food, much of it seasoned Cajun-style. There are also 2 pool tables, a jukebox, and a little stage where musicians sometimes perform. $–$$.

where to stay

The Cottages at Hackberry Hill. 9880 Lost Ln.; (979) 481-0843; hackberryhillcottages .com. These country cottages offer comfortable accommodations with some country flair. The decor includes antiques and lots of old-fashioned florals. There's plenty of room for lounging indoors or outside on the porch, where you can breathe in some fresh air and watch the longhorn cattle graze. $$.

The Stagecoach Inn. 4950 Main St. (FM 1155); (979) 830-8861; thestagecoachinn.com. Back in the 1850s, this historic inn was considered a luxurious place to spend the night while traveling between Houston and Austin. Today, antiques dealer Eileen Evans and her husband, Steve Evans, a retired Air Force pilot, call the spacious inn home; they rent out well-furnished rooms in the Weems House and the Coach House—2 smaller houses on the property. A lovely little garden and the shade of the large pecan and oak trees make this a great retreat for an evening or a weekend. No matter how long you're staying, be sure to

just like the pioneers

Want to see the area as some of Texas's earliest settlers did? Drive north from Chappell Hill along FM 1155 toward the Washington-on-the-Brazos State Historic Site (Northwest Day Trip 02). Not only will you enjoy some beautiful landscapes; you'll mimic the route—minus the cars and concrete—used by some of the state's pioneers as they traveled to the birthplace of Texas independence.

check out the 18th- and 19th-century antiques and reproductions in The Stagecoach Inn's shop. One night's deposit is required in advance. $$.

brenham

German immigrants began settling in Brenham in the 1860s, and though the town remains small today, people continue coming here for the day or longer. That's largely because Brenham—the seat of Washington County—packs just as much charm and hospitality as its neighbor, Chappell Hill.

Brenham is known as home of the best ice cream in the country (Blue Bell, of course). It's also filled with enchanting shops and restaurants, two wineries, historic homes, an old carousel, 5 acres of greenhouses, and a miniature horse farm. And in the spring, all roads here lead to—or rather, are lined with—bluebonnets and other wildflowers. Each May, Brenham welcomes people from miles away to the spirited Maifest, which celebrates the town's German roots.

In other words, there's a lot to see and do here. If you want to do it all (or even most of it), make a reservation at one of the dozens of bed-and-breakfasts in the area, where you'll enjoy views of the rolling hills that seem to go on forever.

getting there

To get to Brenham from Chappell Hill, you have a couple of options. If you're in a hurry, follow US 290 West about 7.5 miles and then veer left onto Feeder Road for about a mile. Take a right at South Day Street; then take a quick right at West Tom Green Street and a quick left onto South Austin Street. Stay on South Austin for roughly three-quarters of a mile; then take a right at West Alamo Street, and you'll find yourself in Brenham.

Alternatively, you can pack in a little extra country scenery, though you'll end up tacking an extra 3 miles onto your trip. Up for it? From Chappell Hill, head north on FM 1155/Main Street toward Chestnut Street North/FM 2447 East and drive about 2.5 miles. Then take a left at CR 83/South Meyersville; take two rights to continue on this road. After going about

> ## floral inspiration
>
> *Here's a fun fact: Back when Blue Bell Creameries was founded in 1907, it was called the Brenham Creamery Co. But in 1930 the owners had a change of heart and decided to rename the company Blue Bell in honor of the wildflower of the same name, which blooms here each summer.*

4.7 miles on CR 83/South Meyersville, take a left at TX 105 West and drive about 6 miles until you reach East Main Street.

where to go

Antique Carousel. 910 N. Park St.; (979) 337-7250; cityofbrenham.org/parks/antique carousel.php. Bring the kids to Brenham's Fireman's Park for a ride on a rare antique carousel. While the carousel's origins were long uncertain, it has been determined that hobbyhorse manufacturer Charles W. Dare's New York carousel company carved the horses between 1867 and 1901. A stamp on the carousel indicates that Kansas's C. W. Parker Company manufactured the carousel, which was found near some railroad tracks about 20 miles northeast of Brenham in 1932. The carousel was subsequently moved to Fireman's Park, where it makes its home today. Fully restored, the carousel is open for riding from March through October.

Blue Bell Creameries. 1101 S. Blue Bell Rd. (off US 290); (800) 327-8135 or (979) 830-2197; bluebell.com. If you've ever been forced to choose an ice-cream brand outside of the Lone Star State, you probably know those commercials are right: Blue Bell *is* the best ice cream in the country. Apparently, the Blue Bell staff haven't let their reputation go to their heads, though, because they still welcome guests with small-town hospitality. Tours are offered on weekdays—and yes, visitors get to sample the ice cream. There are no weekend tours. Show up early because this is the hottest ticket in town, and guests are admitted on a first-come, first-served basis. If you're visiting during Easter or spring break—or you're visiting in a group of 15 or more any time of year—you must make reservations in advance.

Brenham Heritage Museum. 105 S. Market St. at Main Street; (979) 830-8445; brenham heritagemuseum.org. Visit this renovated 1915 federal government building to learn about the history of Brenham. The museum exhibits a number of special shows throughout the year. Be sure to stop into the museum showroom to see restored fire trucks, including an 1879 Silsby steam fire engine. Closed Sunday through Tuesday.

Ellison's Greenhouses. 2107 E. Stone St.; (979) 836-6011; ellisonsgreenhouses.com. With its 5 acres of greenhouses, Ellison's is considered one of the Lone Star State's best wholesale nurseries. While there's a seemingly endless variety of plants here, Ellison's is known for its hydrangeas, poinsettias, and Easter lilies. Stop in to purchase some plants for your garden or simply tour the greenhouses. During your visit, stop at the gift shop, where you can find some unique jewelry, garden art, home decor, and Christian gift items. Visit in late fall to see gigantic poinsettias at the annual Poinsettia Celebration (see the Festivals & Celebrations appendix later in this book).

Historic Homes Tours. (979) 836-1690; giddingsstonemansion.com. The Heritage Society of Washington County offers tours of 2 historic homes in the area: the **Giddings Stone Mansion** (2203 Century Circle) and the **Giddings-Wilkin House Museum** (805 Crockett St.). Both homes were owned by attorney and surveyor Jabez Deming Giddings, who came to Texas from Pennsylvania in 1837. He built the Giddings-Wilkin House in 1843. Now fully restored to include original Giddings family heirlooms, it is believed to be the oldest house still standing in Brenham. Giddings built his second house—the Giddings Stone Mansion— in 1869, hoping to protect his family from a yellow fever epidemic in Brenham. Tours for groups of 10 or more are offered Monday through Friday for $10 per person.

Home Sweet Farm. 7800 FM 2502; (979) 251-9922; homesweetfarm.com. This small family farm is run by former Texas Organic Farmers & Gardeners Association president Brad Stufflebeam, his wife, Jenny, and their children. They never use synthetic materials on their crops but rather trust in only all-natural fertilizers and pest controls. Once a month, the farm hosts Monthly Market Day, when guests can tour the farm for free and purchase Texas olive oil, local cheeses, raw local honey, baked goods, chicken, beef, pork, and seasonal foods. Home Sweet Farm also offers workshops for people interested in learning about sustainable and organic farming techniques. Call or visit the website to learn about upcoming events.

Horseshoe Junction. 2080 US 290 West; (979) 251-8701; horseshoejunction.com. If you've got a carload of kids who need a place to work off some excess energy, point your trusty steed to Horseshoe Junction. This fun park offers a host of diversions guaranteed to provide a family-pleasing experience. Park attractions include traditional rides like bumper boats, miniature golf, and go-karts as well as laser tag and a 3-story climbing wall with multiple difficulties. The Outpost Arcade boasts over 50 video games, both old and new. Since Horseshoe Junction is primarily aimed at the younger set, its hours of operation reflect the school year. Generally, the park is open weekends, except for spring break, Christmas break, and mid-August when it opens daily. It's a good idea to call ahead for hours before going. While most attractions at the park can be purchased a la carte, you can also buy an all-day wristband for unlimited access to everything.

Pleasant Hill Winery. 1441 Salem Rd.; (979) 830-VINE; pleasanthillwinery.com. If you think there's nothing better than sipping a glass of vino while staring out at some breathtaking

> ## something to tweet about
>
> *While many small Texas towns are still working on getting their websites up to par with those of big cities, Brenham is a big exception. Not only do Brenham and Washington County share a slick website (brenhamtexas.com), they're on Twitter, posting tons of updates about the latest happenings in town. If you're on Twitter, follow them at @chamberwashco and @visitbrenham so you're in the know before your day trip.*

scenery, plan to stop at Brenham's Pleasant Hill Winery. The wines here range from a tangy white to a fruity rosé to caramelized port wines made with locally grown grapes. Their Collina Bianca label won a silver medal at the 2010 Lone Star Wine Competition, International, and their Rosso Forte also won silver at the 2011 Lone Star Wine Competition, Texas. The winery is open for tours and tastings on Saturday and Sunday.

Unity Theatre. 300 Church St.; (979) 830-1460; unitybrenham.org. Guests come from as far away as Houston, Austin, and College Station to see professional actors from the area perform 4 different plays on the Main Stage and 2 other plays on the Studio Stage. The intimate theater itself is part of the draw: It's located in a restored warehouse that seats just 125 people. Advance tickets are available for $27 (Main Stage) and $25 (Studio Stage). If you're willing to risk missing a performance, though, you can purchase tickets for $15 at the window 15 minutes before the curtain rises. You can also meet the director if you show up early for a show's second Saturday performance; see the website for show dates so that you can plan accordingly.

Windy Hill Winery. 4232 Clover Rd. (east off FM 50); (979) 836-3252; windywinery.com. If you want a true Texas wine, visit this 20-year-old winery. It is one of the few wineries in the Lone Star State to use only Texas grapes, and it bottles all of its wines on-site. Windy Hill's wines include a mix of reds, whites, rosés, and ports. Stop in to taste the wines or take a tour. And don't worry if you don't know much about wine; the owners will gladly teach you how to taste, swirl, smell, and judge a wine. Closed Monday and Tuesday.

where to shop

The Barnhill House Toys and Books. 606 S. Austin St.; (979) 836-1817. The toys here are a mix of remakes of old pedal cars, dolls, and games and newer finds; the store also sells books and children's dress-up clothes. The Barnhill House is open only a few hours a week, so call before you stop by to make sure they'll be open.

Beadboard UpCountry. 101 S. Baylor St.; (979) 830-8788; beadboardupcountry.com. Want your home to show a bit of Euro-country style? This restored bank building–turned–upscale interior design shop is the place to go. Here you'll find antiques, upholstery, fine linens, candles, Italian soaps, garden accessories, and unique gifts. Closed Sunday and Monday, but if you're visiting during the holiday season, call to find out about additional seasonal hours.

Bluebonnet Pottery & Gift Gallery Studio. 12341 LBJ Dr.; (979) 289-3765; bluebonnet pottery.com. Before you buy here, watch the potters at this studio make colorful, contemporary dinnerware, as well as sculptural pieces. The studio also offers classes and workshops. The gallery is open Tuesday through Saturday, but it often closes to sell its products at shows, especially in the spring. Be sure to call before you stop by, to make sure they're open.

Dona Lynn's Unique Gifts. 100 E. Alamo St.; (979) 830-7222; donalynns.com. Owner Dona Lynn (Vrazel) Parker and her family take pride in hand-selecting an eclectic array of gift items from home decor to cigars. The collection changes frequently but will typically include jewelry, quirky accessories, bath and beauty items, and gourmet foods. They will even put together a gift basket for you if you like.

Glissman's Gift Gallery. 106 W. Main St.; (979) 830-9100. Housed in a historic building dating back to the 1860s, this gift shop touts collectibles, including some old soda fountain and drugstore finds. Glissman's is open Thursday through Saturday.

Hermann Furniture and Brenham Antique Mall. 213 W. Alamo St.; (979) 836-7231 or (888) 836-7237; hermannfurniture.com. Since 1876, the Hermann family has been furnishing area homes. But around here "furnishing" doesn't just mean beds, couches, and chairs: The shop also sells an array of home decor items, including drapes, lamps, home accessories, and gifts. Also on-site are a craft mall, a general store selling specialty foods and other items, and a 6,000-square-foot antiques mall.

Leftovers Antiques. 3900 US 290 West; (979) 830-8496; leftoversantiques.net. Don't let the name fool you: The items sold at this gift shop are by no means unwanted. In fact, you may have to keep yourself from buying too much during your visit to this enchanting 10,000-square-foot showroom. Leftovers is filled with antique and antique-inspired items sure to bring charm to any bedroom, kitchen, bathroom, or living room.

The Pomegranate. 203 W. Alamo St.; (979) 836-1199. Since this shop shares space with the coffee shop Wired and Inspired (see below), feel free to nurse a cup of java while you check out The Pomegranate's bath products, Texana, gifts, and home decor.

The Silversmith Shop. 205 E. Main St.; (979) 251-7747; pesilversmith.com. Visit this unique shop to find one-of-a-kind jewelry creations, hollowware, wineglasses, and sculptural pieces—most created with silver. Be sure to check out the ceramics upstairs. The gallery is closed Sunday through Tuesday, as well as a chunk of the summer, so call before visiting.

Westwood Gifts. 2160 US 290 West; (979) 830-0830; westwoodgifts.com. No matter the occasion, odds are you can find a unique gift here. Westwood's diverse selection includes everything from Waterford crystal to artist-made jewelry, candles, home decor, and wind chimes. If you need to satisfy a sugar craving, stop at Scoops (see below) and get some Blue Bell ice cream.

where to eat

BT Longhorn Saloon & Steakhouse. 205 S. Baylor St.; (979) 421-6700. If you can't stand a long wait, don't come here. But if you have time to spare—especially for a good burger, pulled-pork sandwich, and Cajun fries—BT Longhorn Saloon & Steakhouse is worth a visit. True to its name, the restaurant has a rustic aura, with animal heads and Old West paintings dotting the walls. $$–$$$.

Ernie's. 103 S. Baylor St.; (979) 836-7545. Enjoy contemporary cuisine in a historic building dating back to the 1940s. Ernie's offers beautiful gourmet dishes such as sautéed crawfish tails and jumbo shrimp on fettuccine, pan-seared veal scallopini with mushroom Marsala sauce, and baked spinach salad with portobello mushrooms and swiss cheese. The kitchen strives to use fresh, seasonal produce and herbs, so the menu changes regularly. All of the sauces, desserts, and breads are prepared on-site. Closed Monday. $$$.

Funky Art Cafe. 202 W. Commerce St.; (979) 836-5220; funkyartcafe.com. The art's not the only funky thing at this charming restaurant. The frequently changing menu here includes warm dishes such as chorizo corn tart, chicken and spinach enchilada pie, sand-wiches, salads, wraps, and soups. The restaurant is open only for lunch and closed on Sunday. $–$$.

Las Fuentes Mexican Restaurant and Bar. 201 US 290 Loop East; (979) 836-3910; lasfuentesmexrest.com. If you are craving some authentic Tex-Mex dishes, you can't go wrong at Las Fuentes. They offer daily specials seven days a week including Fajitas Pob-lanas for Two on Tuesday, a choice of shrimp dishes on Friday, and Tomatillo Enchiladas on Saturday. The place gets extra lively on Thursday evenings, which brings Karaoke Night and jumbo margaritas. $$.

Must Be Heaven Sandwich Shoppe. 107 W. Alamo St.; (979) 830-8536; mustbeheaven .com. For 25 years, locals have been coming here for great sandwiches, soups, salads, and quiches. Save room for a slice of homemade pie topped with Blue Bell ice cream. Come equipped with patience; there's often a wait to get a table. $.

Nathan's BBQ. 1307 Prairie Lea St. (exit Blinn College/FM 389 at the US 290 bypass); (979) 251-9900; nathansbbq.com. Formerly Big Daddy's BBQ restaurant, Nathan's is owned by

b&b country

Day trips are great, but let's be honest: Sometimes it takes a night away from home to rejuvenate. There's no place better in Southeast Texas to soak up some extra down-home hospitality than Brenham and the surrounding towns. The area is home to more than 40 bed-and-breakfasts, a handful of which we've included in this section and in the towns that follow for this trip. For more options, call the Bed & Breakfast Registry at (888) BRENHAM. Sweet dreams!

Nathan Winkleman, "the Big Daddy of Texas BBQ" who opened the original barbecue joint in an old gas station. Now enlarged and spiffed up, Nathan's still serves the same flavorful chicken, brisket, chops, and stuffed potatoes for which Big Daddy's was locally famous. Some of the recipes on the menu were passed down to Nathan from his grandmother. $–$$.

Scoops at Westwood. 2150 US 290 West; (979) 830-0266; scoopsbrenham.com. Don't have time to visit the Blue Bell Creameries? Head to Scoops, which serves Blue Bell ice cream delivered straight from the creamery. You'll have your choice of 32 flavors—a few of which you can't even find at the store year-round. Scoops serves up ice cream in waffle cones, shakes, banana splits, floats, and smoothies. $.

Volare. 102 S. Ross St.; (979) 836-1514; volareitalianrestaurant.com. Foodies, take note: This is a restaurant you don't want to miss. Located in an enchanting saltbox-style house, Volare serves Italian food. Chef Silvio DiGennaro crafts a wide range of beautifully presented classic Italian dishes, infused with flavors from the Basilicata region of Italy. The menu includes seafood, pasta, poultry, and meat options, as well as homemade desserts such as tiramisu, spumoni, and the chocolate-lover's favorite—*torta al cioccolato*. Volare offers a long list of wines from Italy and California, as well as a few from Texas. Ask your waiter for pairing recommendations. Closed Sunday and Monday. Call for reservations. $$–$$$.

Wired and Inspired. 203 W. Alamo St. (in The Pomegranate); (979) 836-1199. Whether you want to get online or just need to caffeinate, this coffee bar is the place to go. Wired and Inspired serves great coffee, espresso, tea, and smoothies, and every paying customer gets free wireless Internet access. The coffee shop shares space with The Pomegranate gift shop (see above). Closed Sunday. $.

Yumm! Sweets & Eats. 106 E. Alamo St.; (979) 836-4447. One visit here and you'll appreciate the name! Yumm! Sweets and Eats specializes in brick-oven baked pizzas, but they also offer Italian sandwiches and burgers. If you arrive for breakfast, check out the delicious crepes, waffles, and cinnamon rolls. $.

where to stay

Ant Street Inn. 107 W. Commerce St.; (800) 481-1951; antstreetinn.com. Feel like royalty when you stay in one of this enchanting inn's 15 guest rooms, all of them with high ceilings and decorated with antiques. After your day or night on the town, sit on the veranda and gaze out at the garden. Every room includes free wireless Internet and breakfast at the inn's Brenham Grill. $$.

BlissWood Bed and Breakfast Inn. 13300 Lehmann Legacy Ln., Cat Spring (about 27 miles south of Brenham; follow TX 36 South to get there); (713) 301-3235; blisswood.net. For a great escape from the big city, stay in one of the 9 guesthouses on this 650-acre working farm. The property is lined with stately live oaks, and rocking chairs on the porch make it easy to take in the scenery and gaze at the horses, cattle, camels, alpaca, miniature donkeys, antelope, and peacocks. Every cottage is private and filled with antiques. There are plenty of opportunities for outdoor recreation, including horseback riding, fishing, trap-shooting, birding, and nature walks. $$.

The Brenham House. 705 Clinton St.; (979) 251-9947; thebrenhamhouse.com. Built on the foundation of Brenham's first German Lutheran church, this B&B epitomizes southern charm. The guest rooms are filled with antiques and furniture dating back to the 1920s, and the new owners, Susan and James Lopez, recently renovated the place. Guests here enjoy a southern breakfast every morning, and the innkeepers are happy to accommodate special dietary needs. $$.

burton

There's not a ton to see and do in Burton, but if you're intrigued by Texas's early days, it's worth a stop. Founded in 1870, the town was named after one of its early settlers, John M. Burton. Soon after, it became home to a terminal on the Houston and Texas Central Railroad. Today, you can visit the old depot—as well as two old cabooses—at the Old Depot Museum, thanks to the Burton Heritage Society's efforts to preserve the town's history.

These aren't the only artifacts of old Burton worth seeing. The town is also home to the country's oldest operating cotton gin. And at the Mt. Zion Cemetery and Historical Chapel, you can see the final resting place of some of the town's early residents, including Confederate soldier and Texas Ranger Leander M. McNelly.

getting there

Get back on US 290 West and drive 10 miles until you reach the East Mulberry/TX 125 Spur West sign. Take a right and then follow the signs to North Main/TX 125 Spur West.

where to go

Burton Cotton Gin and Museum. 307 N. Main St.; (979) 289-3378; cottonginmuseum .org. This 9-acre museum is home to the oldest operating cotton gin in the country. Thanks to the help of the Smithsonian Institution and the National Trust for Historic Preservation, the 1914 Burton Farmers Gin has been fully restored to operate like a 1930s model, processing cotton from wagon to finished bale. The gin is listed in the National Register of Historic Places and has been designated a Texas Historic Landmark and a National Historic Mechanical Landmark. Also at this free museum are a cotton warehouse and the Wehring Shoe Shop and Residence. The museum hosts a cotton festival each April (see the Festivals & Celebrations appendix). Closed Sunday and Monday.

Mt. Zion Cemetery and Historical Chapel. FM 1948 at the intersection with FM 390; (979) 353-0050; burtonheritagesociety.org. Often dubbed McNelly Cemetery, this historic cemetery is the final resting place of Confederate soldier and Texas Ranger Leander M. McNelly and other early Texans. In 2006, the cemetery was designated a Historic Texas Cemetery. The Burton Heritage Society maintains the cemetery and chapel; call to schedule a tour and get directions.

Old Depot Museum. 507 N. Railroad St.; (979) 289-2031; burtonheritagesociety.org. Back in the 1870s, passenger trains stopped here en route to La Grange, Bastrop, Austin, San Marcos, New Braunfels, and San Antonio. Today, thanks to the Burton Heritage Society, visitors can see a metal caboose and a wooden caboose, as well as some railroad memorabilia. Tours are available by appointment.

where to eat

Brazos Belle Restaurant. 600 Main St.; (979) 289-2677; brazosbellerestaurant.com. The Brazos Belle bills itself as "a true Country-French Restaurant." To that end, the menu includes the likes of scampi Provençal (large shrimp seasoned in a lavender-seed flower marinade, then grilled and topped with aioli sauce), pâté maison (pâté with spicy Dijon mustard), and cassoulet (duck and smoked country sausage, slow-cooked with white beans and vegetables). The chef will also make vegetarian and children's dishes upon request. To dine here, you must time your visit just right: Brazos Belle is open for dinner on Friday and Saturday and for lunch on Sunday. Credit cards are not accepted. $$–$$$.

Pig and Whistle. 12607 W. Washington St. (next to Railroad Depot); (979) 289-2319. This casual English-style pub and grill serves up pub food basics, which can be eaten inside at the bar or outside on the deck overlooking the rose garden or at tables under the trees. The Pig and Whistle also has a covered pavilion, where guests have been known to dance. $–$$.

where to stay

Inn at Indian Creek. 2460 Boehnemann Rd.; (979) 289-2032; innatindiancreek.com. Guests who stay here rest their heads in 1 of 2 guesthouses built from Texas limestone and surrounded by pecan and oak trees. Whether you stay in the Tepee Guesthouse or the Wig-wam Guesthouse, you'll enjoy a full kitchen and bathroom, plenty of privacy, a continental breakfast, and on Saturday, wine and cheese. Both guesthouses are beautifully decorated and stand on the site of an 1800s farmhouse. $$.

Knittel Homestead Inn Bed & Breakfast. 520 N. Main St.; (979) 289-5102; knittelhome stead.com. Take a trip to the early 20th century during your stay here. All 6 guest rooms are reminiscent of the early 1900s in their decor, though some look like log cabins while others are decorated more elegantly. Guests enjoy private bathrooms and wireless Internet, as well as a continental breakfast and newspaper each morning. $$.

day trip 02

northwest

independence day:
hempstead, independence, washington, navasota

hempstead

Hempstead started as a railroad town when it was established in 1856. At the time, the Houston and Texas Central Railroad began running a line through Hempstead, which proved important to shipping during the Civil War a few years later. As a result, a number of camps were set up around the area during the war.

If railroads defined Hempstead's early identity, violence defined the town at the turn of the 20th century, earning it the nickname "Six Shooter Junction." Notably, US congressman John Pinckney and three other people (including Pinckney's brother) were shot and killed while meeting with Prohibitionists at the courthouse in 1905.

These days, Hempstead's violent image is a thing of the past. Now, Hempstead is essentially a country town, with agriculture making up a big part of the economy and luring visitors. The town is home to a variety of farms and orchards, and a great farmers' market selling huge Hempstead watermelons. Each July these same melons are the guests of honor at the town's annual Watermelon Festival (see the Festivals & Celebrations appendix at the end of this guide).

getting there

Travel about 50 miles northwest of Houston on US 290 West.

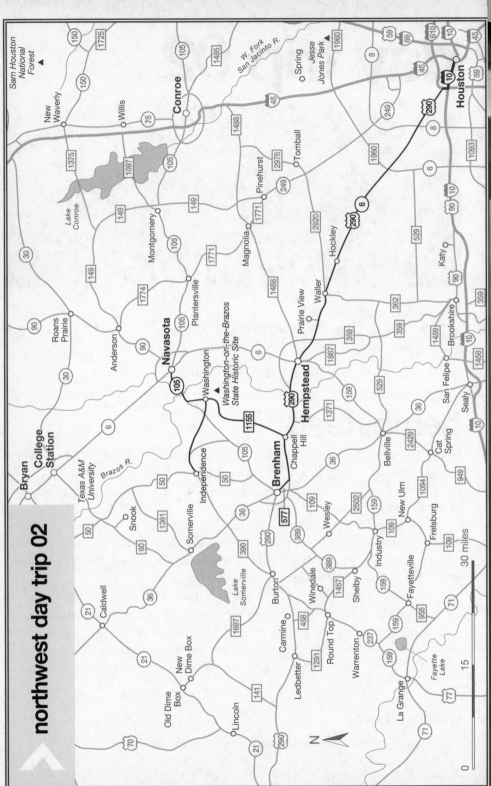

northwest day trip 02

where to go

Bluebonnet Herb Farms. 2015 13th St.; (979) 826-4290; bluebonnetherbfarms.com. If you're a gardener, be sure to take a stroll through the gardens here, and then stop into the garden shop. You'll find a variety of perennials, annuals, and herbs for your garden, as well as antiques, ceramics, and other gifts for your home. If you're hungry, visit the Garden Cafe for some soup, salad, homemade pimento cheese, paninis, burgers, or a homemade dessert. Closed Sunday.

Dilorio Farms and Roadside Market. 750 US 290 Business East; (979) 826-2688; diiorio farms.com. This huge open-air farmers' market sells a little of everything—nuts, flowers, barbecue, outdoor furniture, homemade jellies and jams, animal feed, honey, and, of course, fresh fruits and vegetables, including Hempstead's famous watermelons.

E & B Orchards. 28268 Clark Bottom Rd.; (979) 826-6303; eandborchards.com. If you love summer produce, grab the family and visit E & B Orchards. From mid-May through mid-July (plus or minus a week or two), you can pick you own peaches, nectarines, and blackberries here. You can also have a picnic and snack on E & B Orchards' homemade peach and blackberry ice cream.

Liendo Plantation. 38653 Wyatt Chapel Rd. (about 2.5 miles from FM 1488 Northeast); (979) 826-3126; liendo.org. This lovely historic manse was one of the Lone Star State's first cotton plantations when it was built in 1853. Like most other southern plantations, Liendo was self-sufficient and had an air of generosity. Still, the plantation was built by slaves and depended on the work of more than 300 to maintain its day-to-day operations. When the Civil War—and by extension, slavery—ended, Liendo faced the possibility of destruction. It's rumored that General George A. Custer actually saved Liendo Plantation. While staying there near the war's end, Custer was wowed by the beauty of the plantation and the generosity of the people there. So he vowed to ensure that Liendo wouldn't be destroyed.

From 1873 to 1911, sculptor Elisabet Ney and her husband Dr. Edmund Montgomery lived here. Ney commuted to Austin, where she created a number of sculptures, including those of General Sam Houston and Stephen F. Austin that stand at the Texas Capitol today. Both Ney and Montgomery are buried at Liendo, which is now listed in the National Register of Historic Places and has been deemed a Texas Historic Landmark.

Today, Liendo is a private residence, but it is open to the public for tours on the first Saturday of most months. On the weekend before Thanksgiving, Liendo hosts Civil War Weekend, complete with costumed hosts, folk life demonstrations, music from the 1860s, and artillery, cavalry, and infantry demonstrations.

Peckerwood Garden Conservation Foundation. 20571 FM 359 (just south of FM 359 and the US 290 Business intersection); (979) 826-3232; peckerwoodgarden.com. With Peckerwood occupying 3 different climactic zones, this exquisite garden is home to more than 3,000 rare plants from the US, Mexico, and Asia. Fine arts expert John G. Fairey has

> ## bargain hunters' paradise

*Love a good deal? Kick your trip off with a stop at the **Houston Premium Outlets** in Cypress. This is the newest outlet mall in the area, and it's also the best. The 120 outlet stores here include the likes of Burberry, Calvin Klein, Elie Tahari, Kate Spade, Banana Republic, Michael Kors, Nike, and Coach, and deliver plenty of bargains year-round. The mall is located at 29300 Hempstead Rd. in Cypress. Call (281) 304-5820 or visit premiumoutlets.com for more information.*

carefully designed the 19-acre garden to appeal to all 5 senses and to highlight a variety of textures and colors. Fairey's artistic savvy is also evident in the unique outdoor sculptures in the garden and in the collection of contemporary and Mexican folk art found on-site in the Peckerwood Gallery. Several times a year, Peckerwood hosts Open Days and Plant Sales days, when guests can visit the garden and purchase plants without taking a tour. The rest of the time, you must participate in a tour to visit the garden and the Mexican Folk Art Collection. Garden tours start at 1 and 3 p.m., and gallery tours begin at 2 p.m. Garden tours cost $10 per person; Mexican Folk Art tours cost $15. You can take both tours for $20. Advance reservations aren't required. Because many of the plants here are sharp and/or delicate, Peckerwood does not allow small children, pets, or baby strollers in the garden.

where to shop

Frazier's Ornamental and Architectural Concrete. 23200 TX 6 (Bryan–College Station exit); (979) 921-2906; fraziersconcrete.com. If you're looking to beautify your garden, stop by Frazier's. With acres upon acres of concrete decor products, you've got your pick of garden accents, fountains, and statues, as well as some metal Texana and gifts. Closed Wednesday.

where to eat

Garden Cafe and Brazos Bakery. 2105 13th St.; (979) 826-0404; gardencafebrazos bakery.com. This restaurant offers an upscale lunch experience in a small-town setting. The Garden features dishes that blend traditional southern favorites with a Santa Fe–inspired twist. The handmade soups, sandwiches, and entrees are satisfying without being too filling. A good thing, because you'll want to leave room for a slice of the Garden's homemade pie for dessert. Closed Sunday and Monday. $$.

Las Fuentes Mexican Restaurant. 601 10th St.; (979) 826-2548; lasfuentesmexican restaurant.net. A longtime player on this small town's equally small dining scene, Las Fuentes is no Mama Ninfa's. But the service and margaritas are good and the food isn't bad, considering you're outside the big city. $–$$.

independence

Independence wasn't always the name of this historic town. When John Coles settled the area as part of Stephen F. Austin's colony in 1824, it was called Coles Settlement. But after Texas won its independence from Mexico in 1836, this live oak tree–lined town celebrated by changing its name to Independence. In those early days, Independence was quite a force in the area, losing its 1844 bid to be the seat of Washington County to Brenham by just one vote. It was also selected as the site of Baylor University's first campus, which is nothing more than ruins now.

Today, remnants of Independence's early days line the town, with highlights including the 1833 Seward Plantation, the old Baylor campus-turned-park, the old town square, and one of the state's oldest Baptist churches. Even the roses sold at the rose emporium here are old. Together, these sites offer a rare opportunity to see Texas as some of its earliest settlers did.

getting there

From Hempstead, take 10th Street/US 290 Business West for just over a mile, then take a left to merge onto US 290 West toward TX 6. Stay on there for about 17.5 miles; then take a right at FM 577/Gun and Rod Road and follow it for 3 miles. Take a right at TX 105 East and drive for 1.8 miles. Take a left at FM 50, drive about 8 miles, and you're in Independence.

where to go

Antique Rose Emporium. 10,000 FM 50, Brenham; (979) 836-5548 or (800) 441-0002; antiqueroseemporium.com. Whether you're looking to spruce up your own garden or just want to stop and smell the roses, the Antique Rose Emporium should be on your list of places to visit on this trip. Old and antique roses are the specialty at this exquisite garden and nursery, which was built on the site of an 1840s homestead, but many other lovely blooms line the pathways here. The gift shop here sells unique gifts, many of them featuring—what else?—roses. **Take note:** Antique Rose Emporium technically has a Brenham address, but it is very much a part of Independence, as it sits about 10 miles northeast of downtown Brenham.

Independence Baptist Church and Texas Baptist Museum. 10405 FM 50 at FM 390; (979) 836-2929. Learn about the third-oldest Baptist church in the Lone Star State—the same congregation that lays claim to General Sam Houston's conversion and baptism in

evening light

There might not be much action in Independence after 5 p.m., but it's worth sticking around past sundown to see the town at night. That's when several historic structures—including the Independence Baptist Church (10405 FM 50 at FM 390), Liberty Baptist Church (10655 FM 50), the General Store (9400 Lueckemeyer Rd.), and the Independence Historical Society at Old Baylor Park—are lit up, creating an enchanting contrast against an otherwise dark backdrop.

1854. In its early years the church didn't have a building of its own. After the congregation was organized in 1839, services were held at a nearby school; 6 years later, after Baylor University was established in Independence, services were held on the campus. The church finally got its own building in 1872. Today, that building stands near a free museum that exhibits the original 1856 church bell, old records and manuscripts, and other artifacts telling the story of the church's early days. Sam Houston's wife, Margaret Lea Houston, and her mother, Nancy Moffette Lea, are buried across from the church. Closed Sunday and Monday.

Independence Town Square. (888) 626-8051; independencetx.com. From the town's December 1835 founding to the early 1860s, life in Independence revolved around the town square. In fact, it's believed that General Sam Houston—who'd previously opposed secession from the Union—delivered a speech declaring his allegiance to what he called "the southern Confederacy" here on Town Square on May 10, 1861.

Independence's original Town Square is easy to visualize: The town, initially composed of 78 acres, was laid out in a grid configuration. There were 60 regularly shaped blocks, as well as 4 L-shaped blocks that met in the middle of town to form Town Square.

By walking around Town Square today, you can see old properties such as the 1940 school, McKnight Drug Store, and the Blanton Block (a hotel, stagecoach, mail depot, residence, and general store complex built of native limestone in the late 1820s or early 1830s). From the square you can also see the house in which Sam Houston's widow lived after the general's death. Sometimes dubbed "Mrs. Sam Houston House," it sits 1 block east of old Baptist church on FM 390 and is now listed in the National Register of Historic Places. Unfortunately, the house—now a private residence—is off-limits to visitors.

While some of the buildings that surrounded Independence's Town Square in the town's heyday have been restored and repurposed, others have disappeared altogether. A few new buildings have cropped up as well.

get your ride on

*For a unique view of the terrain—and, in the springtime, the bluebonnets—bring your bike and ride the back roads from Independence to Washington-on-the-Brazos State Historic Site (see below). Begin the 30-mile journey at Old Baylor and head past old cemeteries, historic buildings, and stretches of the Brazos River Valley. Much of the terrain is hilly, so you'll get a good workout as an added bonus. **Warning:** The roads can be a little bumpy and don't have a shoulder for bikers to ride on. To get detailed directions for this trip or for a bike trip from Washington-on-the-Brazos State Historic Site to Independence, visit the Independence Preservation Trust's website (independencetx.com/BikeTour.htm) or call (888) 626-8051.*

Old Baylor Park and Old Baylor University. Intersection of FM 50 and FM 390; (888) 626-8051; independencetx.com. In 1845, Independence was selected as the original site of Baylor University, which moved to Waco in 1886. Today, the spot where the Baptist university once stood is occupied by old trees, 4 extremely tall stone columns, picnic tables, and a playground area. The area, known as Old Baylor Park, is also home to Mound Hill Schoolhouse and 2 of Washington County's earliest houses—the 1839 Independence Log Cabin and the 1825 John P. Coles home, which was moved here from another location. The bluebonnets bloom here en masse each spring, so bring your camera if your journey brings you to the neighborhood in March or April. On a few weekends in March and April, visitors can also tour the houses and school for free. Call the Independence Historical Society (216-524-5274) for more information.

Seward Plantation. 10005 FM 390 (less than 1 mile west of FM 50); (979) 830-5388; independencetx.com/SewardPlantation.htm. For more than 175 years, the Seward family has owned this plantation. When Samuel Seward first settled on the property in 1833, it spanned some 1,700 acres. Later, Seward added another 300 acres to his property, making this the largest residence in Washington County until 1900, when the infamous September 1900 storm damaged the property and blew away 5 barns. The property now consists of a horse barn, a corncrib, a double-pen haymow, old slave quarters, a well house, and a cabin attached to a blacksmith's shop. The plantation is open by appointment only for group tours for 10 or more people.

where to eat

Lueckemeyer General Store. 9400 Lueckemeyer Rd.; (979) 836-4211; independencetx
.com/GeneralStore.htm. When the Lueckemeyer family acquired this general store in 1926,
they added a facade inspired by the place every Texan is told to remember—the Alamo.
Today, the general store is still family-run, but it's in the hands of a different family—that of
Mike and Brenda Bentke Meadows, who purchased the business in 2000. The couple has
since expanded the store to include a grill and a larger seating area, so in addition to finding
basic items here, you can grab sandwiches and other lunch offerings. During your visit, take
a look across the street, where you'll see the remains of the Lueckemeyer Cotton Gin that
was demolished in the 1980s due to its obsolescence. $.

washington

Call it what you will: Washington, Washington-on-the-Brazos, Old Washington. It's all the
same Brazos River town with the same storied history. In 1836, just 2 years after it was
established near a Brazos River ferry, Washington earned its place in Texas history. This is
where the Texas Declaration of Independence was signed, and soon after, the Constitu-
tion of the new Republic of Texas was drafted. In 1842, Washington became the capital
of the Republic of Texas, a distinction it held until 1845, when Texas became a state and
the capital moved to Austin.

Today, the town's role in Texas history is commemorated at Washington-on-the-
Brazos State Historic Site, where a living history museum, a replica of Independence Hall,
and other activities will make you an expert on all things related to Texas independence.

getting there

From Independence, head east on FM 390 East/La Bahia Trail East for about 4.5 miles; then
take a left at CR 93/William Penn Road and travel another 4.5 miles. Take a left at TX 105
East and continue following the road for about 3.5 miles. Take a right on FM 1155 East;
after about a mile, you'll find yourself in Washington, Texas. Yee-haw!

where to go

Rio Red Ranches. 16747 FM 1155 Rd. East; (936) 878-9997; rioredranches.com. This
ranch breeds miniature horses—that is, horses that are typically between 25 and 34 inches
tall. Rio Red's colt Chips Ahoy was the 2007 World Grand Champion Weanling Colt; the
ranch has also produced a number of National Top 10 Mares. If you're interested in buying
a miniature horse or just want to take a look, call ahead.

Washington-on-the-Brazos State Historic Site. FM 1155 (off TX 105); (936) 878-2214; birthplaceoftexas.com. Situated on the Brazos River, this picturesque park is a great place to picnic, frolic, and bird-watch. It's also *the* place to learn about Texas's beginnings. Washington-on-the-Brazos, after all, is where Texas formally declared its independence from Mexico on March 2, 1836.

To that end, this 293-acre park offers plenty of opportunities for those who are intrigued by history: Tour the replica of Independence Hall and imagine the state's forefathers in this same space nearly 175 years ago. When you wander the park's trails, you can see where the town of Washington once stood. Also be sure to visit the **Barrington Living History Farm** (21300 Park Rd. 12; 936-878-2214). The museum revolves around a working farm that was inhabited by the Republic of Texas's last president, Dr. Anson Jones, in the 1850s. The staff here dresses up in period costumes and uses Dr. Jones's journals and other memorabilia to give you a trip back to the former cotton farm's glory days. Guests are invited to join in the old-fashioned fun by making soap, harvesting, planting, plowing, and participating in other aspects of farm life. Also at the park is the **Star of the Republic Museum** (23200 Park Rd. 12; 936-878-2461; starmuseum.org), where you can learn about life in the Republic of Texas. Some 20,000 artifacts appear in interactive exhibits, multimedia presentations, and the museum's research library.

The visitor center houses additional interactive exhibits, a gift shop, a restaurant, and conference and classroom space. There is also limited wireless Internet access here.

The park itself is open every day of the year from 8 a.m. to dusk, though the museums are typically closed on holidays and maintain different hours. Call for more information.

where to eat

The Inn at Dos Brisas. 10,000 Champion Dr.; (979) 277-7750; dosbrisas.com. Visit this beautiful inn for a meal you're sure to remember. Setting the scene are an 18th-century fireplace from France's Loire Valley and floor-to-ceiling windows looking out onto ponds and seemingly endless meadows. Every dish here is made with herbs, spices, and seasonal produce grown in Dos Brisas' organic garden. For dinner, the restaurant offers 8- and 5-course tasting menus, which include dishes such as Dover sole, Hawaiian hearts of palm, cardoons and artichokes with truffle and fried chicken mushrooms, and Oregon plum with squab and foie gras. There's also a vegetable tasting menu. Visit on Sunday for a 5-course brunch. Ask your waiter to pair your meal with one of the 3,500 bottles of wine in Dos Brisas' cellars. Call for reservations, and watch what you wear: Shorts and T-shirts aren't appropriate here, and men are encouraged to wear jackets. $$$.

R Place at Washington-on-the-Brazos. 23254 FM 1155 East; (936) 878-1925. Located just a short walk from Independence Hall, R Place is housed in the barn-looking structure that was once home to H.A. Stolz Groceries. Many families come here for the barbecue, sandwiches, and hand-dipped Blue Bell ice cream. R Place also serves cold beer and wine. $–$$.

where to stay

Barrington B&B. 14808 Whitman Rd.; (936) 878-2844; barringtonbb.com. Located on a working ranch, Barrington B&B guests can stay in the aptly named Honeymoon Cottage or in one of the private rooms inside the main house. With natural light filling every room and wildflower fields and ponds decorating the property, this B&B offers a true escape from the city. Guests enjoy a full breakfast each day. $$.

Brazos Bed & Breakfast. 20251 Pickens Rd.; (936) 878-2230 or (979) 251-2719; brazos bedandbreakfast.com. The 2 suites here make rustic chic. Guests enjoy private patios, wireless Internet access, a home-cooked breakfast, and an antiques-filled country setting that's sure to charm. $$.

The Inn at Dos Brisas. 10,000 Champion Dr. (off FM 1155); (979) 277-7750; dosbrisas .com. Stay in one of the Spanish-style casitas here, and you'll feel like royalty. The first-class accommodations include use of your own personal golf cart (seriously!), a free bottle of champagne, remote-controlled fireplaces, a mini-kitchen stocked with free snacks, wireless Internet, satellite HDTV, L'Occitane bath products, and a breathtaking backdrop of meadows and ponds. During your stay, be sure to schedule a meal at the inn's restaurant (listed in the Where to Eat section above). $$$.

Lillian Farms Country Estate. 12570 FM 1155 East; (979) 421-6332 or (877) 421-6332; lillianfarms.com. This 230-acre estate features 6 Victorian-inspired guest rooms, each with a private bathroom. Visit during the spring and you can look out onto fields full of bluebonnets from your room. Guests here have access to the library, a spa, wireless Internet, and a fishing lake stocked with bass. Lillian Farms offers a romantic getaway package and a culinary weekend package, complete with small, hands-on cooking classes. $$.

navasota

For centuries, people have been passing through Navasota. Several Native American tribes chased and harvested buffalo in the area hundreds of years ago, and French explorer René-Robert Cavelier, Sieur de La Salle, passed through shortly before he was shot to death just outside of town. In 1822, Navasota began attracting its earliest Anglo settlers, when Francis Holland purchased land here. This area was subsequently called Hollandale. Only in 1854, when the town got its first post office, was it renamed Navasota, after the river on which it sits.

A few years later, Navasota became a stop on the Houston and Texas Central Railroad, allowing it to play a big role in the shipping and cotton industries. But within a few years, the town's luck seemed to swing the other way, with a yellow fever outbreak killing a chunk of the population and inspiring many others to flee. The town also suffered from a series of violent incidents, ranging from the spread of the Ku Klux Klan to western-style shoot-outs.

Today, Navasota offers a peaceful change of pace with farms of the organic and livestock varieties, two wineries, and plenty of lovely Victorian homes and buildings. If you can't decide what to do, spend the night at one of Navasota's bed-and-breakfasts, which hark back to the 1930s and 1940s.

getting there

Navasota is only about 8 miles northeast of Washington. To get there, head northwest on FM 1155 East toward CR 100/Washington Cemetery Road for about 1.5 miles. Veer right onto TX 105 East and stay on it for about 6 miles; then take a right at South LaSalle Street.

where to go

Historic Homes and Buildings Tours. Navasota is home to many houses, churches, and other buildings that have been deemed landmarks by the Texas Historical Commission. The **Grimes County Chamber of Commerce** offers walking- and driving-tour brochures. You can stop by 117 S. LaSalle St. or call (936) 825-6600 to pick one up.

If you're looking for historic buildings while you're out and about, here are a few worth keeping your eyes peeled for: the 1880s **Old First National Bank of Navasota** (107 W. Washington Ave.), which features Renaissance Revival architecture and has housed a hotel, a telephone company, and a variety of other businesses over the years; the 1876 Victorian-inspired **First Presbyterian Church of Navasota** (302 Nolan St.); the 3-story **Giesel House** (113 Railroad St.), which was built in 1860 by Confederate veteran R. H. Giesel, who briefly served as the mayor of Navasota; the baby-blue 1898 **Norwood House** (207 Ketchum St.), which reflects Queen Anne influences; and the 1902 **Sangster House** (1113 E. Washington Ave.), which was built in the Queen Anne Revival style, partly with funds from a winning lottery ticket.

Horlock History Center. 1215 E. Washington Ave. (TX 105); (936) 825-7055; navasotatx .gov. Learn about Navasota's heyday—the Victorian era—with a visit to this history center, which can be found in a Victorian house dating back to 1892. Exhibits highlight the tools, art, furniture, letters and other artifacts from Navasota residents who lived during that period. Tours are available by appointment; call ahead.

Krause Farm. 5369 FM 2988, Whitehall; (936) 825-4156 or (936) 870-6393. This small family farm occupies 10 acres just south of Navasota in Whitehall, but the Krause family uses just 1 acre for farming. They apply organic methods to grow fruits, vegetables, and pecans. Chicken and duck eggs are also available for purchase. Call before your visit to find out what items they have available at the moment.

> ## commemorating the fallen

On the East Washington Avenue esplanade (near Main Street) stands a statue of French explorer René-Robert Cavelier, Sieur de La Salle, who was shot and killed near Navasota on March 19, 1687. The man most Americans know as "La Salle" became the first European to travel the length of the Mississippi River in 1682. Citizens of Navasota, along with the Texas Society of the Daughters of the American Revolution, commemorated his life and accomplishments by putting up a 14.5-foot bronze statue of the explorer on the esplanade in 1930. Also on the esplanade is a Veterans of Foreign Wars memorial honoring residents of Grimes County who were killed in war.

Navasota Blues Alley. 129 E. Washington Ave.; (936) 870-3331; navasotabluesalley.com. Honoring native son Mance Lipscomb, a seminal figure in the history of the blues, this free downtown museum is the work of local historian Russell Cushman. The museum's exhibits include photos and artifacts about Lipscomb's place in the evolution of this uniquely American music. An attached record store sells music-related items as well as collectibles.

Navasota Livestock Auction Company. 7846 TX 90 South; (936) 825-6545; navasota livestock.com. Few auction companies sell more livestock than this one. So if you want to see how the bidding's done—or get some horses and cattle of your own—stop by on Saturday starting at 11 a.m.

Navasota Theatre Alliance. Sunny Furman Theater, 104 W. Washington Ave.; (936) 825-3195; navasotatheatrealliance.com. This community theater group puts on a few family-friendly plays each year. Shows are held at the Sunny Furman Theater. Call or visit the website to find out about upcoming performances.

Retreat Hill Winery and Vineyard. 15551 FM 362 Rd.; (936) 825-8282; retreathill.com. Although this new winery has yet to harvest and process its own wines, the Retreat Hill tasting room opened in 2009, presenting its award-winning Blazin' Blush, Vintner's Blend and dry rosé using grapes from other Texas grape growers. It also offers tastings of wines by other vineyards, including dry reds, sweet and dry white wines, and dessert wines. The winery plans to offer dining options in the future. Call or visit the website to find out about tastings and other new additions to the winery's offerings.

where to shop

The Wood Factory. 113 Railroad St.; (936) 825-7233; thewoodfactorymillwork.com. Housed in what was once the P. A. Smith Hotel, this Victorian millworks factory opens its doors to guests who are interested in buying Victorian wood trimmings. The Wood Factory is closed on weekends.

where to eat

Cow Talk Steak House. 7846 TX 90 South; (936) 825-6993; cowtalksteakhouse.ambz .com. This local favorite serves hamburgers, steaks, and breakfast dishes. Unfortunately, Cow Talk Steak House only serves breakfast and lunch, except on Friday and Saturday, when they also serve dinner. Closed Monday. $–$$.

Mallett Brothers Barbeque. 9339 TX 6; (936) 825-9440; mallettbrothers.com. This family owned and operated restaurant has a loyal local following. These regulars swear by the Mallett brothers' tried-and-true beef, pork, chicken, and rib barbecue recipes. Stop by on weekdays for the daily specials. $–$$.

Martha's Bloomers and Cafe M. Bloomers. 8101 TX 6 Bypass; (936) 870-3277; marthas bloomers.com. Get a two-for-one deal on your visit here: Shop for unique gifts and garden items at Martha's Bloomers, a store that's won praise from *Southern Living* magazine, and then enjoy lunch in the tearoom. Cafe M. Bloomers serves up tasty quiches, sandwiches, and salads such as Estella's Special Strawberry Salad (strawberries, feta cheese, and toasted pecans on spinach with a raspberry vinaigrette). Save room for the homemade cobbler. Cafe M. doesn't take reservations, but they will put your name on the list if you have 8 people or fewer in your party and call 30 minutes or less before you plan to stop in. $$.

where to stay

Bogart's Casa Blanca. 1302 E. Washington Ave.; (936) 825-1969; bogarts.org. This luxurious, 1940s-inspired bed-and-breakfast is fit for the movies. Guests stay in one of 2 decorated mansions or the Honeymoon Cottage. There's a heated swimming pool here, and massages are available. Those who don't stay here can tour the mansion on the first Sunday of each month from 2 to 5 p.m. $$.

Red Door Bed & Breakfast. 915 E. Washington Ave.; (936) 825-7482; reddoorbedand breakfast.com. Bob and Nell Young open their vintage 1932 home to guests. There are 2 rooms, each with its own bathroom, as well as sitting rooms upstairs and down. Breakfast is served daily, and you can choose whether you want to feast in the dining room or on the patio outside. $$.

day trip 03

northwest

> > > **all the president's memos:**
bryan–college station

bryan–college station

Surely you already know that Bryan–College Station is home to Texas A&M University and the very spirited Texas Aggies. In fact, the university—the oldest public one in the Lone Star State—practically put College Station on the map with its 1871 founding, though College Station did not actually become a city until 1938. You probably even know that the campus is home to George H.W. Bush's presidential library. But did you know that College Station's neighboring town, Bryan, was named in honor of Stephen F. Austin's nephew William Joel Bryan when it was founded in 1855? Or that you don't have to be an Aggie to find something to like here?

The twin cities, as they're often called, are located in the Brazos Valley, a fertile tract where farms and vineyards, as well as fishing, hiking, and other outdoor recreational opportunities, are abundant. So, too, are museums detailing the area's history, cute shops, restaurants, and bed-and-breakfasts. And though many of these attractions have cropped up to cater to Texas A&M University's nearly 47,000 students and their visiting families, they're increasingly attracting Houstonians and other Texans who've discovered that Bryan–College Station is more than a college town.

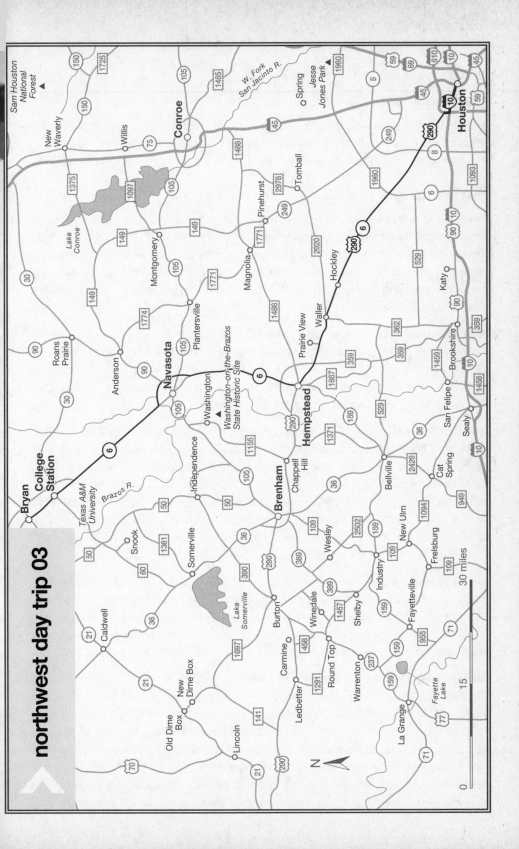

Sam Houston
National
Forest

150 1725

105

W. Fork
San Jacinto R.

1960 Jesse
Jones Park

59 69
610 10

45

8

Houston

New
Waverly

150

Willis

75

Conroe

1485

45

Spring

Jesse
Jones Park

249

45

10
290

59

1375

1097 105

Lake
Conroe

149

1488

Pinehurst

2978 Tomball

249

1960

8

1093

30

149

1774

Montgomery

105

1771

149

1771

2920

Hockley

6

290

6

529

Katy

90

10
90 10

Roans
Prairie

90

Anderson

90

Navasota

105

Plantersville

Washington

Washington-on-the-Brazos
State Historic Site

1488

Prairie View

Waller

6

362

6

359

Brookshire

10

1458

Sealy

10

30

105

Bryan

College
Station

6

Texas A&M
University

Brazos R.

Independence

105

1155

290

Hempstead

2 90

1887

1371

159

529

36

San
Felipe

36

2429

Cat
Spring

949

10

Bellville

Chappell
Hill

Brenham

50

50

36

109

Wesley

2502

159

New Ulm

1094

Frelsburg

109

Snook

1361

Somerville

390

290

389

Industry

109

Fayetteville

Burton

389

Winedale

1457

Shelby

159

159

955

71

50

60

Lake
Somerville

Caldwell

36

21

1697

New
Dime Box

Carmine

458

Round Top

237

Warrenton

159

La Grange

71

Old Dime
Box

21

1291 Ledbetter

159

Fayette
Lake

77

Lincoln

141

21

70

290

N

0   15   30 miles

getting there

College Station is about 95 miles northwest of Houston on TX 6. To get there, follow US 290 West for about 44 miles; then take the TX 6 North exit toward College Station and follow TX 6 for about 39 miles. Bryan is just 4 miles west of College Station on TX 6 Business North.

where to go

Brazos Valley Museum of Natural History. 3232 Briarcrest Dr., Bryan; (979) 776-2195; brazosvalleymuseum.org. Learn about the region in which Bryan–College Station and the Brazos River make their home by checking out exhibits about old-fashioned survey and farming equipment and fossils. You'll also find some sculptures, interactive exhibits, and more than a dozen live animal displays, one of which features a beehive with a glass front. Closed Sunday and Monday.

Carnegie Center of Brazos Valley History. 111 S. Main St., Bryan (across from the LaSalle Hotel); (979) 209-5630; bcslibrary.org. The Carnegie Foundation funded the building of this library in 1903. Today, the restored building is the oldest Carnegie Library in the Lone Star State and home to a collection covering the Bryan fire department from 1881 to 1993. The grounds feature a xeriscape garden. Closed Sunday and Monday.

The Children's Museum of the Brazos Valley. 111 E. 27th St., Bryan; (979) 779-KIDS; cmbv.org. This museum packs in lots of fun, interactive exhibits for kiddos of all ages. Toddlers can hang out in the Mrs. Giggly's Garden exhibit featuring a fun tree fort full of toys while older children will enjoy getting creative at Build Your World! where they can make stuff from plastic pipes and other construction materials. Other exhibits include the Kids' Market (sponsored by local supermarket chain H.E.B.) with play shopping carts and pretend groceries and the Healthy Kids area when children can check their heart rate and eyesight or enjoy playing doctor. Closed Sunday.

Gendron Homegrown. 6150 Zweifel Rd., Bryan; (979) 775-9500 or (979) 777-9344. You don't have to be a locavore to appreciate the pick-your-own fields at Gendron Homegrown. During May and June, pick your own tomatoes, okra, cucumbers, peppers, squash, zucchini, and other veggies here. Along with promoting sustainability and eco-consciousness, these fields also provide some tasty veggies for your next meal! Closed Monday.

George Bush Presidential Library and Museum. 1000 George Bush Dr. West, College Station; (979) 691-4000; bushlibrary.tamu.edu. Former president George H.W. Bush—that's number 41, not 43—picked Texas A&M University to house his presidential library. Located on the campus's southwest corner, the library and museum contain memorabilia from the first Bush presidency, including the former president's personal papers and official records. The museum, which houses replicas of the former president's offices on *Air Force One* and at Camp David, hosts special exhibits throughout the year. Recent exhibits have covered subjects such as human genome mapping, national elections, and cancer research.

Gibbons Creek Reservoir. About 30 minutes east of College Station (From Bryan–College Station, take TX 30 east toward Huntsville and go 18 miles to Carlos; turn north on FM 244. The entrance is about a half-mile on the right, beside Yankees Tavern.); (936) 873-2424; gibbonscreek.com. This park is a great place to fish, camp, Jet Ski, and participate in other water activities. The reservoir spans more than 2,700 acres and is stocked with catfish, crappie, largemouth bass, bluegills, and sunfish. The park's hours vary seasonally, so call before going.

Lake Bryan. 8200 Sandy Point Rd., Bryan (22 miles east of Bryan on CR 164 off F.M. 244, 1 mile north of TX 30); (979) 361-0861; tpwd.state.tx.us. Spanning more than 800 acres, this park area offers hiking, camping, picnicking, biking, and fishing opportunities. The lake is stocked with largemouth bass, sunfish, and catfish.

Messina Hof Winery & Resort. 4545 Old Reliance Rd., Bryan; (979) 778-9463 or (800) 736-9463; messinahof.com. You don't have to leave Texas to learn how wine is made in Italy and Germany. At this Texas vineyard, you'll see how the winemakers borrow from the winemaking traditions of Hof, Germany, and Messina, Italy, to produce wines that you can sample during your visit. Award-winning Messina Hoff also boasts the upscale Vintage House restaurant as well as The Villa bed-and-breakfast; see the Where to Eat and Where to Stay sections below, respectively.

Texas A&M University. Joe Routt Boulevard and Throckmorton Street, College Station; (979) 845-5851; tamu.edu. Visit the Appelt Aggieland Visitor Center in Rudder Center to pick up a campus map and get the skinny on goings-on around one of the state's largest universities. The visitor center is open Monday through Friday.

where to shop

Benjamin Knox Gallery. 405 E. University Dr., College Station; (979) 691-2787 or (800) 299-5669; benjaminknox.com. Located in the 1900 College Station Depot, this gallery is where Texas A&M alum and distinguished artist Benjamin Knox sells his images of Texas, landscapes, and universities around the area, including his alma mater. Stop in to find a unique fine-art gift. Closed Sunday.

Catalena Hatters. 203 N. Main St., Bryan; (979) 822-4423 or (800) 976-7818; catalena hats.com. Since 1983, this family-run operation has been making custom felt and straw hats. Each is shaped to fit the customer perfectly. The shop also offers hat restorations, and their technicians can work miracles on favorite hats that their owners can't bear to part with. The hats are lovingly cleaned and steam-blocked, then trimmed with a new sweatband, decorative trim, and a silk lining. Complete restorations take 3 to 6 weeks to complete. Closed Sunday.

Living Water Pottery. 101A Dowling Rd., College Station; (979) 820-3864. Living Water Pottery, which also has a shop on Etsy.com (etsy.com/shop/livingwaterpottery), sells handmade pottery, much of it country- or Christian-inspired. The shop recently expanded to include studio space where pottery lessons are offered. Visit on the second and fourth Friday of each month from 6 to 8 p.m. for raku demonstrations.

Old Bryan Marketplace. 202 S. Bryan Ave., Bryan; (979) 779-3245; oldbryanmarketplace .net. Located in a historic downtown building dating back to 1908, this now-22,000-square-foot marketplace sells unique gifts, linens, clothes, art, furniture, dishes, and home decor by Sugarboo Designs, Bella Notte Linens, Pine Cone Hill, and others.

U Paint It. 900 Harvey Rd., College Station; (979) 695-1500; upaintit.com. Here is a gift shop with a twist: you can design and paint your own unique dishware under the expert assistance of the studio staff. Once you've created your masterpiece, U Paint It glazes and fires it for you and has it ready to pick up within 6 days. The shop furnishes all the equipment and supplies you need. Closed Monday.

where to eat

Blue Baker. 201 Dominik Dr., College Station; (979) 696-5055; 800 University Dr., College Station; (979) 268-3096; bluebaker.com. Every morning, the kitchen staff at Blue Baker's 2 locations make bread dough and pastries from scratch and then bake the breads—including pizza dough—in a brick oven. The result? Some mighty good sandwiches, pizzas, salads, and desserts. Both locations have free wireless Internet. $–$$.

Christopher's World Grille. 5001 Booneville Rd., Bryan; (979) 776-2181; christophers worldgrille.com. If you want a fancy meal in the Bryan–College Station area, Christopher's World Grille is your best option. This elegant restaurant makes its home in a restored hundred-year-old ranch, where each room is decorated with antiques and filled with personality. The menu, which changes seasonally, includes gourmet dishes with Mediterranean, coastal French, South Pacific, and southern influences. That makes for dishes like the New Orleans stuffed fillet (blackened beef tenderloin on smoked tomato-andouille sauce, stuffed with blackened oyster, spinach and mushrooms, and wrapped in bacon), shrimp bisque, blueberry ginger duck, and pastramied salmon. Closed Monday for dinner. Reservations are recommended. $$$.

Dixie Chicken. 307 University Dr., College Station; (979) 846-2322; dixiechicken.com. This bar is a can't-miss College Station institution. Students come here for the cheap beer and food, as well as dominos, pool, and plenty of country music. The menu includes burgers, chicken-fried steak, and other bar food. It's nothing fancy, but the food's inexpensive and served in a charming honky-tonk atmosphere. $–$$.

El Vale. 1305 W. William J Bryan Pkwy., Ste. 300, Bryan; (979) 779-6065. The staff at this small restaurant serves up some of the best Mexican food in the area for breakfast, lunch, and dinner. The menu includes a long list of plates and specials, as well as tacos, shrimp cocktails, and more traditional Mexican (as opposed to Tex-Mex) meat and seafood fare. $–$$.

keep your pennies

Save money on your trip to Bryan–College Station (and on a trip to The Woodlands)
by opting for a travel package on TravelTex.com, the Official Site of Texas Tourism.

Koppe Bridge Bar & Grill. 11777 Welborn Rd., College Station; (979) 764-2933; 3940 Harvey Rd.; (979) 776-2833; koppebridge.com. In 2009, the *Houston Press* deemed the burgers here among the 10 best in the Lone Star State. If a great burger doesn't tempt you, rest assured: The menu at both Koppe Bridge locations is filled with other popular options, including the chicken-fried steak, catfish, salads, and barbecued sandwiches. $–$$.

Madden's Casual Gourmet. 202 S. Bryan Ave., Bryan; (979) 779-2558; pmaddens .com. What do you get when you mix southern hospitality with southern gourmet cooking? Madden's, a restaurant that's won the attention of *Southern Living* magazine for its great breakfast, lunch, and dinner food. People swear by the fried chicken and meat loaf here, but the menu is also filled with more-gourmet options such as seared sea scallops with roasted corn risotto and chocolate, chile, and coffee–rubbed beef tenderloin with white cheddar polenta. While the food is a bit fancy, it's perfectly okay to wear jeans. $$–$$$.

Mr. G's Pizzeria. 201 W. 26th St., Bryan; (979) 822-6747; gotomrgs.com. Mr. G's uses hand-tossed dough, a secret sauce recipe, cheese imported from Italy, and fresh ingredients to make some of the best pizza in the area. Closed Sunday. $–$$.

Must Be Heaven Sandwich Shoppe. 1136 E. Villa Maria Rd., Bryan; (979) 731-8891; 100 S. Main St., downtown Bryan: (979) 822-7722; 1700 Rock Prairie Rd., College Station: (979) 764-9222; mustbeheaven.com. All 3 locations in the Bryan–College Station area serve up great sandwiches, soups, salads, and quiches. Closed for dinner on Saturday and all day Sunday. Hours vary slightly by location, so call ahead. $–$$.

Revolution Cafe & Bar. 211B S. Main St., Bryan; (979) 823-4044. As its name suggests, this eclectic coffee shop is almost everything that other area bars are not. Regulars come here to sit on the patio and drink sangria, cheap beer, or coffee while listening to live music every night of the week. There's free wireless Internet, too. $.

The Vintage House Restaurant at Messina Hof Winery. 4545 Old Reliance Rd., Bryan; (979) 778-9463 or (800) 736-9463; messinahof.com/vintage.php. Messina Hof Winery's restaurant, The Vintage House, serves beautifully presented gourmet salads, pizzas, pastas, seafood, burgers, sandwiches, and beef. Every dish is made to be paired with the winery's wines. Call for reservations. $$–$$$.

where to stay

There are many bed-and-breakfasts in the Bryan–College Station area. Only a small sampling is provided below. For more help in finding a B&B that suits all your needs (pets included!), visit **Aggie B&B Finder** at 115 Lee Ave., College Station, call (866) 745-2936, or go online to aggiebnb.com.

Kelumac. 10379 Taylor Rd., Bryan; (979) 279-3931; kelumac.com. Wake up to the smell of pine when you stay in one of the 2 rooms at this bed-and-breakfast, which sits on a 23-acre Christmas tree farm. Guests have the opportunity to fish in a private pond and enjoy occasional wildlife sightings. $.

LaSalle Hotel. 120 S. Main St., Bryan; (979) 822-2000; magnoliahotels.com/college-station/bryan-college-station.php. This boutique hotel dates back to 1928 and is a registered National Historic Landmark. Now part of the Magnolia Hotels group, the LaSalle boasts an attractive interior, great service, and top-notch rooms. Guests enjoy complimentary breakfast, a complimentary evening reception with wine and beer, and free wireless Internet. $$.

The Nest Bed, Breakfast & Spa. 16424 Royder Rd., College Station; (979) 693-5562. There are 4 guest rooms at this bed-and-breakfast, which sits on 20 acres. Guests enjoy a 3-course gourmet breakfast and have the opportunity to fish in the pond and feed the miniature donkeys their favorite treat—homemade oatmeal cookies. Spa services are also available. $–$$.

7F Lodge & Spa. 16611 Royder Rd., College Station; (979) 690-0073; 7flodge.com. Each of the rustic cottages is decorated to represent some part of Texas culture. Guests enjoy Jacuzzi tubs, a continental breakfast, down comforters, private porches, and a location that promises plenty of seclusion and opportunities to get in touch with nature. If you can't live without TV or a landline, though, stay elsewhere: The rooms here don't have televisions or phones. $$.

The Villa at Messina Hof. 4545 Old Reliance Rd., Bryan; (979) 778-9463 or (800) 736-9463; messinahof.com. Located on the grounds of the Messina Hof Winery, this bed-and-breakfast has 11 guest rooms, each decorated with beautiful antiques. Two rooms include whirlpools, and all of the other rooms include a patio or porch that looks out onto the vineyard, forest, or pond. Your stay includes a tour of the winery and a tasting, as well as a champagne breakfast and a wine and cheese reception before dinner. Individual and couples' massage packages are available. $$$.

worth more time

There's plenty of history to be found in Bryan and College Station, but not too much of it covers more than the last 50 to 100 years. So if you want to go back a little further in time and stretch this trip out a little more, head northwest from Bryan to **Calvert.**

During the late 1800s, Calvert was the fourth-largest city in Texas. As a result, it is filled with large and attractive Victorian churches, homes, and businesses. Many of these have been restored and are listed in the National Register of Historic Places. If you stop at one of the businesses in downtown Calvert, you can pick up a self-guided driving tour book, which will direct you to some of the most stunning Victorian structures in Calvert's historic district.

Calvert is located about 29 miles northwest of Bryan and about 125 miles northeast of downtown Houston. To get there from Bryan, head north on North Texas Avenue toward East 24th Street; then take TX 6 North/US 190 West about 15.5 miles to South Market Street. Continue on TX 6 North/Colbert Street for about 8 miles.

For more information on Calvert, contact the Calvert Chamber of Commerce at (979) 364-2559 or visit 704 S. Main St. (TX 6) or calverttx.com.

day trip 04

northwest

>>>

antiquers' heaven:
bellville, round top & winedale

bellville

Welcome to Bellville, where, as the chamber of commerce's slogan suggests, "Cowboys are still Cowboys, and children can still be children." The roads here are lined with blue-bonnets each spring and dotted with farms breeding cattle and growing hay, oats, rice, and sorghum year-round. And the town square is filled with antiques shops, galleries, and restaurants where the owners know their customers' names.

When James Bell settled the area in 1822, it was one of Stephen F. Austin's first colonies. In 1848, after Texas had become a state, it became the seat of Austin County. But it was not until the Santa Fe Railroad arrived here in 1880 that the town's population really grew. As you'll discover when you walk or drive around Bellville, the area is filled with restored homes and buildings from the turn of the 20th century, including the old Austin County Jail, which is now a museum.

The Bellville Historical Society offers docent-led tours of many of the town's historic buildings. For more information call (979) 865-9116 or (979) 865-3530 or visit bellvillehis toricalsociety.com.

getting there

Bellville is about 65 miles northwest of downtown Houston. To get there, follow I-10 West to exit 720 (TX 36/Sealy/Bellville); then head left at Meyer Street/TX 36 North and follow the

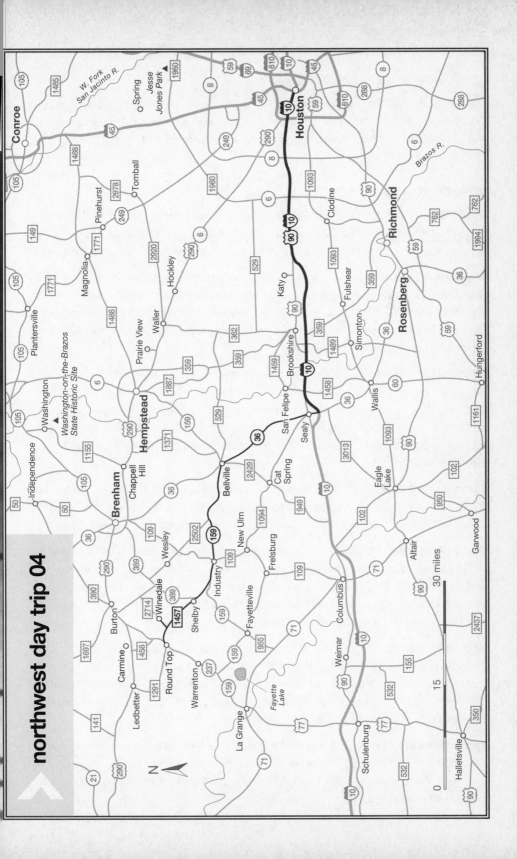

road for 13.3 miles. Alternatively, for a more rural route, take US 290 to the TX 6 exit for College Station/Bryan, follow the signs for Brenham, take a left at US 290 Business East and a quick right at Austin Street, and then take a left at 13th Street/TX 159 West and follow the road for 15.6 miles.

where to go

Austin County Jail. 36 S. Bell St.; (979) 865-9116. The building that housed the Austin County Jail from 1896 until 1992 is now a museum featuring exhibits about Austin County. The free museum is open to visitors on Saturday from 11 a.m. to 3 p.m. and by appointment.

Bluebonnet Farm. 8260 FM 529; (979) 865-5051; bluebonnetfarm.com. This 140-acre farm breeds horses—specifically the American saddlebred horse—and trains them for shows. Because much of the farm is irrigated, Bluebonnet Farm is able to produce all the hay it needs. Riding lessons are available. The farm welcomes visitors who want to learn to ride or train horses; by appointment only.

Historic Building Tours. Bellville is filled with many homes and buildings dating back to the 1800s. For an informative self-guided tour of some of the most notable historic buildings, download a tour guide brochure online at bellvillehistoricalsociety.com or stop by the Bellville Chamber of Commerce (10 S. Holland St.; 979-865-3407) to pick one up. To schedule a docent-led tour of some of these buildings, call the Bellville Historical Society (979-865-3530).

Lavande. 9665 Loop Rd.; (713) 715-8392; lavandetexas.com. Walk through the fields of this lavender farm to clear your mind (or your sinuses) and cut a bundle of lavender to take home. Lavande also sells a variety of bath products and home items made with lavender.

Market Days on the Square. East Main Street between Holland and South Bell Streets; (979) 865-3407; bellville.com/marketday.htm. On the first Saturday of each month, vendors descend upon the Bellville town square to sell their art, antiques, novelties, flowers, and food at this Bellville Chamber of Commerce–sponsored event. Market Days last from 9 a.m. to 4:30 p.m. Parking and admission are free.

Newman's Castle. (979) 865-9804; newmanscastle.com. Believe it or not, this small Texas town is home to a castle—and one with its own drawbridge at that! Mike Newman, the owner of Newman's Bakery, built this castle almost entirely on his own beginning in the late 1990s. Today, he makes it available for tours and parties. Call or stop by Newman's Bakery (504 E. Main St.) to schedule a tour.

Phenix Knives. 305 E. Main St.; (713) 724-6813; phenixknives.com. Visit this blacksmith shop, and watch Cowboy Szymanski make knives the old-fashioned way, using techniques from Asia, Europe, and the US. Tours are offered Tuesday through Saturday; knives are available for purchase.

where to shop

The best way to shop in Bellville is to walk around the square at East Main Street between Holland and South Bell Streets. There you'll find many shops selling arts and crafts and antiques. A small sampling of the stores around the square follows.

Amy's Unique Boutique. 3 E. Main St.; (979) 865-8888; facebook.com/amyuniqueboutique. Stop in here to find novelty items and gifts that range from kitschy Texana and souvenirs to delightfully scented candles. Don't worry if you're not quite sure what you're looking for: Each of the friendly staff will be happy to share an expert opinion. Closed Sunday.

Buck Fergeson Originals. 4 S. Holland St.; (979) 865-2167 or (800) 585-1244; buck fergesonoriginals.com. This shop sells western-inspired sculptures, jewelry, furniture, and home decor. Closed Sunday.

Holland Street Gallery. 14 N. Holland St.; (979) 865-4278; hollandstgallery.com. This art gallery sits on the Bellville town square and sells paintings, glass, pottery, and other works by more than 160 artists from the area. Closed Sunday and Monday.

where to eat

Bellville Meat Market. 36 S. Front St.; (979) 865-5782; bellvillemeatmarket.com. Warning: Your eyes and stomach may go crazy here. This family-run meat market is the home of Poffenberger's Bellville Smoked Sausage, as well as its turkey and beef jerkies, dry stick sausage, fresh and dry sausage, fresh rich beef, and cheeses. Bellville Meat Market also processes meat. Closed Sunday. $–$$.

Golden Pagoda. 201 E. Main St.; (979) 865-9754. This Chinese restaurant is popular among locals, who give the lo mein and General Tso's chicken high marks. The service can be slow, though. $–$$.

The Hill. 758 W. Main St.; (979) 865-3607; thehillrestaurant.com. Come here to feast on the most popular burgers and shakes in town. Other options include a fish sandwich, chopped beef, grilled cheese, and grilled chicken. $.

Newman's Bakery. 504 E. Main St.; (979) 865-9804; newmanscastle.com/bakery. Newman's Bakery is known for its cooked breakfast, as well as its desserts. Visit during lunch to dine on soup and sandwiches. $.

where to stay

Dove Cottage Bed & Breakfast. 519 S. Masonic St.; (979) 865-9360 or (979) 885-8799; dovecottagebb.com. Stay in either a private cottage or in a guest room in the main house at this bed-and-breakfast. You'll sleep surrounded by floral country decor, as well as a few crosses. Free wireless Internet and satellite TV are included. Cottage keeper Shirlene Harper serves breakfast every morning according to her guests' schedules. $.

Somewhere In Time Bed and Breakfast. 1034 S. Tesch St.; (979) 865-9547; somewhere intimebb.com. True to its name, Somewhere In Time offers a charming trip back in time. Guests sleep in either the main house, which dates back to the early 20th century, or can choose from the Carriage House, Garden Cottage, or the Roses and Rosemary Cottage. The property sits on 5 acres filled with flowers and magnolia and oak trees. The B&B is just 1.5 miles from town square. $$.

Texas Ranch Life. 10848 Cactus Ln., Chappell Hill; (979) 865-3649; texasranchlife.com. If you're looking for a really unique experience, spend the night at one of the houses on this 1,800-acre working ranch. It'll cost you a little more than many other B&Bs and hotels in the area, but you're guaranteed a memorable experience seasoned with some history. The ranch itself dates back to 1823, when it was settled by one of the 300 settlers who received a land grant in Stephen F. Austin's first colony in what was then Mexico. Guests have their choice of 8 houses dating back to the 1850s. The owners have spent thousands upon thousands of dollars to restore them and decorate them with appropriate period antiques. The houses also feature much of the original decor and paint. During your stay, you can ride horses, rope the cattle, go fishing, study the wildlife, and hunt for birds, raccoons, and coyotes. $$.

round top & winedale

With a population of just 78 people in 2009, Round Top is one of the smallest—if not *the* smallest—towns in Texas. But this Fayette County town more than makes up for its size in art, antiques, and a commitment to the preservation of local sites and history.

Four times a year, swarms of people descend upon Round Top to buy and sell antiques at the winter, spring, summer, and fall antiques festivals. If there's anywhere in the world you'd find that totally obscure antique you've been looking for your whole life—or better yet, never knew you wanted because you didn't know it existed—this is the place to find it. The rest of the year, you can find antiques, art, and unique gifts at Round Top's many little shops. To find out about upcoming antiques shows, call (512) 237-4747 or (800) 947-5799 or visit roundtoptexasantiques.com or roundtop-marburger.com.

But there's more to Round Top and Winedale culture than antiques. Though Anglo-American plantation owners began settling here in 1826, it's the German immigrants that arrived in the late 1840s whose influence continues to be seen around town. You can spot it, for instance, at Bethlehem Lutheran Church, Henkel Square Museum Village, and Winedale Historical Center, a 215-acre, 19th-century German farmstead that serves many functions—museum, historical site, and host of theater performances, including the Shakespeare at Winedale festival, which takes place in July and August. Winedale is an unincorporated community, but it's often referred to as if it were a town.

how round top got its name

Most towns are named after the people who settled them or notable residents or politicians. Round Top, however, was supposedly named after what stagecoach drivers referred to as "the house with the round top." The house, in case you are curious, was located about a mile northeast of where Round Top currently lies.

getting there

To get to Round Top from Bellville, take West Main Street and then take a slight left at Nelsonville Road/TX 159 West, which you should follow for 17 miles. Take a right at FM 1457 West and stay on the farm-to-market road for almost 13 miles, until you reach East Mill. Take a right there and another quick right onto North Washington, and you're in the heart of Round Top. To reach the hamlet of Winedale from Round Top, follow FM 1457 northeast for 2½ miles then turn left on FM 2714 for 1½ miles.

where to go

Bethlehem Lutheran Church. 409 S. White St. (1 block west of TX 237); (979) 249-3686. This church dates back to 1867, making it the oldest active Lutheran church in Fayette County. The church, built in a German architectural style, is made of stone and is home to a pipe organ constructed of hand-shaped cedar. While the building may be historic, congregants insist they're modern. As the church slogan goes, "We may worship in an antique building, but we are not antique people." Tours are available by calling the church office; you can also stop in to take a self-guided tour.

Henkel Square Museum Village. 110 Live Oak St.; (979) 249-3308. This living-history museum celebrates the German immigrants who came here in the 1850s and made Round Top home to a vibrant German-Texan community. On-site are several restored homes, a church, and an apothecary that date back to those early days. Together, they tell a story of pioneer life in the second half of the 1800s. The museum, which is the work of the Texas Pioneer Arts Foundation, is open Thursday through Sunday.

Round Top Family Library. 206 W. Mill St.; (979) 249-2700; ilovetoread.org. Housed inside an old church, the Round Top Family Library does more than lend books to local residents. It also houses the Bybee Texas Heritage Collection's books, periodicals, and written and oral accounts of Texas history, folklore, architecture, furniture, and decorative arts in the Round Top area in the 1800s. Throughout the year, the library offers story times and other special activities for children. The library also hosts used book sales every week,

Tuesday through Sunday from 1:30 to 5:30 p.m. This hub of Round Top activity has a community garden outside.

Round Top Festival Institute. 248 Jaster Rd.; (979) 249-3129; festivalhill.org. The 210-acre Festival Hill campus is home to performing arts facilities, beautiful gardens and parks for hiking, old homes, and a library full of rare books, photographs, music, and other materials. The campus is perhaps best known for the highly prestigious 2-month Festival Institute held each June and July, when young musicians come here to work with distinguished classical and chamber musicians and put on a series of performances in the Festival Concert Hall. See listing in the Festivals & Celebrations appendix for more information on this popular event.

Throughout the year the Round Top Festival Institute also hosts classical musical forums as well as special theater events. In the spring the institute educates the public about different herbs at the annual Herbal Forum; see listing in the Festivals & Celebrations appendix for more information.

Texas Basketball Museum. 107 Augsburg Ave. (1 block south of US 290), Carmine; (979) 278-4222; texasbasketball.com. This museum celebrates high school basketball players and coaches from the Lone Star State with a Hall of Fame Room, as well as autograph and trophy collections. See if you're Hall of Fame–worthy by shooting some baskets on the court outside.

Winedale Historical Center. 3738 FM 2714; (979) 278-3530; cah.utexas.edu/museums/winedale.php; shakespeare-winedale.org. The plantation homes, log cabins, and barns that sit on this restored 19th-century German farmstead are filled with antique decorative items, furnishings, and 85 quilts collected by the late philanthropist Ima Hogg. Today, the 225 acres that comprise the Winedale Historical Center are owned by the University of Texas at Austin's Briscoe Center for American History. The Winedale Historical Center is open for public tours by appointment only, so call ahead. School groups regularly come here to learn about early Texas history, as well as theater and horticulture. Throughout the year Winedale also sponsors special events, including theater performances in the Theatre Barn. The most notable of these is Shakespeare at Winedale, a series of Shakespeare performances presented by the University of Texas English Department in late July and early August. To learn more about Shakespeare at Winedale, please see the listing in the Festivals & Celebrations appendix.

where to shop

Antiques at the Village Green. TX 237 at Wantke Street (2 blocks south of Round Top Square); (254) 563-6308; villagegreenroundtop.com. Beautiful gardens surround rustic old buildings in this historic shopping village. Peruse the shops for folk art, collectibles, furniture, antiques, and more. If you need to refuel, grab a cup of java at Coffee Connection.

calendar matters

When the Round Top Antiques Fair takes place, this tiny town can get pretty congested. So if you're not interested in Round Top's antiques offerings, you're probably better off avoiding the area during these weekends. Before your visit check the Round Top Antiques Fair website (roundtoptexasantiques.com) or call (512) 237-4747 to find out whether the show's in town.

Bybee Square. 307 E. Austin St.; bybeesquare.com. The historic buildings in this square house a number of art galleries, gift shops, and artisans' shops, including Comforts, Thunderbird Ranch Fine Art Gallery, Mimi Bella, Cowgirl Junky, and Southern Grace.

D. Little Gallery. 108 N. Washington St.; (979) 249-3770. Artist Dorothy Little sells her oil paintings in this gallery, which doubles as her studio. The gallery is open Thursday through Sunday, and by appointment.

The Glass Anvil Art Foundry. 285 E. Thigpen St., Carmine (about 7 miles north of Round Top, take TX 237 to TX 458); (979) 278-3688 or (713) 419-8757; theglassanvil.com. Glass artist Diane Tovey creates mosaic, stained, and fused glass art and jewelry in her studio here. The Glass Anvil Art Foundry is open by appointment only for shoppers interested in ordering custom pieces.

Green Peck Gallery. 311 N. Live Oak St.; (979) 249-3972 or (979) 249-6452; greenpeck .com. This art gallery features the work of several artists working in a variety of media, as well as antiques, cards, and fine linens. Green Peck Gallery is open Friday and Saturday and occasionally on Sunday.

Lyn Foley Artistry in Glass Jewelry at The Gallery at Round Top. 203 E. Austin St.; (979) 249-4119; lynfoley.com and thegalleryatroundtop.com. Husband-and-wife team Lyn and Jim Foley work together to create beaded jewelry at their studio in Round Top. The author of *Wearable Art: Born in Fire* creates glass bead necklaces and earrings that are sold at many regional shows as well as in this gallery.

where to eat

Round Top Tavern. 101 S. Washington St.; (979) 249-5696; roundtoptavern.com. Located just across the street from Round Top's historic town square the Tavern offers down-home menu favorites. Sit back and enjoy bar food, enjoy some adult beverages, or listen to live music. Closed Monday and Tuesday. $–$$.

Royers Round Top Cafe. 105 Main St.; (979) 249-3611 or (877) 866-PIES; royersround topcafe.com. Feast on gourmet comfort food at this Round Top dining sweetheart. Be sure to save room for one of Royers's pies, which have been featured on the Food Network's *Road Tasted*. Vegetarians, take note: The chef here will work with you to cook up something delicious sans meat. Royers is open Thursday through Sunday. $$–$$$.

Scotty and Friends. 109 Bauer Rummel Rd.; (979) 249-5512; scottyandfriends.com. Scotty and Friends is nestled among giant live oaks, including the 13th-largest live oak in Texas. Diners can eat indoors or outside on the deck while admiring the view. Owner Scotty Lynch has created a favorite place to eat while in the Round Top area. The menu here includes a variety of salads, burgers (including those of the vegetarian variety), and sandwiches (including one composed of fried green tomatoes), as well as fish, steak, and grilled chicken. The restaurant is open Wednesday through Sunday. $–$$.

The Stone Cellar. 204 E. Mill St. on Bybee Square; (979) 249-3390; stonecellarwines.com. Part wineshop, part pub, The Stone Cellar serves gourmet pizzas and pub food. There's also plenty of wine and beer to go around. The Stone Cellar is open Wednesday through Sunday. $–$$.

where to stay

There are dozens of hotels and B&Bs in and around Round Top to accommodate all of the merchants and buyers who come for the antiques shows. If none of the inns listed below have rooms available or you'd just like more options, you can find a complete list of area lodging options at roundtop.org.

Belle of Round Top. 230 Days End Rd.; (936) 521-9300; belleofroundtop.com. This Victorian mansion is within walking distance of shops, restaurants, and other sights in town. The B&B includes 3 rooms, and guests enjoy Blue Bell ice cream before bed and freshly brewed coffee in the morning. $$.

Cole Cottage. 203 W. Wantke St.; (888) 922-4179; colecottage.com. You'll get this modernized 19th-century farmhouse to yourself—kitchen included. The cottage is in walking distance of Round Top's many shopping, entertainment, and dining offerings. $$.

Round Top Inn. 407 S. White St.; (979) 249-5294; roundtopinn.com. Several old buildings have been restored as guesthouses with private bathrooms and porches. Breakfast is included in your stay at this tree-lined site. $$ ($$$ during antiques shows).

appendix a:
regional information

north

day trip 01

Old Town Spring Visitors Bureau
606 Spring Cypress Rd., Spring
(281) 288-2355
shopspringtexas.com

The Woodlands Convention & Visitors Bureau
2801 Technology Forest Blvd., The Woodlands
(281) 363-2447 or (877) 963-2447
thewoodlandscvb.com

day trip 02

City of Montgomery
101 Old Plantersville Rd., Montgomery
(936) 597-6434
historicmontgomerytexas.com

Greater Conroe/Lake Conroe Chamber of Commerce and Conroe Convention & Visitors Bureau
505 W. Davis St., Conroe
(936) 756-6644 or (936) 522-3500
conroe.org or conroecvb.net

day trip 03

Huntsville Visitors Bureau
7600 TX 75 South, Huntsville
(936) 291-9726
huntsvilletexas.com

Sam Houston Statue and Visitors Center
TX 75, just north of Huntsville State Park, Huntsville
Exit I-45 at exit 109 or 112
(936) 291-9726
samhoustonstatue.org

northeast

day trip 01

Coldspring–San Jacinto County Chamber of Commerce
31 N. Butler St., Coldspring
(936) 653-2184
coldspringtexas.org

Greater Cleveland Chamber of Commerce
102 Hill Top Sq., Cleveland
(281) 592-8786
clevelandtxchamber.com

Lake Houston Area Chamber of Commerce
110 W. Main St., Humble
(281) 446-2128
lakehouston.org

day trip 02

City of Onalaska
372 S. FM 356, Onalaska
(936) 646-5376
cityofonalaska.us

Livingston–Polk County Chamber of Commerce
1001 US 59 Loop North, Livingston
(936) 327-4929
lpcchamber.com

Woodville–Tyler County Chamber of Commerce
717 W. Bluff St., Woodville
(409) 283-2632
tylercountychamber.com

day trip 03

Big Thicket National Preserve
6044 FM 420, Kountze
(409) 951-6700 (visitor center and information)
(409) 951-6800 (headquarters)
nps.gov/bith

City of Liberty
1829 Sam Houston St., Liberty
(936) 336-3684
cityofliberty.org

Kountze Chamber of Commerce
800 Redwood St. (inside Kountze Public Library), Kountze
(409) 246-3413 or (866) 4-KOUNTZ
kountzechamber.com

Liberty-Dayton Chamber of Commerce
1801 Trinity St., Liberty
(936) 336-5736
libertydaytonchamber.com

Lumberton Chamber of Commerce
826 N. Main St. (US 96), Lumberton
(409) 755-0554
lumbertoncoc.com

Silsbee Chamber of Commerce
545 N. 5th St., Silsbee
(409) 385-5562
silsbeechamber.com

east

day trip 01

Anahuac Chamber of Commerce
603 Miller St., Anahuac
(409) 267-4190
anahuacchamber.com

Baytown Chamber of Commerce
1300 Rollingbrook St., Ste. 400, Baytown
(281) 422-8359
baytownchamber.com

City of La Porte
604 W. Fairmont Pkwy., La Porte
(281) 471-5020
ci.la-porte.tx.us

La Porte–Bayshore Chamber of Commerce
712 W. Fairmont Pkwy., La Porte
(281) 471-1123
laportechamber.org

Pasadena Chamber of Commerce
4334 Fairmont Pkwy., Pasadena
(281) 487-7871
pasadenachamber.org

day trip 02

Beaumont Convention & Visitors Bureau
505 Willow St., Beaumont
(409) 880-3749
beaumontcvb.com

day trip 03

Nederland Chamber of Commerce
1515 Boston Ave., Nederland
(409) 722-0279
nederlandtx.com

Port Arthur Convention & Visitors Bureau
3401 Cultural Center Dr., Port Arthur
(800) 235-7822
visitportarthurtx.com

day trip 04

Orange Convention & Visitors Bureau
803 W. Green Ave., Orange
(409) 883-1011 or (800) 528-4906
orangetexas.org

southeast

day trip 01

Alvin Convention & Visitors Bureau
200 Depot Centre Blvd., Alvin
(281) 585-3359
alvintexas.org

Bay Area Houston Convention & Visitors Bureau
913 N. Meyer Rd. at TX 146, Seabrook
(281) 474-9700
visitbayareahouston.com (covers Clear Lake, Webster, Kemah, League City, and
Seabrook)

Kemah Visitor Center
604 Bradford St., Kemah
(877) 775-3624
kemahtourism.com

Santa Fe Chamber of Commerce
12408 TX 6, Santa Fe
(409) 925-8558
santafetexaschamber.com

day trip 02

Galveston Island Convention & Visitors Bureau/Galveston.com & Company
(409) 797-5145 or (866) 505-4456, ext. 145
galveston.com

Galveston Island Visitors Center
2328 Broadway, Galveston
(888) 425-4753

south

day trip 01

Brazoria Chamber of Commerce
202 W. Smith St., Brazoria
(979) 798-6100
brazoriachamber.net

Brazosport Area Chamber of Commerce

300 Abner Jackson Pkwy., Brazosport
(979) 285-2501
brazosport.org (serves Lake Jackson, Freeport, and Brazosport)

City of Angleton
121 S. Velasco St., Angleton
(979) 849-4364
visit.angleton.tx.us

southwest

day trip 01

Central Fort Bend Chamber Alliance
4120 Ave. H, Rosenberg
(281) 342-5464
cfbca.org

City of Rosenberg
2110 4th St., Rosenberg
(832) 595-3300
ci.rosenberg.tx.us

West Columbia Chamber of Commerce
202 E. Brazos Ave., West Columbia
(979) 345-3921
westcolumbiachamber.com

west

day trip 01

Katy Area Chamber of Commerce
23501 Cinco Ranch Blvd., Ste. B206, Katy
(281) 391-5289
katychamber.com

Sealy and Historic Austin County Convention & Visitors Bureau
309 Main St., Sealy
(979) 885-3222
visitsealy.com (for information on San Felipe and Sealy)

West I-10 Chamber of Commerce
907 Bains St., Brookshire
(281) 375-8100
westi10chamber.org (for information on Brookshire)

day trip 02

Columbus Chamber of Commerce
425 Spring St., Columbus
(979) 732-8385
columbustexas.org

day trip 03

The Greater Schulenburg Chamber of Commerce
618 N. Main St., Schulenburg
(979) 743-4514 or (866) 504-5294
schulenburgchamber.org

La Grange Area Chamber of Commerce
171 S. Main St., La Grange
(979) 968-5756 or (800) LA-GRANG
lagrangetourism.com

northwest

day trip 01

Brenham and Washington County Chamber and Convention and Visitors Bureau
115 W. Main St., Brenham
(979) 836-3696, (888) BRENHAM
visitbrenhamtexas.com (Also visit downtownbrenham.com for information about Burton, Brenham, Chappell Hill, and other Washington County towns.)

Chappell Hill Chamber of Commerce and Visitors Center
5145 Main St., Chappell Hill
(979) 337-9910
chappellhilltx.com

day trip 02

Hempstead Chamber of Commerce
1116 Austin St., Hempstead
(979) 826-8217
hempsteadtxchamber.com

Independence Preservation Trust
20 Briar Hollow Ln., Houston
(888) 626-8051
independencetx.com

Navasota and Grimes County Chamber of Commerce
117 S. La Salle St., Navasota
(936) 825-3699
navasotagrimeschamber.com

Waller Area Chamber of Commerce
1110 Farr St. (next to city hall), Waller
936-372-5300
wallerchamber.com

Washington County Chamber of Commerce
314 S. Austin St., Brenham
(979) 836-3695 or (888) BRENHAM
brenhamtexas.com

day trip 03

Bryan–College Station Convention & Visitors Bureau
715 University Dr. East, College Station
(979) 260-9898 or (800) 777-8292
visitaggieland.com

day trip 04

Bellville Chamber of Commerce
10 S. Holland St., Bellville
(979) 865-3407
bellville.com

Round Top Area Chamber of Commerce
205 N. Live Oak St., Round Top
(979) 249-4042 or (888) 368-4783
roundtop.org

appendix b:
festivals & celebrations

Stopping at site after site, shop after shop, can be a fun way to see a small town, but let's face it: Sometimes it's easier to just head to a festival or special event, where you can park the car and find a variety of fun options in one spot. Luckily, you're sure to come across several festivals taking place around the Lone Star State on any given weekend—or in many cases, weekday. In the pages that follow, you'll find a sampling of annual festivals and events that are held within a couple hours' drive of Houston. These include just about every kind of festival and event imaginable: watermelon festivals, birding festivals, mosquito festivals, rodeos, music festivals, architectural tours, wine and beer festivals, mushroom festivals, and history-related events. You name it; Texas has it. No matter your likes or age, you're sure to find at least a few appealing events here. To find additional festivals, visit traveltex.com or request a print copy of the Texas Department of Transportation's quarterly events calendar by calling (512) 486-5876. Have fun!

january

The Ice Rink at Woodlands Town Center. (281) 363-2447; thewoodlandscvb.com. Indulge your winter fantasies with a trip to the outdoor ice-skating rink at Woodlands Town Center. This Rockefeller Center–inspired rink is open from the week of Thanksgiving through Martin Luther King Jr. Day in January.

Katy Home & Garden Show. (281) 392-2177; katyhomeandgardenshow.com. Head to Katy, and visit more than 300 exhibits to figure out how to fix up your home and garden. The 2-day show is held the last weekend of January.

february

Gulf Coast Music Hall of Fame Show. (409) 548-4444. Once known as the Janis Joplin Birthday Bash, today the fund-raising show at the Robert A. "Bob" Bowers Civic Center in Port Arthur salutes all Southeast Texas music greats with performances and memorabilia.

Katy ISD FFA Rodeo. katyrodeo.org. Avoid the big crowds at the Houston Livestock Show & Rodeo with a trip to this annual Katy event, which supports agricultural education in the Katy Independent School District. There's a carnival, parade, livestock show, and rodeo, which includes a number of youth events. The rodeo typically takes place over 3 days in late February.

Mardi Gras! Galveston. (888) GAL-ISLE; mardigrasgalveston.com. Enjoy a party like no other at Galveston's most popular event, which takes place over about 11 days in February or March, depending on the date of Easter Sunday. The colorful festivities include 11 parades (complete with bead throwing), a carnival, more than 50 galas, live music of all varieties, and Gulf Coast and Cajun cuisine aplenty.

Southeast Texas Mardi Gras. (409) 721-8717; mardigras.portarthur.com. Head to downtown Port Arthur for this family-friendly Mardi Gras celebration. The weekend-long event, held in February or March, depending on the date of Easter, includes live music, carnival rides and foods, street entertainers, arts and crafts, and, of course, parades and beads galore.

Yachty Gras Night Boat Parade. (713) 882-4040; yachtygras.com. Celebrate Mardi Gras nautical-style on the Kemah Boardwalk. Watch brightly decorated boats sail along the boardwalk—and be prepared to have beads and doubloons thrown your way.

march

General Sam Houston's Birthday. (936) 294-1832. Celebrate Sam Houston's birthday in Huntsville on March 2 by marching from the campus of Sam Houston State University to Oakwood Cemetery, where the legendary Texas statesman is buried. A ceremony is held at Houston's grave. Those who make advance reservations can also attend a commemorative luncheon.

German Heritage Festival. (281) 379-6844; tomballgermanfest.org. Whether you've got some German blood or you're just looking for a good time, head to the German Heritage Festival in Tomball, typically held during the last week of March. You'll find folk dancers clad in traditional German garb, sausage and beer, carnival games and rides, 4 stages of live music, arts and crafts, and fireworks.

Nederland Heritage Festival. (409) 724-2269; nederlandhf.org. Celebrate Nederland's Cajun and Dutch roots at this family-friendly, 6-day festival. Highlights include a Battle of the Bands, an art and photography show, a chili cook-off, pageants, a treasure hunt, a country music show, a washer tournament, and a cuisine walk.

Parade of Quilts. (361) 865-3920; flatoniachamber.com. You'll know spring is in the air when you wander around downtown Flatonia in March. Throughout the month, shop owners hang quilts of every hue and style in their windows for passersby to admire.

Round Top Herbal Forum. (979) 249-3129; festivalhill.org. Learn how to grow and cook with different herbs at this annual Round Top event, held over 2 days in mid-March. You can also pick up some fresh herb plants for your garden. Visit the Thyme Well Spent shop to purchase art, herb-scented lotions and soaps, and some tasty herb treats.

Springfest Wine & Art Festival. (281) 353-9310 or (800) OLD-TOWN; oldtownspring .com. Sample wines, listen to live music, and admire the art exhibits as you stroll through Old Town Spring during this annual festival, held in late March.

Texas Independence Day Celebration. (936) 878-2214; birthplaceoftexas.com. Discover how early Texans lived at this commemoration of Texas's independence from Mexico. Held at Washington-on-the-Brazos State Historic Site, the festival features reenactments, old-timey craft demonstrations, and Texas music. It takes place on the weekend closest to Texas Independence Day (March 2).

Tyler County Dogwood Festival. (409) 283-2632; tylercountydogwoodfestival.org. Celebrate the blossoming of dogwood trees in Woodville. The festival, which spans 3 weekends in late March and early April, includes an art show and festival in Heritage Village Museum, a rodeo, parade, a western dance, fireworks, a pageant, and the coronation of the Dogwood Festival Queen.

april

Burton Cotton Gin Festival. (979) 289-3378; cottonginmuseum.org. Learn about Texas's glory days as a cotton exporter for 2 days in mid-April at the Cotton Gin & Museum in Burton. Tours of a real cotton gin, a tractor pull, a petting zoo, and demonstrations are among the old-timey draws. There's also music, contests, and food for those looking to get their 21st-century fix.

Clear Lake Crawfish Festival. (281) 488-7676; clearlakearea.com. Fill your belly with crawfish and gumbo on a Saturday in early April. Among the biggest draws at this Clear Lake festival are the crawfish eating contests, the gumbo cook-off, arts and crafts activities, a silent auction, live music, and games for kids.

Eeyore's Birthday Party. (979) 278-3530; shakespeare-winedale.org. Celebrate the birthday of Winnie the Pooh's donkey sidekick at Winedale Historical Center in Round Top. The late April festivities include children's games and costume contests, a Shakespearean comedy, and food.

Folk Life Festival. (281) 396-2460. Learn how Texas pioneers lived at this annual Katy festival, held at the Outdoor Learning Center on a Saturday in early April. The family-friendly event features blacksmithing and pioneer cooking demonstrations and opportunities to make corn husk dolls and learn calligraphy.

Fruehling Saengerfest. (979) 865-3407; texasgermansociety.com. Enjoy German music as you feast on sausage, sauerkraut, and homemade desserts. There's also a cakewalk. Bellville's 1-day festival is held on a Sunday near the end of the month.

Galveston FeatherFest. (832) 459-5533 or (888) 425-4753; galvestonfeatherfest.com. The avian spring migration takes place in April, making this 4-day event the perfect opportunity to watch for more than 200 species of birds. This family-friendly fest offers bird-watching expeditions by boat, bus, and kayak to several different habitats around the area.

Good Oil Days. (281) 446-4140; goodoildays.com. For more than 3 decades, the residents of Humble have invited visitors to a day that's rich in good, old-fashioned family fun complete with arts and crafts, live entertainment, and tasty treats.

Marburger Farm Antique Show. roundtop-marburger.com. Whether you're an amateur or pro antiquer, this show is the place to get your fix in late March and early April. Held at Marburger Farm in Round Top, the 5-day event features antique jewelry, art, furniture, textiles, silver, and more from over 350 dealers from around the world.

Migration Celebration. (866) 403-5829; migrationcelebration.org. Grab your binoculars and head to Lake Jackson mid-month to celebrate the migration of more than 600 bird species around Brazosport. The 3-day event includes nature tours, birding seminars, kayaking and crabbing, and other activities for kids.

Montgomery County Fair & Rodeo. (936) 760-3631; mcfa.org. This family-friendly event in Conroe features a rodeo (complete with youth stick-horse races), a barbecue cook-off, a beauty pageant, a country store featuring arts and crafts, and petting zoo. The 10-day event is usually held in mid-April; a 2-day trail ride precedes the fair.

Official Bluebonnet Festival of Texas. (979) 836-6033 or (888) 273-6426; chappellhill museum.org. Celebrate the fields full of bluebonnets at this popular Chappell Hill festival for 1 weekend in mid-April. You'll find more than 250 juried vendors selling bluebonnet-inspired home and garden decor, jewelry, and gift items. Live music, food, and other entertainment are also part of the fun.

Round Top Antiques Fair. (512) 237-4747; roundtopantiquesfair.com. Antiques dealers from around the country sell a wide range of jewelry, art, decor, furniture, silver, and other finds at this 4-day show. Considered one of Texas's best antique shows, this Round Top event is held the first weekend of April.

Sam Houston Folk Festival. (936) 294-1832; samhoustonfolkfestival.org. Visit Huntsville's Sam Houston Memorial Museum Complex to see how Sam Houston and early Texans lived. The event features museum tours, folklife demonstrations, arts and crafts activities, a Living History Theatre, costumed historical figures, and live music.

San Jacinto Day Festival. (281) 479-2421; sanjacinto-museum.org. See how Texas revolutionaries defeated Santa Anna's army during a historical reenactment at the San Jacinto Battleground State Historic Site in La Porte. The family-friendly event, which takes place on the Saturday closest to San Jacinto Day (April 21), also includes live music, food, and games.

San Jacinto Festival. (979) 345-3921; westcolumbiatx.org. If historical battle reenactments aren't your thing, you've got another option for commemorating San Jacinto Day: On the weekend before or after San Jacinto Day, West Columbia celebrates Texas's victory with a barbecue cook-off, live music, a carnival, arts and crafts, a pet parade, a washer contest, and food.

Sylvan Beach Festival & Crawfish Jam. (281) 471-1123; laportechamber.org. Kick off the beach season at this annual festival, held at Sylvan Beach Park in La Porte on a Saturday at the end of April. You'll enjoy crawfish cook-offs, arts and crafts activities, carnival rides, live music, and plenty of kid-friendly fun.

Texas Crawfish & Music Festival. (800) OLD TOWN; texascrawfishfestival.com. Spring hosts this palate-pleasing festival during the last 2 weekends in April. You'll enjoy crawfish and Cajun food while listening to live country, rock, and zydeco music. There's also a carnival.

Wine and Roses Festival. (979) 778-9463; messinahof.com. Celebrate the blossoming of the roses and grapes with a visit to Bryan's Messina Hof Winery on a Saturday at the end of April. The festival boasts free wine and food tastings, arts and crafts demonstrations, live music, and a grape-stomping competition.

may

Airing of the Quilts. (936) 291- 9726; huntsvilletexas.com. The state's largest outdoor quilt festival is an opportunity to see the more than 300 new and antique quilts that are offered for sale in downtown Huntsville. Stitching classes are also offered.

Bay Day. (281) 332-3381; galvbay.org. Celebrate all that Galveston Bay has to offer with hands-on activities, a children's scavenger hunt, a photo contest, live animal exhibits, and a cruise through Galveston Bay on the RV *Karma*. This 1-day event takes place mid-May in Kemah.

Blessing of the Shrimp and Pleasure Boat Fleet. (713) 545-5246; kemah.net/blessing .html. Visit the Kemah Boardwalk on the first Sunday in May to see decorated boats get blessed for the upcoming boating season. There's a boat parade, awards ceremony, and live entertainment. A gumbo cook-off is held the day before the blessing.

Galveston Historic Homes Tour. (409) 765-7834; galvestonhistory.org. Tour some of Galveston's oldest homes on this tour held during the first 2 weekends in May. You'll discover mansions of national importance, Craftsman-style bungalows, and an array of other restored buildings.

General Sam Houston Folk Fest. (936) 291-5920; huntsvilletexas.com. The first weekend of May, Sam Houston Folk Fest celebrates the Huntsville's most famous resident with exhibits, food, demonstrations, and music.

Hardin County MusicFest. (409) 246-3413; hcmusicfest.com. Known as "The Big Light in the Big Thicket," the tiny town of Kountze will shine a spotlight on Texas songsmiths during the annual Hardin County MusicFest, which also features a barbecue cook-off, a washer tournament, and helicopter rides.

Maifest. (888) BRENHAM; maifest.org. For more than a hundred years, the Brenham community has celebrated its German heritage with Maifest, held in early May. The festivities include Junior and Senior King and Queen coronations, parades, a children's carnival, arts and crafts activities, and, of course, German food and music.

Pasadena Strawberry Festival. (281) 991-9500; strawberryfest.org. Take a bite out of the world's biggest strawberry shortcake at this 3-day festival mid-month. Other attractions at the family-friendly event include carnival rides, pageants, a pig race, and live music.

SLAVNOST. (888) 785-4500; czechtexas.org. Hosted by the Texas Czech Heritage & Cultural Center, this La Grange event celebrates Czech culture in the Lone Star State. The lineup includes Polka and Czech music, pastries, a silent auction, and a tour of Czech Village Houses. SLAVNOST is held on a Sunday in May.

Texas Crab Festival. (409) 684-5940; texascrabfestival.org. Show your Gulf Coast love at this Crystal Beach festival, held the last weekend of May. The biggest draws may be the Crab Legs Contest, Weiner Dog Nationals, Crab Races, and eating crab and seafood dishes, but there's also plenty of fun to be had playing volleyball, participating in the horseshoe tournament, and checking out the arts and crafts vendors. Kiddie activities abound, too.

Texas Music Festival. texasmusicfestival.org. A fixture on Galveston County's calendar since 1954, League City invites fans of Texas tunes to enjoy 3 days of concerts, carnival fun, a barbecue cook-off, a safari run, and a karaoke showdown.

The Weimar Gedenke! Festival. (979) 725-9511; weimartx.org. Pay homage to Weimar's German heritage at the town's largest event, held each May on Mother's Day weekend. Between the *biergarten,* live music, games, arts and crafts activities, a 5K run/walk, and a Texas-inspired barbecue cook-off, there's something for everyone in your family.

june

Freedom Festival. (979) 532-1862; whartonfreedomfest.org. On the last Friday and Saturday in June, Wharton hosts a barbecue cook-off, a car and motorcycle show, street dancing, and a fireworks show.

Galveston AIA Sandcastle Competition. (713) 520-0155; aiasandcastle.com. Ever wonder what an architect's sand castle might look like? You can find out when you visit Galveston's East Beach for one of the world's largest sand castle contests during a Saturday in early June. An awards ceremony is held around dusk.

Grimes County Fair. (979) 218-5617; grimescountyfair.com. During the first part of June, Navasota hosts the Grimes County Fair, complete with a rodeo, livestock show, arts and crafts activities, dancing, and a Fair Queen pageant.

Juneteenth celebrations. Attend one of the many Juneteenth celebrations in the area to commemorate the day that word reached Galveston that Abraham Lincoln had freed the slaves. Some of the biggest celebrations occur in Galveston, of course, with events including an Emancipation Proclamation reading and prayer breakfast, a Jubilee parade, and live music events. Information: galveston.com/juneteenth. In Brenham, the Washington County Historical Juneteenth Association holds a parade downtown, which is followed by a festival at Fireman's Park. Information: (979) 836-9438. Additional Juneteenth events around the state can be found at juneteenth.com. Please note that some Juneteenth events are held on the actual day of Juneteenth (June 19); others are held a few days before or after. Call or go online for more exact dates.

Round Top Music Festival. (979) 249-3129; festivalhill.org. From early June through the second week in July, about a hundred student musicians accompany world-renowned conductors and soloists in orchestra and chamber-music concerts at the Festival Institute. Purchase season or individual tickets to the shows.

Sealy KC June Music Fest. (979) 885-6786; visitsealy.com. Get your fill of polka tunes and dancing at this annual Sealy event, held the fourth Sunday in June. Hosted by the Sealy Knights of Columbus Hall, the day features polka and country bands, a polka Mass, and home-cooked food.

Summer Music Festival & CPRA Rodeo. (979) 865-5995; austincountyfair.com. On the fourth Saturday in June, this Bellville festival serves up arts and crafts activities, live music, a barbecue cook-off, a Little Miss Pageant, and a Hawaiian Tropic Model Search. A fireworks show caps off the day.

july

Crush for Fun at Pleasant Hill Winery. (979) 830-8463; pleasanthillwinery.com. During 8 days in July and August, visit Brenham's Pleasant Hill Winery for wine tastings, food sampling, tours, and other grape-inspired fun.

Fourth of July. Want to skip out on the big-city July 4 celebrations? You've got plenty of other fun options around the area: In Beaumont, Riverfront Park fills up with blankets and lawn chairs as thousands of people listen to country, jazz, and blues music and eat barbecue, cotton candy, funnel cake, and other snacks. A fireworks show caps off the evening. Information: (409) 838-3435; beaumontcvb.com. Chappell Hill hosts what it bills as the "Best Small Town Parade in America," complete with cowboys, antique cards, and the Marching Kazoo Band. Information: (979) 337-9910; chappellhilltx.com. Columbus hosts Texas's "Oldest Independence Day Celebration." The free evening event features live music and, after sundown, fireworks. Information: (979) 732-8385; columbustexas.org. The Kemah Boardwalk hosts a fireworks show on Galveston Bay. Information: (877) AT-KEMAH; kemahboardwalk.com. In Richmond, George Ranch Historical Park holds a vintage baseball game—that is, one played by the 1890s rules. Information: (281) 343-0218; georgeranch .org. At Washington-on-the-Brazos State Historic Site in Washington, you can celebrate both Texas's and the US independence with a fireworks show, patriotic tunes, and Blue Bell ice cream. Information: (936) 878-2214 or (888) BRENHAM; birthplaceoftexas.com.

The Great Texas Mosquito Festival. (800) 371-2971; mosquitofestival.com. For 3 days in late July, mosquitoes get a surprising amount of love in Clute. The family fun here includes a barbecue and fajita cook-off, horseshoe tournaments, a haystack dive, a 5K run, a Mr. and Mrs. Mosquito Legs Contest and a Mosquito Calling Contest, and a baby crawling competition.

Gulf Coast Jam. (409) 548-4444; portarthurtexas.com. Enjoy an evening of tunes performed by Gulf Coast musicians at Port Arthur's Bob Bowers Civic Center. Recent acts have included Percy Sledge, Jerry LaCroix, and the Boogie Kings.

Hempstead Watermelon Festival. (979) 826-8217; hempsteadtxchamber.com. Hempstead hosts its biggest festival on the third Saturday in July, and watermelon is the guest of honor. Highlights include a parade, a Watermelon Queen competition, artists and craftspeople selling gifts, a vintage car show, and a barbecue cook-off.

Lunar Rendezvous Festival. lunarrendezvous.org. Celebrate the accomplishments of space scientists in the Clear Lake/Bay Area through a series of events held in July. Among these activities are a fun run, a fashion show, and a coronation ball. A golf tournament, tennis tournament, and kickoff party are held in April and May to get the community excited about the festival.

Sealybration. (877) 558-7245; visitsealy.com; sealycommunityfoundation.org. Have some fun with Sealy locals at the town's major celebration. The festival's highlights include games and water activities for the kids, arts and crafts, a carnival, a barbecue cook-off, a softball tournament, live music, and fireworks.

Shakespeare at Winedale. shakespeare-winedale.org. Shakespeare fans, Winedale is calling: Visit Round Top to see some of the great bard's plays onstage at the Winedale Historical Center during the last 2 weekends in July and the first 2 weekends in August. The program, sponsored by the English department of the University of Texas at Austin, features performances Thursday through Sunday, as well as special performances throughout the year.

august

Chappell Hill Lavender and Wine Fest. (979) 251-8114; chappellhilllavender.com. Breathe in delightful scents as you cut lavender and browse vendors' artistic creations during the Chappell Hill Lavender Farm's annual festival, held on a Saturday in August.

Navasota Blues Festival. (936) 870-3331; navasotabluesfest.org. On the first Friday and Saturday in August, Navasota's Grimes County Expo Center comes alive with one great blues concert set after another. A cocktail hour with the musicians and guitar lessons are also offered.

Schulenburg Festival. schulenburgfestival.org. Nicknamed the "National Party of Texas," this Schulenburg extravaganza boasts 3 days of nonstop entertainment. Among the offerings are a fun run, horseshoe pitching, a carnival, a volleyball tournament, a chili cook-off, craft and antiques vendors, and a golf tournament.

Shakespeare at Winedale. shakespeare-winedale.org. Shakespeare fans, Winedale is calling: Visit Round Top to see some of the great bard's plays onstage at the Winedale Historical Center during the last 2 weekends in July and the first 2 weekends in August. The program, sponsored by the English department of the University of Texas at Austin, features performances Thursday through Sunday, as well as special performances throughout the year.

september

Fiestas Patrias. (281) 342-6478; fortbendmuseum.org. Celebrate Mexican culture during this festival commemorating Mexico's independence from Spain. Held at the Fort Bend Museum in Richmond on the Saturday nearest September 16, Fiestas Patrias features *folklórico* dancers, a festival queen coronation, Mexican food, and authentic mariachis.

Galveston Island Wild Texas Shrimp Festival. (409) 762-6676; yagaspresents.com/shrimpfestival. Get ready for a crustacean-themed sensation as Galveston's annual ode to its oceanic gifts serves up a virtual gumbo of entertainment for the entire family, complete with a free boat and RV show, live music, a 5K fun run, a shrimp gumbo cook-off, a children's Lil' Shrimp Parade, and much more.

Longhorn Rod Run. (800) OLD-TOWN; (281) 353-9310; oldtownspring.com. Check out vintage cars along the street as you shop in Old Town Spring during the last weekend of September. The cars—or rather, their owners—also compete for prizes at this annual event.

Mexican Heritage Festival. (409) 982-8300 or (409) 724-6134; portarthurtexas.com. Honor Texas's southern neighbor at Port Arthur's annual celebration of Mexico's independence from Spain. The colorful festivities include tamale and costume contests, Tejano music, a coronation, *folklórico* dancers, and, of course, Mexican food. The festival is held at Bob Bowers Civic Center.

Montgomery Food and Wine Trail. (936) 597-5004; experiencemontgomery.com. Sample Texas wines and foods at this family-friendly festival in downtown Montgomery. Other activities include grape stomps, face painting, and shopping.

Oktoberfest Festival. (281) 415-8019. Held at the end of October, this popular Woodlands festival kicks off with a keg tapping ceremony. Subsequent activities include yodeling contests, dance lessons, live music, and opportunities aplenty to fill up on bratwurst, sauerkraut, strudel, and German beer.

South West International In-Water Boat Show. (561) 842-8808 or (281) 334-0515; southwestinternationalboatshow.com. During the last weekend in September, League City's South Shore Harbour Marina hosts the state's largest in-water boat show. Live music and other entertainment create a festive atmosphere while buyers, sellers, and enthusiasts check out the boats.

Texas Gatorfest. (409) 267-4190; texasgatorfest.com. Take the family to Anahuac—aka the "Alligator Capital of Texas"—for this 4-day festival in mid-September. You'll find something for everyone: airboat rides, a carnival, live music, waterborne tours, a coronation, and the requisite Alligator Round-up.

Texas Pecan Festival. (409) 962-3631; texaspecanfestival.com. Celebrate the harvesting of pecans from the more than 2,500 pecan trees that were planted in Groves around the turn of the 20th century at the town's annual celebration. Held in Lyons Park for 4 days in mid-September, the state's official pecan festival features a carnival, live music, pie-eating and pecan-toss contests, a pet show, a parade, arts and crafts activities, and the crowning of the Pecan Queen.

Washington County Fair. (979) 836-4112; washingtoncofair.com. You'll find fun for the whole family at this county fair, held in Brenham over 9 days in mid-September. Highlights include a rodeo, a Fair Queen coronation, a carnival, arts and crafts activities, livestock and poultry auctions, music, and other live entertainment.

october

Austin County Fair & Rodeo. (979) 865-5995; austincountyfair.com. Austin County Fairgrounds are the place to be in Bellville over 5 days in early October. A shrimp boil and dance kick off the festivities, which include a livestock show and rodeo, carnival, parade, live music, and a queen pageant.

Ballunar Liftoff Festival. (281) 488-7676; ballunarfestival.com. Watch dozens of hot-air balloons lift off and fill the sky over NASA's Johnson Space Center in Houston during 3 days in late October. Other draws at this rainbow-hued event include arts and crafts exhibits, live music, skydiving exhibits, and children's activities.

Bellville Antiques Festival. (979) 865-0625; bellvillehistoricalsociety.com. Go antiquing on the Austin County Fairgrounds in Bellville during the last weekend in October. You'll find unique pieces from more than 60 dealers, as well as homemade desserts, sandwiches, and soups.

Brazoria County Fair. (979) 849-6416; brazoriacountyfair.com. Dubbed "The Largest County Fair in Texas," this family-friendly extravaganza is held over 9 days each October. Attend and you'll be treated to a carnival, livestock exhibits and a rodeo competition, live music, arts and crafts, and greasy and sugar-laden food aplenty. The fair takes place at the Brazoria County Fairgrounds in Angleton.

Cajun Catfish Festival. (936) 539-6009 or (800) 324-2604; conroecajuncatfishfestival .com. For 3 days in mid-October, Conroe throws a big family-friendly party—and catfish are invited. The festival highlights Cajun food; a Go Texan wine and food area; a catfishing (catfish-catching) contest; a kid zone complete with video games, movies, inflatables, and a climbing wall; and live music of the Cajun, zydeco, blues, and Texas country varieties.

Clear Lake Celtic Music Festival. (713) 365-9648; celticmusicassociation.com. Get your fill of Celtic music, Irish dancing, games, face painting, sweet treats, and other vendors at this daylong Clear Lake festival in mid-October.

Czhilispiel. (361) 865-3920; flatoniachamber.com. On the fourth full weekend in October, downtown Flatonia hosts its popular chili festival. Activities include a jalapeño-eating contest, chili and barbecue cook-offs, an egg toss, a mechanical bull, live music, a pageant, a carnival, a petting zoo, a car and truck show, arts and crafts, and a washer tournament. Admission is free on Friday and Sunday.

Fair on the Square. (936) 295-8113; chamber.huntsville.tx.us. Get a head start on your holiday shopping with a visit to Huntsville's downtown square on the first Saturday in October. You'll find more than 300 vendors, many of them artisans peddling jewelry, home decor, and other arts and crafts. There's also a beer garden, arts and crafts activities, children's activities, food, and live music.

Fall Antiques Fair. (512) 237-4747; roundtopantiquesfair.com. Find out why antiques collectors and dealers love to go to Round Top for this 4-day antique extravaganza. Held at the beginning of October, the fair spans multiple venues and features antiques from hundreds of dealers from around the world.

Father of Texas Birthday Celebration. (979) 885-2181; colonialcapitaloftexas.com. Celebrate the birthday of one of Texas's founding fathers with a trip to the Stephen F. Austin State Park in San Felipe on the weekend nearest Stephen F. Austin's November 3 birthday. Events include a children's archaeological dig, colonial-era activities, historical presentations and opportunities to look at 1800s period equipment, and tours of the area and San Felipe Cemetery.

Harvest Festival & East Texas Folklife Festival. (409) 283-2272; heritage-village.org. East Texas's biggest folklife festival takes place in Woodville during the third weekend of October. The period costumes, pioneer demonstrations, and food, music, and dancing of old will take you back to the days of the area's settlers.

Katy Rice Harvest Festival. (281) 391-5289; riceharvestfestival.org. Join upward of 50,000 Houstonians in celebrating Katy's agricultural contributions to the area at this popular 2-day festival. Held in Katy during the second weekend of October, the festival boasts a carnival, live entertainment, arts and crafts activities, artists peddling their work, funnel cake, roasted corn, kettle corn, and other snacks.

Lighted Pumpkin Stroll. (281) 934-3276; dewberryfarm.com. Take a Saturday evening walk through Brookshire's Dewberry Farm in October and see brilliantly carved pumpkins light up. Then pick your own pumpkin from the patch or traipse through the 6-acre corn maze.

PetFest. (281) 528-7070; petfestoldtownspring.com. Dress up your pets and take them to Old Town Spring to support efforts to find homes for other 2- and 4-legged animals. In addition to the PetFest Costume Contest, you and your pets will find live music, demonstrations, and a chance to meet with a pet psychic.

Scarecrow Festival. (979) 836-6033; chappellhillmuseum.org. Get in the fall spirit at Chappell Hill's Scarecrow Festival during the second weekend of October. Check out an array of scarecrows, find the perfect pumpkin in the pumpkin patch, shop at more than 250 juried vendors' booths, enjoy live music, and decorate a pumpkin to scare off any ghouls.

Texas City Music Fest By The Bay. (409) 643-5990; bythebayfest.com. Pay tribute to blues legend and Texas City native Charles Brown at this live music festival in Texas City, where you'll hear tunes ranging from zydeco to country to alternative to blues. The festival typically takes place in late October. You'll also find plenty of kids' activities and food.

Texas Mushroom Festival. (877) 908-8808; texasmushroomfestival.com. Madisonville—aka the "Mushroom Capital of Texas"—fetes its beloved fungi on a Saturday in October. Wine tastings, cooking demonstrations, the Shiitake 5K Run/Walk, craft and food vendors, a photo contest, and kids' activities are all part of the celebration.

Texas Reds Steak and Grape Festival. (979) 209-5528; texasredsfestival.com. Wine tastings, steak cook-offs, live music, and a grape stomp are par for the course at this popular Bryan event. The 2-day festival also offers children's activities and chef demonstrations.

Texas Renaissance Festival. (800) 458-3435; texrenfest.com. Plantersville may be 65 miles from Houston, but it feels much farther—about 5 centuries farther—when you visit for the Texas Renaissance Festival, which takes place for 8 weekends in October and November. Renaissance-era music, food, games, rides, dancing, demonstrations, and costumes are all part of the fun.

Texas Rice Festival. (409) 296-4404; texasricefestival.org. Visit Winnie to celebrate the rice harvest during the first week of October. Rice Festival highlights include rice-cooking competitions, pageants, parades, a longhorn show and a horse show, a barbecue cook-off, street dancing, an antique car show, and plenty of rice and Cajun dishes.

Texian Market Days. (281) 343-0218; texianmarketdays.com. This living-history festival serves up a day of fun for the whole family in late October. Hosted by the George Ranch in Richmond, Texian Market Days is a great chance to brush up on your Texas history with Civil War camps and battle reenactments, historic home tours, hands-on activities, and live entertainment.

november

Civil War Weekend. (979) 826-3126; liendo.org. On the weekend before Thanksgiving, Liendo Plantation in Hempstead offers a trip back to the Civil War era. The event includes artillery, cavalry, and infantry demonstrations, as well as spinning, weaving, soap-making, quilting, and furniture-making demonstrations. Adding to the festive aura are demonstrators dressed up in period clothing and the sound of 1860s tunes.

Harvest Festival at Armand Bayou. (866) 417-3818 or (281) 474-2551; abnc.org. Get a taste of life circa 1900 as you watch volunteers dressed in period costumes churn butter, make soap, and bale hay. Held at Armand Bayou Nature Center in Pasadena, the festival also features wagon rides, a pie-eating contest, live music and dancers, and children's games and crafts. The festival takes place over a weekend in mid-November.

Home for the Holidays. (281) 353-9310; oldtownspring.com. Visit Old Town Spring to do some holiday shopping and get some added cheer. Beginning in mid-November, Spring's historic shopping district features train rides, musicians and barbershop quartets, and carriage rides along the lit-up streets. There are also opportunities to have your photo taken with Santa. The festivities kick off with a mid-month tree lighting.

The Ice Rink at Woodlands Town Center. (281) 363-2447; thewoodlandscvb.com. Indulge your winter fantasies with a trip to the outdoor ice-skating rink at Woodlands Town Center. This Rockefeller Center–inspired rink is open from the week of Thanksgiving through Martin Luther King Jr. Day in January.

Live Oaks and Dead Folks. (979) 732-3392; library.columbustexas.net. During the first weekend in November, Columbus's Nesbitt Memorial Library offers a unique tour of Odd Fellows Rest Cemetery either the Old City Cemetery or the Odd Fellows Rest Cemetery. At 7 p.m. each evening the tour begins, with actors playing the parts of some of the town's deceased personalities.

Poinsettia Celebration. (979) 836-6011; ellisonsgreenhouses.com. The weekend before Thanksgiving, Ellison's Greenhouses in Brenham celebrates the flower of the season.

Admire poinsettias of every hue and size as you tour the greenhouse and listen to talks by garden and floral design experts. Also on the agenda are arts and crafts activities, food, and plenty of family fun.

San Felipe Colonial Heritage Day. (979) 885-3613. In early November, San Felipe's Stephen F. Austin State Park serves up an array of activities that reveal how early Texans lived.

Taste of the Town. (281) 487-7871; pasadenachamber.org. Travelers with an appetite for culinary adventure can enjoy palate-pleasing presentations of American and ethnic food, seafood, and desserts prepared by 30 Pasadena area restaurants at the Pasadena Convention Center. A live auction is also on the menu.

december

Brenham Christmas Stroll and Lighted Parade. (979) 836-3696 or (888) BRENHAM; downtownbrenham.com. Sip hot cider as you walk through a beautifully lit downtown Brenham during the first weekend in December and enjoy seasonal entertainment.

Chappell Hill Holiday Home Tour and Teddy Bear Parade. (979) 836-6033; chappell hillhistoricalsociety.com. Tour quaint old houses decorated for Christmas in Chappell Hill. Bring the kids and their favorite teddy bears, whom they can dress up and march with in the Chappell Hill Teddy Bear Parade. Rudolph and Mrs. Claus are also on hand for some added fun. The home tours take place about 2 weekends before Christmas; the Teddy Bear Parade takes place on the Saturday of the tours.

Christmas Bird Count. audubon.org. Birds' southern migration makes the Texas coast a great place to see—and count—birds in December. Visit Freeport on the Christmas Bird Count assigned by the Audubon Society and you're likely to see more birds there than anywhere else in the country. Check the website for the date.

Christmas Boat Lane Parade. (281) 488-7676; clearlakearea.com. On the second Saturday evening in December, watch more than a hundred festively decorated boats sail through Clear Lake from the South Shore Harbour Marina in League City to Galveston Bay. The best-decorated boats receive prizes.

Christmas Homes Tour. (979) 364-2559; calverttx.com. See some of Calvert's finest old homes, all decked out for Christmas during this 2-day tour, held in early December.

Christmas in Historic Montgomery. (936) 499-3786 or (936) 597-8940; historic montgomerytexas.com. On a Saturday in mid-December, Montgomery hosts its Christmas extravaganza, complete with a holiday marketplace selling arts and crafts, a Christmas parade, a Cookie Walk, a Candlelight Home Tour, horse-drawn carriage rides, and an opportunity for kids to drop off their letters to Santa at Santa's Post Office.

Christmas in Rosenberg. (832) 595-3525; ci.rosenberg.tx.us. Celebrate the holidays in Rosenberg's historic downtown area, where kids can climb a rock wall, run through an obstacle course, and ride a trackless train at the children's carnival, courtesy of the Rosenberg Railroad Museum. You can also meet Santa and Mrs. Claus and mull over the merchandise at vendor booths.

Christmas on the Brazos. (936) 878-2214; tpwd.state.tx.us. On the second Saturday in December, visit Texas's birthplace—Washington-on-the-Brazos—for some caroling and a walk down the candlelit path to Independence Hall. During your visit, you'll learn how residents of old celebrated Christmas.

The Christmas Train. (281) 331-9517; thechristmastrain.org. If you're looking for a truly "moving" holiday experience for the whole family, you'll be on the right track if you head to Alvin, where a choo-choo chugs its way through a winter wonderland filled with over 300,000 lights. At the Christmas Village kids can have their pictures taken with Santa and hear Mrs. Claus read a story.

Dickens on the Strand. (409) 765-7834; galvestonhistory.org. This popular Galveston event will take you back to Christmas in Charles Dickens's 19th-century London. Held the first weekend in December, Dickens on the Strand features parades, carolers, bagpipers, and vendors selling Victorian-inspired crafts, food, gifts, and decorations. Show up in costume, and you'll fit right in. There are also several special events and galas for which you'll need special tickets.

German Christmas Market. (281) 379-6844; tomballsistercity.org. German and Texan traditions mingle at Tomball's open-air holiday market, held on the second Saturday in December. About 150 vendors line the streets to sell Christmas crafts and other holiday wares. You'll also find live music, a beer garden, a kids' area, and food vendors selling traditional German treats.

The Ice Rink at Woodlands Town Center. (281) 363-2447; thewoodlandscvb.com. Indulge your winter fantasies with a trip to the outdoor ice-skating rink at Woodlands Town Center. This Rockefeller Center–inspired rink is open from the week of Thanksgiving through Martin Luther King Jr. Day in January.

Las Posadas and Bethlehem on the Boardwalk. (409) 985-7822 or (409) 365-8722; visitportarthurtx.com. Using live animals and professional performers, this Port Arthur event honors Hispanic culture with a reenactment of Jesus's birth. A Christmas parade follows the reenactment, which is held downtown mid-month.

Moody Gardens Festival of Lights. (800) 582-4673; moodygardens.com. This popular event kicks off in mid-November with Santa Claus parachuting into Galveston's Moody Gardens to flick on a light switch—and light up dozens of holiday displays, complete with festive music. The Festival of Lights continues from then through New Year's Day, with holiday flicks shown on the 3-D IMAX, train rides to see the lights, and nightly entertainment. A special Gift of Christmas show and dinner are offered starting a week before Christmas Eve and continuing through the weekend after Christmas.

The Polar Express **Train Ride.** (877) 726-7245; texasstaterr.com. When the conductor calls out "All aboard!" the pages of author Chris Van Allsburg's beloved children's novel come to life as sightseers embark on a steam engine–powered trip to the North Pole, courtesy of Palestine's version of *The Polar Express*. Each weekend from mid-November through December, passengers can enjoy caroling and hot cocoa and meet Santa Claus as the Texas State Railroad train chugs along.

Sealy Fantasy of Lights. info@sealycommunityfoundation.org; sealycommunityfoundation .org/fantasyoflights.html. Sealy packs in some family fun at this community-oriented event. Highlights include a barbecue cook-off, a beanbag tournament, a softball tournament, dancing, arts and crafts activities, a 5K fun run, a softball tournament, a lighted parade, and a perfectly timed snowfall. The Fantasy of Lights is held at B&PW Park and Levine Park during the first weekend in December.

index